# Nobody Grew
but the Business

**Also by Joseph Tabbi**

*Postmodern Sublime: Technology and
American Writing from Mailer to Cyberpunk*

*Cognitive Fictions*

COLLECTIONS

*Reading Matters: Narrative in the New Media Ecology*
(edited with Michael Wutz)

*Paper Empire: William Gaddis and the World System*
(edited with Rone Shavers)

# Nobody Grew
# but the Business

*On the Life and Work of William Gaddis*

✦

## Joseph Tabbi

NORTHWESTERN UNIVERSITY PRESS

EVANSTON, ILLINOIS

Northwestern University Press
www.nupress.northwestern.edu

Printed in the United States of America

10  9  8  7  6  5  4  3  2  1

Library of Congress Cataloging-in-Publication Data

Tabbi, Joseph, 1960– author.
    Nobody grew but the business : on the life and work of William Gaddis /
Joseph Tabbi.
        pages cm
    Includes bibliographical references and index.
    ISBN 978-0-8101-3142-2 (cloth : alk. paper) — ISBN 978-0-8101-3143-9
(e-book)
    1. Gaddis, William, 1922–1998. 2. Authors, American—20th century—
Biography. 3. Gaddis, William, 1922–1998—Criticism and interpretation.
4. Capitalism in literature. I. Title.
    PS3557.A28Z88 2015
    813.54—dc23
    [B]

                                                              2014050148

∞ The paper used in this publication meets the minimum requirements of the
American National Standard for Information Sciences—Permanence of Paper for
Printed Library Materials, ANSI Z39.48–1992.

*In memory of David Markson,*
*friend and mentor*

# CONTENTS

*Gallery follows page 48.*

# ACKNOWLEDGMENTS

I wish to thank all those who knew Gaddis personally and who met with me, spoke by phone, or conversed by e-mail: Kevin Begos, Alan Bigelow, Mary Caponegro, Robert Coover, Alice Denham, Arvid Friberg Jr., Matthew Gaddis, Sarah Meares Gaddis, William and Mary Gass, Mike Gladstone, George Hunka, Bernard Looks, Harry Mathews, and Joseph McElroy. Before I began my formal research, David Markson helped inform me about the Greenwich Village setting that so influenced Gaddis and his generation. Meetings at Markson's apartment at the unlikely intersection of Tenth and Fourth Streets became for me a kind of impromptu postgraduate seminar, as earlier gatherings had been for so many writers during the previous three decades. At the invitation of the Gaddis Estate, I was able to attend the memorial gathering at the New York Academy of Arts and Letters in May 1999. The attendees and speakers that evening gave me a lasting impression of Gaddis's uptown milieu. A stroll afterward with Markson, Caponegro, and Steve Moore took us by chance past the tenement apartment on Horatio Street where Gaddis once lived.

The idea of writing a biography hadn't occurred to me, however, until Mike Levine happened by my university office one afternoon in Chicago. A contributor to Gaddis scholarship in his own right, Mike was an active interlocutor throughout the composition, circulation, and preparation of the manuscript for publication at Northwestern University Press. The managing editor, Anne Gendler, saw the typescript through several passes and corrected some errors; any that remain are my own responsibility.

A grant from the Special Collections at Washington University in St. Louis enabled me twice to visit the Gaddis archive. These visits were supplemented by the generosity of early-career Gaddis scholars Ali Chetwynd, Felix Fuchs, and Sonia Johnson, who shared their findings with me. Carrie Smith of the Wylie Agency sent me PDF versions of the letters and papers which allowed me to reference a vast range of archival resources even when I was away from my paper files. Matt Moraghan, my graduate research assistant at the University of Illinois at Chicago, contacted copyright holders for most of the illustrations and in the process he discovered some new photos that appear in the book.

A number of chapters were tried out at various stages in diverse institutional settings. On the invitation of Birger Vanwesenbeek, I presented an early draft of the chapter "Williams Family Orchestra" at the State University of New York at Fredonia (whose renowned music school and orchestra enriched my own childhood in western New York State). Further materials on Gaddis's childhood were presented at the University of Stockholm's Department of English, on the invitation of Irina Rasmussen Goloubeva and Bosse Ekelund. Brooks Landon circulated a chapter on *The Recognitions* for his University of Iowa honors class, "Postmodernist Pillars," which had the undergrads also reading David Foster Wallace's *Infinite Jest* and Thomas Pynchon's *Against the Day*. On the occasion of the Dalkey Archive Press reprinting of *J R*, Lee Konstantinou organized and Eve Bachrach edited the "Big Read" at the *Los Angeles Review of Books*. Early versions of my chapter on *J R* appeared online at the *LARB* "Occupy Gaddis" blog. Parts of the final chapter, "His Master's Voice," are taken from my afterword to *Agapē Agape*.

# ABBREVIATIONS

| | |
|---|---|
| *AA* | *Agapē Agape* |
| *CG* | *Carpenter's Gothic* |
| *E* | *Excerpts from the Unpublished Files of Muriel Oxenberg Murphy* |
| *F* | *A Frolic of His Own* |
| *J R* | *J R* |
| *L* | *The Letters of William Gaddis* |
| *LS* | *The Last of Something*, ed. Alberts, Liese, and Vanwesenbeek |
| *P* | "William Gaddis: A Portfolio," *Conjunctions* |
| *PE* | *Paper Empire*, ed. Tabbi and Shavers |
| *PR* | *Paris Review* interview, with Zoltán Abádi-Nagy |
| *R* | *The Recognitions* |
| *RSP* | *The Rush for Second Place* |
| *SBB* | *Sleeping with Bad Boys* by Alice Denham |
| *WG* | *The White Goddess* by Robert Graves |
| *WU* | Washington University, St. Louis: Special Collections |

# CHRONOLOGY

**1922**   Gaddis born in Manhattan on 29 December

**1928–34**   Merricourt boarding school in Berlin, Connecticut (age 5–13)

**1934–35**   Worthington Grade School

**1935–40**   Farmingdale High School (grades 7–12) near Massapequa, Long Island

**Summer 1940**   Sails the Caribbean on the SS *Bacchus*

**September 1941**   Enters Harvard, leaves at end of first semester

**1941–42**   On leave from Harvard, he travels in the western United States (age 19–20): Los Angeles (after a brief tour of Panama in December 1941); Arizona (ranch work); Leadville, Colorado (laborer, U.S. Army Camp Hale); St. Louis (river dredging)

**1942–45**   Returns to Harvard, where he stays until after his enforced leave of absence on 21 November 1944 for disorderly behavior (and arrest)

**October 1943**   Has first story, "The Addict," accepted by the *Harvard Lampoon*; becomes its president the following year

**1945–47**   Works for the *New Yorker* as a fact-checker (February 1945 to April 1946), living alternately in Massapequa and Greenwich Village; lives for a time with Helen Parker, on whom he would model the character Esther in *The Recognitions*

**1947–51**   Travels in Mexico and Central America, Western Europe (largely France and Spain), and North Africa (age 25–30)

**1948–50**   Begins writing *The Recognitions*, serially titled "Vanity," "Blague," and "Some people who were naked"

**1949–50**   Works for United Nations organization (UNESCO) in Paris, which he describes thus to his mother: "It's just like the evenings I used to come home with 'a theme to write'—on the same subjects too, the most recent is 'weather forecasting'—and they read like 9th grade essays too. But it's what UNESCO wants—and pays for" (undated letter to Edith Gaddis)

**1951**   Travels to North Africa to work on documentary film on background of fine paper-making

**1951–52**   Returns to the United States, where he supports himself doing freelance work—including assignments (in English) for the U.S. State Department's Russian- and Arabic-language publication *America Illustrated*—while continuing to work on *The Recognitions*

**1952**   Rents Harry Woodburn's farmhouse in Middletown, New York, where he completes a draft of *The Recognitions* and submits it to Harcourt, Brace

**1953–54**   Edits *The Recognitions* while house-sitting for Alan Ansen in Hewlett, Long Island

**1954**   Meets Pat Black at a Greenwich Village party hosted by Millie Brower, whose apartment was the site of many open readings of literary works in progress

**1955**   *The Recognitions* published at age 32 (by Harcourt, Brace, 10 March); marries Pat Black (18 May); through recommendation of Harrison Kinney, finds work and begins a career in business, writing speeches for corporate executives and scripts for government films

**1957–60**   Writes speeches and articles for executives and president of the chemical and pharmaceutical company Pfizer International

**1961**   For the 100th anniversary of the not quite "decisive" Civil War Battle of Antietam, Gaddis undertakes what he later describes as a "rather stilted play" on the subject, *Once at Antietam*, which he recycles for *A Frolic of His Own*

**Early 1960s**   Does film work for industrial concerns and the U.S. Army; shares apartment in East Ninety-Sixth Street with Douglas Wood; lives with wife Pat and two children in a walk-up brownstone at 193 Second Avenue until persuaded by Harrison Kinney to move to a wooded neighborhood in Croton-on-Hudson, a few miles north of Manhattan

**1961–62**   Issue #11 (3 June 1961) of Jack Green's *newspaper* includes a 32-page "Quote-Précis of William Gaddis's *The Recognitions*"; followed in 1962 by issues 12–14, an account of the errors and misapprehensions among the novel's reviewers entitled *fire the bastards!*

**1962**   Paperback of *The Recognitions* (Meridian); English publication follows in autumn; it is later translated into Italian (1967) and French (1973), and a mass market paperback is published by Avon in 1974

**1963**   Receives a National Institute of Arts and Letters award for republication of *The Recognitions*

**1964–68**   Does contract writing for Eastman Kodak

**1965**   Separates from Pat; in October, meets Judith Thompson at her apartment on East Forty-Sixth Street in New York; the couple will live for two years in Croton while Gaddis works on *J R* under contract (initially) for Holt, Rinehart & Winston; conceived in 1956, the novel was "provisionally entitled both *Sensation* and *J. R.*" (letter posted to himself 27 August 1956)

**1966**   National Endowment for the Arts grant (repeated in 1969)

**June 1968**   Marries Judith on the 7th, spends weekend in New York City and observes Robert Kennedy's funeral mass. Now living on income from the book advance, supplemented by freelance corporate film- and speech-writing

**February 1969**   Buys "carpenter gothic" house in Piermont about ten miles north of New York City

**1972**   Receives Rockefeller Foundation grant

**1975**   *J R* published (Alfred A. Knopf, October)

**1976**   Receives National Book Award; asked by the U.S. State Department to visit the Far East as an American Specialist, meeting with writers, journalists, and academics concerned with American writing in Thailand, the Philippines, and Japan

**1976–79**   Teaches at Bard: writers' workshops, one-on-one advising, and an undergraduate class on the theme of "failure" in the American novel; continues piecework for IBM and others

**1978**   Separates from Judith by mutual agreement; in October begins (in a letter to his daughter Sarah Gaddis, 14 October 1978) "thinking seriously about thinking seriously about starting another book," *Carpenter's Gothic* (working title "That Time of Year")

**1979**   Reunites with Muriel Oxenberg Murphy, whom he'd met after completing *The Recognitions* in November 1953; they would live together until 1995

**1980s**   Divides time between Wainscott, Long Island, and East Seventy-Third Street with Muriel

**1981**   Receives Guggenheim grant

**1982**   Receives MacArthur Foundation "Genius Award" in July

**1984**   Elected to the American Academy and Institute of Arts and Letters

**1985**   *Carpenter's Gothic* published (Elisabeth Sifton Books/Viking, July); returns to Bard for a semester. In December travels to Moscow, Leningrad, and Lithuania by arrangement with Pepperdine University and the Moscow Writers Union

**1986**   Attends international meeting in Sofia in October, on invitation of the Union of Bulgarian Writers' conference on "Peace: The Hope of the Planet"

**1987**   Begins taking notes in April for *A Frolic of His Own* (working title "The Last Act")

**1988**   Publishes an interview in the *Paris Review* recorded in Sofia two years earlier, its "purpose after all . . . simply to do one fairly long interview in a 'serious' place & get it out of the way so that when people come with this same threat I can simply direct them to this one without appearing to be some reclusive nut" (letter to Sarah Gaddis, 23 January 1988). In September *Carpenter's Gothic* appears in French translation; speaking engagements in West Berlin, Freiburg, and Bonn

**1993**   Receives Lannan Literary Foundation Lifetime Achievement Award; awarded Edith Wharton Citation of Merit as New York State Author for 1993–95, by appointment of Governor Andrew M. Cuomo

**1994**   Publishes *A Frolic of His Own* (Poseidon, an imprint of Simon & Schuster, January); published in England in June

**1995**   Begins working on *Agapē Agape*, first as a nonfiction book, then as a novel

**1998**   Dies on 16 December at home in East Hampton, New York, two weeks before his seventy-sixth birthday

**2002**   Posthumous publication of *Agapē Agape* and *The Rush for Second Place* (both in October)

# Nobody Grew
# but the Business

# Introduction

—Hate it man like how can I hate it I mean I don't even know
what it's about . . .

> Rhoda in *J R* (604), on hearing passages
> read aloud from *Agapē Agape*

At the start of William Gaddis's literary career in the 1950s, T. S. Eliot
and Ernest Hemingway were still the leading literary lights in America
and the generation of Thomas Pynchon and Ken Kesey was still at university, trying out their art in postwar literature programs. At once a
traditionalist and a pioneer of postmodern innovation, Gaddis has been
hard to place in literary history. "He came of age in perhaps the last historical moment when literature seemed to matter," says Carter Scholz (*P*
403), who contributed one of around twenty-five posthumous tributes to
Gaddis in *Conjunctions*, a journal out of Bard College where in earlier
decades Gaddis had taught occasionally. *The Recognitions* on its 1955
appearance (when Gaddis was thirty-two) seemed designed to topple the
illusions of Western civilization. Misrecognized by reviewers as a belated
*Ulysses*, Gaddis's first novel in fact marked a new beginning for literary
fiction in the United States. Robert Coover, an early adherent, recalls how
so many writers working in completely different areas and coming at their
art from rearguard and avant-garde positions, from their experiences in
World War II and from their residence in lit programs, nonetheless came
together in this period with a common purpose.[1] And they all knew about
Gaddis. The generational feeling was not so much of coming late to modernism; it wasn't about bringing "tradition" and an expatriate sensibility
home to America, as Pound, Eliot, Stein, Dos Passos, and Hemingway had
done. The new beginning was more about opening out to new constituen-
cies, non-Western origins, and (in Coover's case more than Gaddis's) new
collaborations and much contention among those working in print, film,
television, and electronic media. There was no strong sense, at least not
until Marshall McLuhan's work started getting noticed in the mid-1960s,
that literature might be sidelined or even silenced by the new media; no

sense that the large critical canvas, or the worldliness that united writers as different as Gaddis and Donald Barthelme, Saul Bellow and Ishmael Reed, would be broken up into special interests. Few expected that literary writers themselves, those whose fictions didn't get picked up by Hollywood, would be channeled into academia and compelled to engage their audience not through major publishing houses but increasingly through promotional book tours, public readings, performances, and blogs.

Against the grain of American celebrity culture, Gaddis kept himself in the background: in interviews, he simply refused to answer biographical questions. While he was living, no author photograph appeared on any of his book jackets; he never read from his work ("How would I do all the voices?" was his reasonable plea); we have only a single television appearance, aired in England in the mid-1980s; and a walk-on part in a blaxploitation vampire film in 1973. Routine comparisons of Gaddis with J. D. Salinger and Thomas Pynchon emphasized the low public profile, not the literary affinities. Those who advanced theories that each of these reticent writers was in fact the other never quite noticed what, for example, *Catcher in the Rye* and Gaddis's second novel *J R* had in common, namely, their presentation of adolescent energies driving and disturbing the headlong business culture in the United States. "Remember at that time," University of Albany professor Tom Smith remarked four decades later when introducing Gaddis to his audience, "the great buzzword was 'phony,' from J. D. Salinger's *Catcher in the Rye*, which was the most popular novel of the 1950s."[2] That was consistent, Smith told his colleagues and students, with the "rich labyrinth of fraud, falsity, forgery, fakery, fabrication, and fantasy" in *The Recognitions*. Two decades later, young J R's own "recurring epithet 'holy shit' is an epic epiphany, or a recognition of our time"; and Gaddis's second novel, like Salinger's first, can be regarded as "an all too realistic vision of what America has become" through the Reagan era, into the 1990s when Smith was speaking, and arguably into the present.

Yet few commentators outside of academia have remarked on the unprecedented imagination by Gaddis of the corporate state itself, its rise in America and its expansion worldwide. That was the signal accomplishment that Gaddis shared with Pynchon and Coover, but with few others on the same epic scale or with the same fine-grained documentary detail. Gaddis might have enjoyed for a time a countercultural approval for his refusal to engage directly with the publicity machine. It was not yet common or considered natural, after all, for sports stars and business leaders to act parts in television commercials, so an author could be forgiven for not wanting to read his work aloud to an audience or write jacket blurbs for other authors. Gaddis never made a principle of absolute withdrawal, which may have brought Salinger and Pynchon even more attention as conscientious objectors. Over time, though, Gaddis more than any of these others tended to be regarded as just "difficult," and that perception of the man was reinforced by the demands of the work itself. By the end of his career, the verdict was in and Gaddis himself seemed to appreciate that nothing he could say or do would change this perception.

"I don't like the word 'difficult,'" he told the *London Observer* in 1994, "although that, apparently is the consensus."[3] He was even less enamored of the term "experimental," since he felt he knew exactly what he was doing at every moment in the writing.[4] Yet these were the terms that continued to stick to him, even after his death in 1998 at the age of seventy-six. Writing in the *New Yorker* in 2002, Jonathan Franzen could simply label Gaddis "Mr. Difficult" and imagine he was banishing Gaddis as an influence—on himself and the very few others of Franzen's generation who had achieved the mainstream success in sales that always eluded Gaddis. That the same could be said about *Don Quixote*, *Moby-Dick*, and *Remembrance of Things Past* counts for little in Franzen's judgment, since all of them have in common the fact that he, Franzen, never finished reading them.[5]

The *New Yorker* for its part never changes, and the coverage given there to Gaddis's posthumous work was consistent with a market-savvy, uptown New York tradition going back to the scathing reviews of *The Recognitions*, half a century earlier: "foul-mouthed," "disgusting," and "evil," according to *fire the bastards!*, Jack Green's 1962 Gaddis defense.[6] But Green's prescient advocacy, self-published in his underground *newspaper*, would also be rehearsed half a century later in *Conjunctions* in the playful and passionate tributes from Gaddis's supporters in the wider literary community. This time, as four decades before, the defenders were writing mostly in academic journals and alternative literary magazines. And many of the same arguments from the 1960s were rehearsed in 2003: that literature, if it was going to last, needed to do more than entertain readers and reprise events of the day; that readers of literary fiction, if they want the experience to *be* literary, need to participate in the construction of meaning; that the political state, the economy, and religion are not just topics for an ambitious writer: these things are themselves fictions that a great writer can inhabit, and imagine—*differently*.

Even among Gaddis's proponents, literary peers, and friends often we find a certain reticence regarding the man himself. "Mr. Gaddis," is how fellow novelist Joy Williams referred to her male elder, not William, certainly never Bill. "He was elegant, urbane, unassuming," writes Mary

Caponegro, who attended one of Gaddis's classes at Bard in the 1970s. "One could not imagine him without his tweed jacket, just as one could not imagine calling him by other than his surname" (P 381). One of his interviewers, Sally Helgesen in *Bookletter*, noted his habit of "distancing himself as he always does when describing his work by the use of an impersonal pronoun." And it does seem as if Gaddis's self-effacement came from a deeply held belief in the author's calling not to impose oneself on the world but to register what is there, independent of the shaping imagination, and resistant to narratives we tell ourselves about ourselves: "One discovers something new each day and says, 'oh, this fits here,'" he told Helgesen. "So one makes a note in the outline from which a situation can be developed."[7]

In this same interview, when asked why he took so many years to write each book, Gaddis cites Mark Twain to the effect that "each work must be set aside for certain periods so it can gather a life of its own." The Roman poet Horace had advised shelving a manuscript for a minimum of nine years before publication, and Gaddis understood that time away, living and accumulating new experiences, and reading more books, was necessary for any book of his own to take on its layers and textures. There was never a question of blockage; he'd have many periods—like the one in Gerona, Spain, in August 1950—when he could expect that the writing would go well for a week or so, and then it wouldn't. Either way, he understood that "the best part of it has been coming back to it, after a year of not touching it but worrying about it, to find that upon returning to it that it does retain its life for me, and still asks to be finished."[8] The twenty-year stretch between his first and second novel may have been just what he needed to let the time of one's living generate exactly what a new work needed to become really new (even if the waiting, and the continual revising, left one feeling old): "nothing to make you wearier of yourself than artfulness when you were 10 years younger."[9]

Apart from the business of making a living, the author, presumably, needed this time for gathering newspaper and magazine clippings. (These alone would fill some ten or twelve cardboard boxes when they were eventually shipped to the Gaddis archive at Washington University in St. Louis.) An extended period of gestation—the time it takes for a news event, a conversation, or an observation from life to find its place in a long-term literary composition—needed to go on separate from the author, who otherwise exercises total responsibility for what goes on the page. An author, Gaddis seems to imply, does not have a special "self" to express or a life narrative that cries out to be told; rather, he composes a life *in* the work, in words on the page. That Gaddis regularly would transcribe conversations whole cloth into his writing was a source of irritation and occasional distress to friends who did not share Gaddis's view that all life experience was fodder for the work.[10]

Not everyone who knew or encountered Gaddis sensed this distance in him, however. Stewart O'Nan was a young writer visiting Cologne during a period when Gaddis was being lionized in Germany after years of comparative neglect in his home country. O'Nan gives us a rare, irreverent, and nuanced perspective on the purportedly aloof Gaddis:

> He was bony by then, and wore a beige suit and carried a walking stick like some down-at-heels country count, a deflated Buddy Ebsen. As the fawning German interviewer lobbed soft ones, he reared back and scourged the American reader, comparing himself to Melville with a crabbed laugh. And then twinkled, Grinchlike, and gave me a wink. He knew the artist's outrage was an old soft-shoe too, a routine he'd played before bigger houses than this. Made me like the guy. (*P* 402)[11]

Buddy Ebsen? At different times, he would collect more flattering comparisons: "the young Leslie Howard" is how he appeared to Jack Kerouac, when the thirty-year-old Gaddis had just had the manuscript of *The Recognitions* accepted "and so acquired a strange grace in my eyes . . . flushed successful young author but 'ironic' looking with a big parkingticket sticking out of his coat lapel. . . ."[12] "A poor man's Frank Sinatra" was how *Playboy* centerfold model and aspiring novelist Alice Denham described him during the period in the mid-1960s when he was doing corporate writing, raising a family, and finding his way toward his second novel, *J R* (1975). In his seventies, he struck Jonathan Coe of the *Guardian* as "a more dapper, ascetic version of Kirk Douglas."[13] The one time I met him, after taking the subway to the Upper East Side apartment he then shared with Muriel Murphy in the late 1980s, he seemed reserved but down-to-earth. I remember giving regards from David Markson in Greenwich Village, Gaddis's friend of thirty years who was then in the process of his own, quite different, extensively allusive literary quest (which Gaddis never quite "got," but then he rarely read fiction by his contemporaries). I remember telling Gaddis that my writing professors a decade earlier at Cornell University, who had Pynchon in their classes, thought that Pynchon never would have written *V.* quite the way he did without *The Recognitions*. I remember Gaddis telling our small group of scholars, two of whom had arrived from Florida, another from New Brunswick, about the occasion when a young woman from Poland flew in to Manhattan, opened a bottle of vodka on arrival, sat *there* (Gaddis pointing to a spot on the floor between us) and proceeded to debate one-on-one into the night on the question of theology in *The Recognitions*.

Before he became the imposing "Mr. Gaddis," on the one hand, vilified for "difficulty, unreadability, unworthiness,"[14] and, on the other hand, inspiring "awe" in subsequent generations of writers seeking to reach his artistic level, he possessed a normal range of personal identities. He was known variously as Billy at his Connecticut boarding school; Willie to his Harvard friends and literary peers; and the "Arizona cowboy" during a year touring the American Southwest.[15] He was William, Willie, or Mr. Gaddis to his wives; Pop or Papa to his children (into their adulthood); and Bill among the U.S. Army generals and corporate executives whose speeches he ghostwrote. There will have been thousands of anecdotes that must go unrecorded: the time, for example, in the 1940s when he came down off the West Side expressway, skidded, and scattered the stalls of the immigrant merchants in the lower Manhattan district. (And his companion for the drive, Sheri Martinelli, announcing above all the shouts: "I don't care what they say, Willie I still think you're the *best* driver."[16]) As those who knew Gaddis pass on, such anecdotes will be lost; but then again, we have Ed Feasley and Otto Pivner in *The Recognitions* doing much the same thing: "[They] were moving at seventy-three miles an hour. But neither of them wanted to go to Connecticut, and when they realized that they were taking that direction the car swung about with a scream, and was saved from what might have been a fatal skid by hitting its sliding rear against a lamppost" (*R* 316). The incident is followed by a visit to a hospital and their removal of an amputated leg (belonging to the mother of Stanley, another habitué of the Greenwich Village scene, circa 1950). The modern viewer of reality TV's *Jackass* will find as much to admire in Gaddis's writing as the modernist literary aesthete. The novels are filled with *life*—and not least the author's own life and the lives, words, and recounted experiences of people he knew and family members he knew about, going back to America's founding in apostasy, migration, speculation, noise, and sheer recklessness.

This book will be a *literary life* and intellectual history, in that I recount the growth of a major writer's art over the course of a lifetime in the context of social and cultural transformations. For reasons that Gaddis elucidates *in* the work, few writers if any can aspire to such an achievement in the United States today. Even Gaddis's own novels, for years under the imprint of major houses, have moved to Dalkey Archive Press, a distinguished small-run literary house. The megaliths can no longer take risks on literature, for reasons that (typically) Gaddis again had worked out *in* his depiction, in *J R*, of publishing as a part of the capitalist machine. Even as publishers and their power continue to grow immensely, the audience for literary work, numerous and avid as ever, is unlikely to back a blockbuster. "Nobody Grew but the Business," the title Gaddis chose for an early release of a thirty-page section from *J R*,[17] can also describe a literary career and a life constrained by corporations.

In his review essay on the occasion of the Dalkey Archive reprint of *J R*, Lee Konstantinou points out how the "big six" publishers worldwide have given up on American literature. Even as the review appeared, the six became five as Bertelsmann that same week bought out Gaddis's former publisher, Viking. The publishing business has certainly grown, but literature in the meantime has *transformed*, as the summer 2012 "Occupy Gaddis" collaborative reading of *J R* demonstrates. With hundreds of pages of close readings and scene-by-scene descriptions by ordinary readers, with occasional mistakes usually corrected within hours by others, or by the reader as he or she kept reading, we are able to see clearly and for the first time how it is that readers with neither specialized training nor a personal, prior interest in the publishing scheme actually negotiate the difficulties of Gaddis's writing. We see it in the *Los Angeles Review of Books*, in the Gaddis Listserv, and in subsequent blogs such as the one started (a year after the *LARBlog*) in June 2013 by a former Bard student of Gaddis's, George Hunka. The tone of such writing, more personal but also more open to the kinds of scholarly, collegial, and convivial information needed to appreciate Gaddis, is a far cry from the major media review. Without the reviewer's need to measure up to the author under discussion (or under attack), and without a stake in academic positions or posturing, participants in dedicated online forums can bring into focus a moment-by-moment, readerly engagement that was never publicly available in Gaddis's lifetime. Such encounters can direct us to the responsiveness Gaddis insisted all along was needed if a reader wanted to overcome the noise of American corporate culture that he faithfully represented in order to transform it (with the reader's participation) into art.

With the emergence of new modes of criticism along with the rise of digital media, we are moving definitively past problems of reception that dogged Gaddis throughout his long career, during what now can be seen as the gradual transformation of literary art in America away from the print paradigm in an era of corporate publishing. In the shared reading context of existing blogs, the problem of "difficulty" in Gaddis's fiction is clearly seen to be no problem for readers who look to novels not for entertainment alone but for *literary value*. What we are in danger of losing despite, or rather because of, unlimited corporate growth is the leisure and educational infrastructure that—alone among cultural institutions—is capable of training young minds of all economic classes across nations in the direction of the literary arts.[18] What we seem to have reached instead, at best, is a developed regime of creative writing. That may have served in Gaddis's time as a ground for recruitment of young talent by New York publishers but today the discipline has become nearly autonomous, a field of writers writing largely for other writers who either publish in small, independent presses or circulate the work in electronic forms among networks whose growth is rhizomatic, not accumulative. The growth of "The Program," identified as such by Mark McGurl, will also be part of Gaddis's life story—somewhat surprisingly given Gaddis's oft-stated aversion to reading from his work and his conviction that writing cannot be taught. He tended to agree with William S. Burroughs, who like Gaddis "had been in teaching situations a few times, and who used to say 'I don't teach creative writing; I teach creative reading.' "[19]

The 2012 "Occupy Gaddis" readings at the *Los Angeles Review of Books*, following on the 2010 "Infinite Summer" reading of David Foster Wallace and formulated after the "Occupy Wall Street" actions in American cities, show not only that Gaddis has survived another generation intact; the terms for his appreciation, at last, may have come into view as the inequities of the corporate system, the historically unprecedented "growth" that empowers "the 1 percent" and nobody else, finally register among ordinary Americans. Where literature might once have appeared elitist—and Gaddis's and Pynchon's Ivy League origins reinforce this perception—by the second decade of the twenty-first century there would be little interest among the business elite in literature as such. Certainly there has been in this upper segment little enthusiasm for an immanent critique of its own ways of doing things. Gaddis could be dismissed as an articulate scold by the 1 percent—as Muriel Oxenburg Murphy, his life partner of sixteen years and longtime Manhattan socialite, dismissed his work in a posthumous memoir when she said that his métier was in pointing out "how rotten everything was, and how unfair" (*E* 95). In a different society, there would be no need for Gaddis's work and we might accept Murphy's verdict. In the present society, an America that (as Konstantinou writes) "is hollowing out the foundation necessary to even read a book like [*J R*], an America that teaches its children via closed-circuit television, an America that thinks democracy means owning a share of profit-maximizing publicly traded corporations," Gaddis's critique starts to make a kind of sense. Who can it be, if not the 99 percent, whose talk makes up the bulk of his written work? In channeling his critique and his world vision through us, through voices we recognize as our own and the voices of those near us, Gaddis offers an alternative to markets and corporate systems that operate without recognition. This is what makes him the novelist for our time.

This is not to say that the work is prophetic, or that Gaddis somehow anticipated the Internet generation. He is among the last generation of authors in any country whose archive is entirely in print, Kodachrome, typed manuscripts, and handwritten letters (some of them done in calligraphy, no less). Yet he is an author (with Pynchon and Coover and—in England—W. G. Sebald and very few others of the postmodern generations) who has helped to resituate print literary culture in the era of new media.[20] En route to *The Recognitions*, Gaddis may have begun with some residual modernist nostalgia for "tradition." "Life is very long" was a frequent affectation of the youthful admirer of T. S. Eliot as he spent his twenties commuting between Europe and the United States. But even as Gaddis entered his thirties and his first novel grew from highbrow satire to a multinational carnival of epical proportions, he had worked through Eliot's traditionalism (and his own premature world-weariness) to something new and different. What he found himself living through, after his years at Harvard and during the gradual, underground social transformations of the 1940s and '50s, was not so easily mapped onto Eliot's earlier postwar sensibility: it was not the destruction of an old order so much as the acceleration of a new, hypertrophied capitalism that emerged with his country's sudden unrivaled ascendance as a world power (and with New York as the center of the art world, overtaking Paris[21]). At the same time, he lived through an unprecedented rise (and sudden drop) in the perceived importance of imaginative literature in American culture. Though his first book did not bring him the celebrity status his title presupposed, *The Recognitions* nonetheless appeared when publishers of commercial fiction were able (through their best sellers) to subsidize serious work, and even in commercial failure Gaddis was allowed in at least one of his corporate jobs to work on his own writing, in the mornings. That was how Gaddis described his position at Pfizer, when he knew David Markson, Alice Denham, and other writers who carried on after his own glory days in New York's West Village: "Pfizer's not too bad," Denham recalls Gaddis saying among friends at one of the downtown bars: "They let Dick [Dowling] and me write all morning on our own stuff and show us off to clients as 'our novelists' " (*SBB* 101).[22]

Hollywood and TV and magazine journalism during these years could instantly transform a Norman Mailer or a Joseph Heller into a celebrity, and peer recognition in Greenwich Village could bring invitations to teach at universities, and to set up programs of one's own (the route taken in mid-career by Barthelme and William Gass). Gaddis of course kept his distance from each of these developments, though not for lack of trying to have a film made of his second novel, *J R*; and he taught more often than people realize. Indeed, the success of celebrity culture and the incorporation of authors into writing programs nationwide spelled the end of an era whose mystique Gaddis enjoyed and cultivated, even as he revealed its many pretenses and itemized its complicities with late-capitalist development.

Gaddis's anticipation of literary postmodernism is well known; his exhaustive account of the world system as it impinges on every aspect of contemporary life is also known, if not sufficiently appreciated. What is less known, and what should contribute to that wider appreciation, is the extent to which Gaddis drew on his own life for his novels, as a way of proving to himself the validity of his perceptions about the course that our shared American life was taking. Any biography of Gaddis, therefore, must also account for the way that his life *entered* his art and is on display there—for anyone, that is, who reads the books and, unlike the teenager Rhoda (in my epigraph), takes the trouble to discover what they're about.

# Chapter 1

# Williams Family Orchestra

—Money . . . ? in a voice that rustled.
—Paper, yes.
—And we'd never seen it. Paper money.
—We never saw paper money till we came east.
—It looked so strange the first time we saw it. Lifeless.
—You couldn't believe it was worth a thing.
—Not after Father jingling his change.
—Those were silver dollars.
—And silver halves, yes and quarters, Julia. The ones from his pupils. I can hear him now . . .

*(J R 3)*

Although Gaddis's 1975 novel *J R* is set in an unrelenting present and the author mostly removes himself from the narrative, we can in fact find much of Gaddis's family history in the conversation of the aunts. Anne and Julia Bast, natives of Indiana currently residing in Massapequa, Long Island, appear at the start of the novel and return periodically; their lilting, aimless but affecting dialogue creates a kind of refrain for the novel, a respite from the noise of contemporary culture. The elderly sisters recall how their brothers, Thomas and James Bast, each made separate careers out of their musical heritage: James as the composer of *Philoctetes*, an opera highly spoken of but never performed (like Gaddis's first novel, *The Recognitions*, which found a small but nonetheless active and communicative audience on its release in 1955); and Thomas as the founder of a company that began producing player piano rolls but has diversified and become incorporated as General Roll. (The sisters remember "back when Thomas started it . . . we thought it was a military friend he'd made" [5].) The distribution of the company estate following Thomas's death is the reason for the lawyer Coen's visit to the elderly

*13*

sisters, who recall that they never saw paper money before coming east
("—You couldn't believe it was worth a thing"), and they still have a
hard time grasping the growth of the family business into a corporate
concern. The life of the young men is what they remember, the family
itself, and not least the *family orchestra* that was their daily pastime and
partial livelihood. Music was also what brought the world to their small
town:

> —The Russian Symphony . . .
> —And Sousa's Band? Of course there was a certain competitive
> spirit between the boys. No one denies that, Mr Cohen.[1] We had
> a family orchestra, you know, and they practiced three and four
> hours a day. Every week Father gave a dime to the one who showed
> the most improvement. From the time they were six, until they left
> home . . . (7)

Rachmaninoff, Ravel, Saint-Saëns—all were recruited by Thomas (using
composer James's professional connections) for performances in which
their first rolls were "cut." Possibly it was not Saint-Saëns himself but
Paderewski playing Saint-Saëns. The aunts' conversation in the novel
can be hard to follow at times, though not nearly so convoluted as the
extant letters from Gaddis's real-life Quaker grandaunts on his mother's
side: Mrs. A. L. Meredith of Salem, Indiana, cousin Hazel from Yellow
Springs, Ohio, and Emma Bond of Vanlue, Ohio. Their letters, sent to
Gaddis's grandmother Ida Williams Way and kept by Gaddis's mother,
Edith Charles Way, put together a kind of "family tree" from memories,
handed-down stories, and rumors concerning the municipal records of
the State of Indiana. Hazel was the sort of housewife and mother whose
idea of a vacation was to visit the Cincinnati library at every opportunity;
writing was clearly one of her chief joys—though this was always done
at the service of her correspondent, not for the furthering of her own
literary ambitions. Hazel, like all the female cousins, was a participant
at yearly conferences of the Daughters of the American Revolution. Her
letters were written during spare hours when her husband wasn't using
the house typewriter, usually during a break from a full day of cooking,
housecleaning, "washing curtains, bedding, and the like."[2] A recipe for
nut bread is given in the letter that Emma Bond sent to Cousin Ida on 21
November 1943, with an update on researches into the whereabouts of
John Stockton Hough. The Indiana and Ohio cousins would have been
happy to know that Edith, the daughter of their eastern relations, would
hold on to these recollections and researches; they could have had no idea

that Edith's only son, William Thomas Gaddis, would transform their letters, and their persons, into the opening lines of one of the twentieth century's great novels of corporate America.

Ida, the one who made it to Massapequa, Long Island, was regarded highly by her cousins. "You are something for us to live up to," wrote A. L. Meredith from Indiana in the 1930s: "Something quite above the rest of us." Ida was one of the "illustrious cousins, the musical Williams [*sic*]."[3] Samuel E. Williams, Gaddis's great-grandfather, was born in 1855 on a farm in Wayne County, Indiana. Samuel studied music during weekly trips to the university in Cincinnati, and from the age of eighteen he divided his time teaching school, keeping up the family farm, and directing bands in his hometown of Fountain City. In 1876 he married Ella Hough, daughter of Moses and Peninah Hough (whose family Gaddis would remember when he named his son Matthew Hough Gaddis). Samuel's ambition from childhood to have a professional musical career was realized in 1887, when he was called by the city of Winchester to direct the town band, which became under his leadership a band and orchestra. Later still, after the death of his wife Ella in 1890 and his retirement at age forty from teaching, Samuel formed the Williams Family Orchestra with the idea of keeping the family together.

The fictional aunts in *J R* recollect, sotto voce, a hint of scandal in the family background; however, the Winchester newspaper obituary expressed only local pride at the marriage of Samuel's great-grandfather, James Meredith of Virginia, to Mary Crews, a Cherokee Indian princess he'd met while they were attending Guilford College in North Carolina. James Meredith served in the Revolutionary War and his son, David Meredith, was among the first settlers of Indiana. (Samuel Williams's maternal grandparents, similarly, were among the first settlers in western Ohio.) David's son, who became General Solomon Meredith, "was 6 feet 7 inches tall and at the age of 19 walked every step of the way from North Carolina to Wayne County, Indiana."[4]

Writing to Gaddis's grandmother Ida, the distant cousin A. L. Meredith was "proud to tell" her that she had secured "certificates of service of James Meredith. They cover the period 1776–1784. He served in N. C. being a resident of what is now Stokes Co." Mrs. Meredith doubted "very much his having been a Quaker since 3 of his daughtersinlaw were turned out of the Quaker Church for marrying out of Meeting. The wife of James may have been [a Quaker]. It is understood she was part Cherokee Indian. What do you know about it?"[5] According to the genealogy at heathcot.org, "the efforts of many of [Mary's] descendants to receive Cherokee citizenship were denied by the Dawes Commission."

The pioneering spirit of his ancestors lived in Samuel's devotion to music, and so to an extent did their unconventional ways. Samuel was the author of three books: *The Inductive Note Reader,* published in 1895, *Nature in Song,* and *Terse Texts for Teachers,* all of which were widely used in the formative years of public music education in America. In a late photo, Samuel stands near a radio set, indicating an interest in music broadcasting and recording. His sons, Ernest and Jan Williams, continued the line as prominent musicians. Ernest, after touring in Australia, India, Egypt, and Europe, would settle for six years as first trumpet in the Philadelphia Symphony Orchestra under Leopold Stokowski, Richard Strauss, George Enesco, Vincent d'Indy, and Ossip Gabrilowitsch. He taught at the Juilliard School of Music in New York and eventually founded a school of his own in Brooklyn along with a summer band camp in Saugerties, deep in the Catskills. His symphony written for band instruments, "the first of its kind in world musical history," was dedicated to his father, who died in 1937, the year of its performance.[6]

In 1922, the Ernest Williams School of Music was founded in Brooklyn. It remained open until Ernest's death in 1945. The "ideal" for the school, in the words of Ernest's obituary, "was to establish in this country a school that should be to America as the famous Kneller Hall is to Great Britain; a school that should give a comprehensive training to instrumentalists, embracing the entire field of ensemble work, both theoretical and practical." Students were attracted from all over the country and one of them, Fred Ross from West Virginia, regarded Williams as a gentleman who knew that the development of talent had to allow for mistakes, but could also be a taskmaster: "Mr. Williams," Ross stated, "understood if a person made an honest mistake while playing, but he became very upset if a performer made a careless mistake. He sometimes would tap the person on the head with his baton."[7]

Though Gaddis himself was never musical—"I can't read music and can't play anything but a comb," as his autobiographical narrator says in *Agapē Agape* (90)—while growing up he absorbed from his family and school environment what was recognized as "most essential" in Ernest's program, namely "thorough and intensive routine. The Ernest Williams School grew amazingly since its inception." It was an "all-year round institution, holding its winter sessions in Brooklyn and its summer sessions in camp at Saugerties, where aspiring musicians may continue their studies. [. . .] Mr. Williams turned a rough mountain site into a modern village, with running water, electric lights, a fine concrete swimming pool and other athletic and recreational facilities as well as a large auditorium and dormitory and cottage accommodations for several hundred students."

The growth of a family, and a business dedicated as much to measurable, material progress as to personal creative development, remained the ideal to which Gaddis held himself, and his country.

Jan Williams would teach at the Juilliard School. He played for the Russian Symphony Orchestra in New York, under Modeste Altschuler, the Goldman Band, and (for nine years) the Metropolitan Opera under Toscanini. In 1927, he was the principal clarinetist at the New York Philharmonic. The oldest daughter, Ida, was no less talented on the organ, though she would be the first in the family to break from the practice of music performance and education, when she left her position as a public school music supervisor in 1920 to start a career in business. Ida's daughter, who was by this time Mrs. Edith Gaddis, would continue in the business field three years after bearing a son, William Thomas Gaddis, and divorcing her husband (whom the boy would not meet until his early twenties).

The incipient feminism in Edith's own pioneering spirit was not lost on the author of the 1941 *New York Times* profile titled "Steam Plant Purchasing Agent Finds Fascination in Her Work: Edith Gaddis's Shopping List Ranges from Huge Mechanical Shovels to Miles of Iron Pipe." Edith inherited some of the height of her male ancestors along with their streak of independence, although this tended to go into her career and avant-garde style more than travel (which she would eventually enjoy mostly vicariously as her son and only child grew to manhood). The will to settle new territories, common to both sides of her family, became in her a will to occupy positions hitherto the domain of men. Coming from Indiana to New York, and having some financial security in the home in Massapequa that she inherited from Ida, what Edith wanted primarily was a "job" and she "found one in the statistical department of a Wall Street firm." She left that to be married and soon after came to New York Steam as an "assistant to the purchasing agent," J. N. Moncrieff, a man who was noted for the time he "took to train his assistants."[8]

In time, Edith was able to move into Moncrieff's position as chief purchasing agent with the New York Steam Corporation (later Consolidated Edison). When asked by her interviewer for advice of use to those aspiring to similar advancement, she offers the following: "Get to the bottom of the job. . . . Know everything concerning it that is in your power to know."[9] Edith's work ethic, derived in part from her Quaker grandfather's teaching, musical, and writing career and consistent with the "thorough and intensive routine" taught at her uncle Ernest's Brooklyn School, would certainly be communicated to the eventual author of exploratory fictions, William.[10]

In her person, Edith struck the *Times* interviewer as having "a magnetic combination of inherent poise and an unstoppable joie-de-vivre."
She came of age as an independent woman, after all, during the 1920s in
America: at the time of her *Times* interview she still wore her hair in a
softly waved bob. Among friends, she displayed her long legs proudly; she
was "a handsome woman" with a "strong nose and a good, firm chin."[11]
She was not afraid of a strong drink; she smoked and went by the nick-
name "Pete."

The Williams Family Orchestra, and Samuel's strength of will that had
held his family together for two generations and across two American
states, gave way in the 1920s to a business ethos and culture of self-
realization that, on one side, made Ida's and daughter Edith's move to the
East Coast possible. But the stable, semiautonomous family that was so
important to so many transatlantic and cross-country migrations, settle-
ments, and resettlements was already under pressure from the need not
just to sustain one's position, but also to grow in wealth and worldly
contacts. From one generation to the next—and across genders also—this
restlessness and sense of displacement defined Gaddis's milieu. It helps
to explain why a young woman such as Edith would be attracted to the
avant-garde in style and the arts, and also in business. That same ethos
would require, during the years when Edith was building her career, her
son's attendance at a boarding school in Berlin, Connecticut. His eventual
placement in Harvard University represented a classic American family
achievement, but this too was unsettled, as Gaddis's residence in Cambridge was often interrupted by illness, and by travel in the West, Mexico,
and New York City. His main participation in university life was as the
editor of a satirical magazine, the *Lampoon*.

In his mature fiction, Gaddis contrasts the family orchestra with
something altogether new and decidedly threatening, the development
of a "family of corporations." One of these, Diamond Cable, would be
presided over by a character named Moncrieff. More broadly, the "J R
Family of Companies" run by a fatherless sixth-grader whose mother is
always away, traces a mid-1970s development that may have been rooted
in these early changes that Gaddis's own family lived through. The corporate turn in the United States was never inevitable, however. Edith and her
son, though separated for much of the boy's childhood, had an unbroken
connection in letters and developed, together, a kind of nonconforming,
wholly modern sensibility that for a time seemed to offer an alternative
to either the patriarchal family (whose musical legacy Edith and her son
valued) or the culture of unbridled individualism whose excesses they
understood as destructive of authentic personal expression.

Gaddis learned from his family to value discipline in the arts and to submerge one's individuality in a collaborative performance, even as the performed work was played, and heard, differently each time according to the individual talents of each family member: the hand's pressure on each string or key, the air in each breath of every member in a large orchestra. Though isolated through much of his childhood, he knew what it was to be together with people in a common effort. But this performative discipline, so central to his great-grandfather's vision of aesthetic and familial integrity, his granduncles' social and cultural experimentation at band camp in Saugerties, and the business ambitions of his mother, would all be subject to the same technological standard that aspired to remove all nuance in the performance and, more important, any risk of *failure*. The latter, the potential for failure, Gaddis came to understand (after the commercial failure of his first novel) to be necessary to the realization of any substantial achievement in business or the arts. But technologies of control, whether they appeared in the player piano roll or its offspring, the punch cards of an IBM computer, were fast removing chance, nuance, and a certain noise and ambiguity necessary to human expression and togetherness. Hence Gaddis's interest, almost from the start of his serious writing career, in the history of the player piano—whose standardized formatting and steps toward the commercial distribution of music seemed to him to capture the counterfeit culture that America was following in his lifetime.

That Gaddis's fiction chronicles the advanced corporatization of American culture more fully and earlier than any other postwar novelist in the United States is well known among his critics and literary peers. What may be less appreciated is the musicality of his presentations. Even where a dialogue is difficult to follow, the words become meaningful as parts in an overall literary composition, nuanced and surprisingly rich. Ed Park, in one of the more perceptive reviews of Gaddis's oeuvre, demonstrates a rare, and correct, capacity to hear music in the "madness" of everyday dialogue in *J R*, as in: "—No no wait Major you're Vern wait you're knocking over the Dan Dan wait."[12] Rhythms abound in the most technical descriptive passages of telephones ringing and cars careening and trains arriving and departing as the narrative moves from one scene to the next. When "sunlight, pocketed in a cloud," momentarily breaks "through the leaves of the trees outside" the aunts' sitting room, there's an echo of the remembered coins "jingling" in their father's pockets. Without explicit "he saids" or "she saids," we may not know at the start of *J R* who exactly is talking, until one of the aunts speaks to "Anne" or "Julia." But do we need to know? The pacing and counterpoint are the main elements that Gaddis communicates in his literary performance. Musicality is accomplished, in the first place, by a prodigious act of *listening* by the author, and then developed in his eventual transcription to the typewritten page of each voice, every person, and each fleeting change it was in Gaddis's "power to know" (to again cite Edith's comment to her *Times* interviewer).

As the mother and son found their separate ways toward a difficult modernity, one in business and the other in authorship, the culture around them turned increasingly toward something else—namely, *modernization*. What drove Edith to immerse herself in "Shovels and Iron Pipes" drove Gaddis also in his desire to know, and make known, the material sources of his American situation. For neither was this engagement in the materiality of corporate life necessarily a negligence of home and family. Elements of Gaddis's life and ancestry, largely unacknowledged by critics and easy for readers to miss, have their part in the overall composition. Gaddis does place extraordinary demands on readers, but these are not so much the demands of erudition or specialized knowledge, as his less sympathetic critics often suppose. They are more demands on our attention, on our ability to *listen* along with the author. When we come to appreciate how close a listener his mother was, in every letter he sent home as a boy from boarding school from the age of five onward, we can begin to appreciate the origin of Gaddis's high expectations, and high regard, for a "very small" audience that nonetheless has been lasting and global in its extent, like the work itself.

# Chapter 2

# Merricourt

—End of the day alone on that train, lights coming on in those little Connecticut towns stop and stare out at an empty street corner dry cheese sandwich charge you a dollar wouldn't even put butter on it, finally pull into that desolate station scared to get off scared to stay on [. . .] school car waiting there like a, black Reo touring car waiting there like a God damned open hearse think anybody expect to grow up . . .

(*J R* 119)

This recollection in *J R* is conveyed by the character Jack Gibbs to Amy Joubert in a cafeteria as she chaperones children on a field trip from the Long Island school where they both teach, children who in one way or another are being groomed for their own itinerant lives. Gibbs's remarks appear on page 119 of the novel; some seventy pages later, when Amy has met her seven-year-old son, the boy tells her that all he had to eat on the train to Penn Station was a sandwich that "cost a whole dollar just bread and cheese" (191). In a book that offers almost no stream of consciousness or third person perspective on a character's psychology, this single coincidence (easy to miss, like countless points and counterpoints worked into every page and each paragraph of Gaddis's fiction) can tell us all we need to understand the affection felt by a still young heiress for a man who has never outgrown the alienation of his boyhood. But if we are to enter fully into the fiction we need to be listening, with at least a portion of the attention that a mother reserves for the small revelations of her child's speech.

The fictional Gibbs's boyhood experience might coincide with Gaddis's own but we should not think that Gaddis himself was damaged by his years at the Merricourt School in Berlin, Connecticut, from age five to thirteen. (His father, following money difficulties on Wall Street, had already left the scene when the boy was three.) When asked by his daughter Sarah late in his life if he ever held any animosity toward his mother for sending him away, Gaddis answered without hesitation: "No, none at all."[1] He needed boys around him, she needed to work if she wanted her son to have the same chance in life that others in her family had until then. It's clear that a cheerful and normal youngster speaks in the early letters, all of them saved by Edith and passed intact to her son at her death (along with the family house in Massapequa, Long Island, and a summer home in Saltaire, Fire Island, that would help to steady him through the material uncertainties of a writing life). The boarding school, which was Congregational, was certainly strict, "with real rules. You made your bed. You swept the walks, you had little jobs," he told an interviewer. There, a certain "desolation" set in. "At 5 you think, this is the way it is," Gaddis recalled. "There is a sense of loneliness and desolation. You think that's what life is—and it *is!*"[2]

Berlin, Connecticut, is also the setting of the first chapter of *The Recognitions*. In the distance, Mount Lamentation will be the site of many such epiphanies of loneliness and desolation, not least for the four-year-old protagonist, Wyatt Gwyon:

> Beyond the roof of the carriage barn, clouds conspired over Mount Lamentation. He looked there with open unblinking eyes as though in that direction lay the hopeless future which already existed, of which he was already fully aware, to which he was conclusively committed. His shoulders were drawn in, as though confirmed in the habit of being cold. (19–20)

"For one dedicate in the Lord's service," as his Aunt May assured the boy he was, his clarity of predestination offered cold comfort indeed. In the novel, Wyatt was given not a nominal Auntie Ruth and Uncle John (as the directors of the school at Merricourt encouraged their charges to call them) but a real aunt and spiritual mentor, sister to a real and present (though increasingly distracted) father who is the minister of the town's church. Wyatt's mother Camilla dies young and is absent from the boy's infancy, though the woman comes to both him and his father in hallucinatory scenes, interrupting the tendency both father and son have toward the construction of theological systems. Camilla would be, like the character Esme in the Village scenes, the figure of the White Goddess, whose pursuit is central to the mythological concerns that Gaddis took over from T. S. Eliot and Robert Graves, while turning these themes explicitly (in the book's later chapters) toward a sexual exploration of the tensions between a patriarchal regime of control and a feminine, mythic disturbance.

Gaddis stayed true to this bleak (but in many ways liberating) child-hood insight in each of his books, true not just to his own experience but also to the perpetual disruptive nature of youth generally. "Desolation," yes, but also a child's sense of immediacy, the capacity to enter into the moment-by-moment flow of life as it unfolds, not trying to make narrative sense of one's situation, and not caring overmuch if the whole setup comes crashing down. That is one reason Gaddis gives (in this same interview conducted in the Hamptons in his eighth decade) for omitting standard punctuation and writing mostly in dialogue. He kept and *cultivated*, throughout his working life, a childlike impatience with the follies of grown-ups. Where others, more conventionally socialized into the company of adults, could put up with their pretenses and mostly unreflective beliefs, Gaddis wanted to "speed things up"; he wants his fiction "to be immediate, as though happening."[3] And everything that happens in his world fiction happens now, not in some hoped-for or, for that matter, dreaded future.

A "Beautiful Location" with "Home Comforts," "Parental Care," "Proper Diet," "Large Play Lawns," orchard, gardens, nature study, handcraft tutoring, character training, and "Music": the offerings at the Merricourt Country Boarding School and Home Camp,[4] unavailable today anywhere in America at any price, were within range of a rising junior executive and single mother in New York City during the Great Depression. The directors, Ruth and John Kingsbury, set up the school just a few miles from John's family home in Berlin. The couple contracted with a man to keep the grounds, a woman to take care of the cleaning, and two or three teachers to develop their courses with the same group of students from one year to the next. School would run, typically, from 8:30 to 11:30 in the morning, and then again from 2:00 to 3:00 in the afternoon. No report cards were needed; the children communicated their own progress in letters sent home every week or two, and Billy understood that these would be read, before being sent on, by "Auntie Ruth" and "Uncle John." As the boy grew, he took on more of the travel arrangements himself, duly noted his purchases (and the price), and indicated what clothes he would need (a practice that would last through his travels as a young man in the American Southwest, Central America, and Europe). It was young Billy who asked his mother for clothes and classroom necessities: "a new pair of every-day shoes?" "a Bible with large print and maps in the back?"[5] (Both arrived within a week.) If elaborations were required, there would be a P.S. or marginal note from one of the directors, along with any reminders about payments or news about the boy's health, play regime, or academic progress. (Billy keeps a regular correspondence also with one Doctor Wilson and lets his mother know when the doctor visited and gave him things like marbles and a telescope lens, and some stamps for his collection;[6] she and the Kingsburys consult one another about how to inform Billy of the doctor's passing.)

He reported each book he encountered, and also his verdict on its worth: at age twelve he thought Sherlock Holmes was "perfect."[7] "I am reading 'Arabian Nights' an its good."[8] If he went with classmates into town to see a movie, he knew his report was expected: *Their First Mistake* was "awfully funny, Hardy fed the milk to Laurel instead of the baby."[9] *The Scarlet Pimpernel* was "neat, a story of the French revolution, and this rich man (The Scarlet Pimpernel) was helping the rich people to escape from France so they wouldn't have their heads cut off by the guillotine."[10] At age eight or nine, he would read with his class *Don Quixote*,[11] Omar Khayyam's *Rubaiyat*, and "the whole poem of Hiawatha + it was 510 pages long."[12] The reading was done collectively, writing lessons were taught every morning, and since the children knew no other regimen and had no television, their literary life was considered entirely natural—though the remark about the length of the Longfellow poem does suggest a developing sense in Billy, at age ten, of his own growing aptitude: "This is the longest letter I have ever writing."[13] His first experience of fiction reading may well have been the stories that appeared in his *American Boy* magazine.

Even going to watch a cartoon, the class would schedule a trip to the local theater, and afterward he could be Popeye in *I Yam What I Yam* while a classmate was the Phantom of the Air. Winter evenings, they might all go to the "Swedish church in New Britain" and hear the choir sing.[14] Viewing and listening were inherently social, not strictly familial or individual acts, and never custodial—not the way future mothers in Edith's position, or daycare laborers, might routinely sit a child in front of a television or equip groups of children with their separate iPads. The church, or the downtown movie house, meant moving through the town, not sitting at home or being transported in a parent's car to a self-contained entertainment or caregiving facility. And imagine the sense of belonging, of at-homeness in the larger world when, on a class excursion to the city, the boy could attend *The Little Minister* at Radio City and see his "Uncle Jan play too."[15] The family "band camp," founded by his grandfather and great-uncles, extended into the larger world, as did the "boarding school and home camp" in rural Connecticut. There was never anything provincial, or impersonal, in the development of his childhood imagination and his sense of belonging. He did indeed find himself alone at train stations, but once when that happened he would listen to the men at the station talking, and he'd read his copy of the *American Boy* until Granga and his uncle Bob "came after a while and got me."[16] Feelings of freedom and connections larger than the nuclear family were instilled in practice, not in abstract phrases about "family values" that would become increasingly strident as the freedoms and allowed contacts for children in America became legally circumscribed, and a child left alone even briefly could be cause for state intervention.

"We went," with the scoutmaster Mr. Woodruff, "to Mt Lamintation. When we got there every body tried to make a fire to pass the fire-building test. We couldn't use paper only wood (twigs, chips, etc) but we made them and passed."

The world away from home and school was there waiting, to receive him in an imagined future. As he reported to his grandmother: "We went to a place where they did 10 neat magic tricks—and the man told me what I was going to be when I was a big man. He said I would either be an orator, lawyer, or some kind of a talker. We had neat fun."[17] If he was allowed to handle "some old muskets brought down from Miss Fiske's house," given him by a Massasoit Indian chief on Thanksgiving, he did not need to fear that either his mother or his grandmother would be unduly concerned.

As he turned eight, he was "making diaries" and scrapbooks filled with "lots of things," learning about Greek gods, making an "airplane book," and also keeping "a book to tell the books that I have read and the names of the books that I have up stares [. . .] so many I have to put some outside the desk."[18] He notices when his mother writes to him in pencil, and in a letter to his great-grandfather he mentions that (for his part) he likes his "good Parker pen."[19] It is an event worth reporting, when "Uncle John" returns from Albany with an Underwood typewriter, which the boys take turns using for letters home.[20] A few years later, he would be given use of his mother's new typewriter for letters to his grandparents, and he used the machine also during vacations to impress school friends. By the age of eleven, he was typing on his own stationery, under the letterhead "William T. Gaddis. Jr. Massapequa Long Island."[21]

When he read the New York papers from his Connecticut outpost (or was given them perhaps by the school directors), he might find a poem by one of his mother's acquaintances: "Is Mr. Keatings first name Paul? If it is here is a poem I found in the New York Tribune, for Sunday."[22] In this same letter, we see Billy at age twelve or thirteen settling into a characteristic narrative style, moving from a newfound personal and

material interest (stamp-collecting, the topic of Keating's poem), carrying the interest to encyclopedic lengths, and following the topic daily in
newspapers only to then observe the entire amassing project subverting
itself by being subjected to a set of inhuman technological and bureau-
cratic absurdities: "Dave got his stamps from Little America. Have you
been reading about it in the newspaper? Well, there was a man down in
Little America, stamping all the letters by hand. There were 7000 letters,
and he never would have gotten done, so they sent a stamping machine
down to him. The ink froze, and the man could[n't] run the machine, so
they sent a man down to show him how. When the man got down there,
the other man had found out how, but had been stamping the wrong
dates on the letters, they thawed out the ink, and finished it. Daves came
out all right."

Solitary though he might be, and focused, he was never lonely, doing
such work: his classmate Dave, he knew, was there all the while in his
own room, at another desk doing something similar. His mother, back in
Manhattan, was likely to be reading the same newspapers, and (increasingly as he grew older) many of the same books.

If he'd been given an assignment—to write the life of Washington, for
example—his mother would be notified of his progress along the way
to the essay's submission on 25 April and his receipt of the Merricourt
certificate of completion on the 28th.[23] He may have learned this way to
trust: not everybody, and certainly not anybody outside his small circle of
classmates, teachers, and friends in town, but these he certainly *did* trust.
The boy knew for example that "Auntie Ruth" and "Uncle John" Kingsbury would conduct his writing from his small desk in Merricourt to its
intended destination (Edith in New York, his "Granga" and grandfather
in Indiana). Once received, his accounts of his own everyday life would be
read, he knew, with as much care as he put into their composition.

Not a bit of the sadness, recollected in adulthood, appears in the 120
extant letters that Billy wrote during his Merricourt years. To his mother
and grandmother, he was all about clothes and postage stamps; parts he
took on in plays; class excursions to nearby towns, museums, and farms;
travel arrangements; a magic trick he's learned; his pride in the tuck-in
shirts the women sent to him. To his great-grandfather, he wrote about
the goggles he got for skiing; his ride on a toboggan; games of football;
gymnastics; mapmaking; and his class trip to see "a sham battle in Hart-
ford."[24] The bleakness of the town railway station at night, recalled by
Gibbs in *J R* (and cited in the epigraph to this chapter), is not typical of
the life in rural New England in the 1920s, where Billy could observe, on
occasion, the appearance on the front lawn of two wild pheasants,[25] an

ostrich egg brought in by one of the teachers,[26] or "a big big turtle on the wharf" in Cape Cod.[27] These were as much a part of the school curriculum as the reading, "writing lessons every morning,"[28] language study, and arithmetic that his teachers and the directors set at a pace conducive to the boys' interest and activity, not to a standard imposed by a state or a corporate concern. And this, too, the disciplined but flexible course of study, inaugurated his lifetime regime in which he never forced his writing, but instead allowed the work to develop at its own pace in the confidence that the world (and not his hard work or imagination alone) would bring to him anything he needed for a project's completion.

As we shall see, Gaddis in later life regarded his early schooling—under teachers who administered grades but never emphasized competitiveness—as providing a firm foundation for later striving not to exceed others but to question them, and in this way to "embrace change" rather than seek certainties in the form of "entrenched beliefs and material interests."[29]

The Kingsburys were trusted by Edith, and she in turn was treated as a valued associate: "We sometimes refer to you, as being a longtime friend to Merricourt," Ruth wrote (in a handwritten note attached to one of Billy's letters[30]). And Edith, evidently, trusted the Kingsburys enough to know that visits from the boy's father would be carefully monitored. Her policy, evidently, of keeping her ex-husband out of her boy's life was known and would be discreetly enforced:

Dear Mrs. Gaddis—

I don't know how much you have heard about Mr G's visit. He came in a car from Middletown, Ct with friends. I did not meet him but saw him + Mr. K. standing in the playroom watching three boys who were playing there—among them B. People come + go here so much that no particular attention was paid to him. One or two asked who he was, + I said it was someone to see the place or Uncle John.

I think he said Billy was a fat baby. Anyway, he was surprised to see him tall + thin. Afterwards they went out + waited around where Wilson + Uncle J had been cutting a branch from a tree. He said he would like to send B. a present which he did at Easter time. It came to Uncle John and I don't think B. even asked who sent it. It contained a soft rabbit and an auto.[31]

Gaddis wouldn't meet his father until his mid-twenties, and had little contact with him after that. In letters to his mother and to his wife Pat in the 1950s, he will mention gifts received, given at holidays or birthdays. Apart from a certificate of the man's death in 1965, nothing concerning William Thomas Gaddis Sr. was saved by the son who never, not after that one time at the age of eleven, went by "Junior," though the fatherless protagonist of his second novel, eleven-year-old J R Vansant, carries that designation in his initials. ("The Award goes to Junior!" announced a late-arriving Mary McCarthy when *J R* was up for the National Book Award; her deciding verdict, among otherwise split judges, carried the day despite her never noticing that J R was the boy's name.[32]) For a while, when at Harvard (and unsure of his social location among the clubs and the cavorting), Gaddis took on a middle name of his own choosing, "Tithonus," from Tennyson's poem of that title. His first mention of his father in his letters indicates that the boy and his mother never, ever, discussed the man who had been living, all this time, in Manhattan or within a few miles of the city. Gaddis was age nineteen, had been to Harvard already for a semester and was staying near Tucson when he raised the topic in a letter, hesitantly:

> And then as you say this slightly ironic setup—about my father. But I suppose we shall do just what might be expected and wait . . . things always do take care of them selves, and as "most of our troubles never happen," by the same token plans and worries after make an unexpected outcome that much harder to meet. As you said it has not been a great emotional problem for me, tho it does seem queer; you see I still feel a little like I must have when I said "I have no father; I never had a father!," and since things have been as they have, I have *never* really missed one—honestly—and only now does it seem queer to me. All I know of fathers I have seen in other families, and in reading, and somehow thru the deep realization I have gained of their importance; of father-and-son relations; and families: not just petty little groups, but *generations*—a *name* and honor and all that goes with it—this *feeling* that I have gained from other channels without ever having missed its actual presence: somehow these are the only ties I feel I have with him. You understand, not so much personal feelings, but the sort of feeling that I feel must exist between the father and son of a family as fine and as able as I feel the name of Gaddis to represent; something far above such stuff as the *Good Will Hour* thrives on.[33]

What he was able, haltingly, to articulate only then, at age nineteen, and what his residence at Harvard made him feel, was the absence not so much of a father as a *paternity*. His mother had helped to ensure in him a feeling of pride and heritage in her side of the family, the Williamses and the Ways and their accomplishments in music, education, and entrepreneurial business. The paternal side would need to be *invented*, based on what he will have seen in "other families, and in reading." He acknowledges the "importance; of father-and-son relations; and families," as though these were titles in a Harvard course in world literature, works by Turgenev or Tolstoy that might be studied but not lived, and not regretted by their absence in his own life. Families, for Bill Gaddis at age nineteen, were "not just petty little groups but *generations*," and this generational development that goes on independently of present fathers and family origins would become central to his own developing vision of an abstract "family" of concerns and corporations that was becoming the reality of his own time and American circumstance. The Merricourt school was a business, after all, and its separation from young Billy's organic family, gentle as it was, set the stage for the imagination of the J R Family of Companies that thrive when actual families are increasingly broken, and dispersed.

The notion of an absent father but active paternity, expressed at the age of nineteen to his mother, was a refinement on a childhood fantasy that Gaddis gives to the character Otto Pivner in *The Recognitions*, his eventual self-parody in fiction:

> As a child, Otto had had a phantasy which, in all of the childish good faith which designs such convictions, he passed for fact to himself and his friends. At about the time he learned that he had a father, or should have one, Albert, King of the Belgians, was killed mountain-climbing. It was not difficult to relate the two: he told that his father had been killed mountain-climbing, and so took upon himself the peculiar mantle of a prince. (507)

Otto has come to an upscale hotel in midtown Manhattan in expectation of meeting his father there for the first time in his life, but through a vaudevillian series of mishaps he will instead find himself at the restaurant sitting across from the counterfeiter Frank Sinisterra. His actual father, Mr. Pivner, wearing a green wool muffler for recognition, has in the meantime lost consciousness at the hotel entrance, having neglected his insulin injection during the excitement of Christmas and his important meeting. Unseen by Otto, Pivner is carried out by the doormen. And a few minutes later, in the company of Sinisterra, Otto loses any childhood notion of "Albert, King of the Belgians, careening gloriously down among the crevices of rock, gone, never to reappear and interrupt legends offered about him, to suffer translation from the fiction of selective memories to the betrayal of living reality" (515).

With characteristic excess, Gaddis had let the metaphor play out in Otto's inebriated imagination while he was at the bar waiting, flirting occasionally with the woman next to him, and as the appointed time passes, flirting also with the idea of just leaving (except that by now he has run up a sizable tab and he's hoping to have from his father a holiday gift that will cover it). Before he misrecognizes Sinisterra (who entered the hotel wearing that selfsame green scarf), Otto flirted also with the prospect of a more dignified paternity. He had noticed down the bar a well-dressed man "of better than middle age" whom he imagines could be his father: "His suit was flannel, too light for the season, but bearing other seasons in other lands, as though it were spring now, in London, and he had stepped in from Saint James's Street for a drink; [. . .] (London and royalty were close in Otto's mind)" (507). Otto looks for resemblances, finds them in the "visage of monarchy," and for a time he contemplates tossing out the wool muffler that his father had sent as a gift and would use, on his side, to identify Otto. But Otto's attention is drawn elsewhere: he "looked and found resemblance [in the man at the bar]. About the eyes, was it? the bridge of the nose? Clearer correspondence than the device hung from his own neck, wool proclamation of plebeian kinship, green signal of the multitude, its verdant undiscriminating growth" (507–8).

Unspoken but understood (by those on both sides, the patrician and the plebeian) is the distinction between a descendant of first settlers and an immigrant;[34] the latter, mostly, are relegated to comic roles in the early fiction: another time in the Village, when he encounters Sinisterra's son Chaby, Otto has the impression he's the sort who would clean his fingernails with a fork tine; the Caribbean prince and current butler Fuller, with a full set of gold teeth, is another vaudevillian figure presented sympathetically in the novel but respected primarily for an unlikely childlike wonder at the events unfolding in the Upper East Side world of his masters. (It is unclear, at the time he was writing *The Recognitions*, how well Gaddis himself knew this world.) In later life, Gaddis would maintain an ironic distance from immigrant culture even when he was living in upper Manhattan with the daughter of a Russian-Jewish founder of a pickled herring fortune, Muriel Oxenberg Murphy. Muriel sometimes felt that Gaddis associated successful immigrants with "cheats and crooks" (*E* 95), though her perception is hard to square with Gaddis's friendship with Saul Steinberg during the years that Muriel and Gaddis were together.

A more likely characterization of Gaddis's racial attitudes at the time, when he was Otto's age, can be gathered from one of the assignments he undertook in Paris when working for UNESCO. In an unpublished short story, Gaddis came up with a character, Ernest, who also worked at UNESCO and who (much like Gaddis) "hoped one day to write an earth-shaking work of some sort, he could not decide which, for it was always a play when he worked at a novel, or poetry when he worked at a play."[35] When it comes to race relations, the Ministry's "most important policy" is to maintain "a universal effort to offend no one," which Ernest thwarts by taking a group of visiting Islamic delegates to see *The Lost Weekend* at the cinema, and he supposes (ironically) that "once whole-hearted understanding is reached over fish, singing and dancing, and Assur Nassirpal, such embarrassing subjects as religion, economic rights, lebensraum, social exploitation, and racial prejudices based on centuries of experience will follow." It is the anodyne, corporate attitude toward real cultural difference (and an avoidance of any acknowledgment of economic and social differences) that concerns Gaddis primarily in this unpublished story, and however he may have felt about "immigrants," in his youth and in later life, we can confidently say that his refusal of the UNESCO directive to "offend nobody" persisted, and deepened, as he came to maturity as a writer.

As for Otto, any doubts he may have had in the restaurant about the decidedly "plebeian" Sinisterra are dispelled when the ersatz father offers a gift of $5,000 in twenty-dollar denominations. The counterfeiter, disguised in a black wig and with chemical drops to alter his eye coloring, had assumed Otto was "the pusher" sent by the organization that would disseminate the fake bills, "the queer" as Sinisterra's criminal colleagues call it. A pursuit ensues across Manhattan and into the bars of Greenwich Village, where Otto goes to show off his newfound wealth (which he claims to have earned by selling a play). At one point, Otto will keep the counterfeit cash between his legs, for safekeeping. The dissemination of forgeries that occurs on each of the nearly one thousand pages of this largely autobiographical first novel, and the "queering" of value that pervades Gaddis's lifework, can be said to originate in the Merricourt boy's unspoken wonder at the absence of his own father; and also in the young man's search for a "paternity" larger than what he could observe in his father, who was listed in a 1940 census registration as a "wage or salary worker in private work," or his father's father, who was a machinist married to a German immigrant.

Gaddis needed the fictions, arguably, to explain that paternal lack and to invent an alternative prehistory for his own life. The insecurity ran deep however and would remain with him throughout his life. It can account in part for the studied superiority in mixed company and even the obsessive devotion to "getting it right" in his work. These are all characteristics that were necessary, in Muriel's view, for "the Scarlet Pimpernel of [American] letters" to feel himself to be "head and shoulders above" people who could have made their fortune, like the sinister businessman Sinisterra, by cheating (E 60, 95). The would-be aristocrat, imagined by the child who went to see *The Scarlett Pimpernel* with his Merricourt class and rehearsed by Gaddis in his self-portrayal in Otto, persisted in ways he could not have fully recognized in himself—in the "slightly ironic" (L 25) distances between the ordinary life and the high aesthetic of his first novel, and in the psychic distances that, if Muriel's recollections are credited, were felt even by those who knew him well and intimately half a century on.

Certainly, an aristocratic aura was conveyed to one of his closest friends, Martin Dworkin, whom Gaddis met in New York when applying for a job with the United States Information Service. In the early 1950s, in the full flush of the downtown scene and with his own plans for a literary career, Gaddis appeared at Dworkin's office with a confidence he would never show so openly after the commercial failure of *The Recognitions*. He came to the interview dressed in "a white linen suit, flower in his lapel and gold watch chain across his vest"[36]—the very outfit worn by the fictional Otto. Gaddis struck Dworkin, the more he got to know him, as essentially an "aristocrat" in temperament and likely in his political outlook. Dworkin and another lifelong friend, Mike Gladstone (whom Gaddis knew at Harvard), both recall the way Gaddis bristled and quit the Harvard Club "in a dudgeon" when he was presented with a bill for his dues.[37]

The psychic scars of his formative years certainly contributed to his adult demeanor and his motivations as an imaginative writer. The patrician "phantasy" (R 507), with its self-consciously archaic spelling, conveys the full confusion of a childhood that was not merely fatherless but one where his father was never mentioned. And this silence, a policy set by Edith and obeyed by the Merricourt schoolmasters, affected the boy deeply and had become internalized by Gaddis, in young adulthood, as a determination to *create* that paternity, in his person and in his literary work. Near the end of his career, Gaddis in his 1994 novel *A Frolic of His Own* would present the ninety-seven-year-old Judge Crease as having cultivated a personal absence precisely by devoting himself to *language*, in published writings that outlast him. Like every patrician father in Gaddis's oeuvre, Crease never physically appears in the novel; but several of his opinions are presented and parts of his will, which stipulates his immediate cremation to avoid public fanfare or familial gathering. Crease's stepdaughter in the novel, Christina, who shares with Muriel a social knowingness and unforgiving view of human nature and creative ambition, explodes when her lawyer husband expresses admiration for the man:

> —Harry he never spared anyone a thing in his life! He was the most, one of the most selfish men who ever lived, the law was the only thing that was alive for him people were just its pawns [. . .]. Father was always coldblooded right to the end ordering up this cremation without even a fare-thee-well? (487)

The cold-blooded ideal denounced by Christina and a cause of much psychic suffering in Crease's son Oscar was nonetheless upheld consistently by Gaddis as an ideal for authorship, at once aristocratic in its removal from petty conflicts and democratic in its embrace of written language as a resource available to, if not mastered by, all.[38]

A legal opinion is usually read only by lawyers and judicial colleagues; that is a large enough audience when one's language is operative, and in this too Gaddis would find a parallel for his own view of literature as primarily a conversation among similar minds, "ever the same" though communicating across centuries.[39] Law, in ways more traceable than literature, nonetheless determines lives and thoughts of those who never have read a legal opinion: the courtroom decisions and corporate contexts (not least the nineteenth-century rulings that granted a fictive but consequential personhood to corporations), shape our lives in ways that are deeper than we know. And this, too, would be Gaddis's signature theme in his fictions, which are not so much about corporations and states and religions as about the fictions on which they are built, in common with works of literature.

Though Gaddis like his characters had his share of psychic suffering in childhood, the Merricourt experience, homogeneous and largely insulated from cultural outsiders, cannot be considered negative on balance. His school days left the boy with more than an inclination toward morbid fantasies and selective memories later to be betrayed by reality. What Gaddis also took from his boyhood was a deep trust in the dedicated service of adults who, even if they were not his real "uncle" and "aunt," would attend and respond to him. Through the gentle regimen of letter-writing imposed by the school, the boy also came to trust that his efforts, detailed, generous, and carefully presented, would be read and received with love by the one immediate family member he knew in reality. That long-lasting, trusting relationship, which made bearable the distance between the boy and his mother, would be carried forward to an unbreakable trust between the author and his audience—a trust strong enough for him to reveal in his books his own youthful fantasies and authorial pretensions, and strong enough to withstand, and make fun of, the misreading of reviewers, miscalculations and misstatements of (mostly immigrant!) publishers, and disappointments in book sales. As his religious faith, never intense, waned with his childhood experience, he would keep that unquestioning faith in himself and in the existence of an attentive audience. The trust, cultivated in the playgrounds, desks, and boarding rooms of Merricourt, would support him over an extended period of university studies, travel in the Americas and Europe, and eventually two years of semi-seclusion in his native New York when he converted his experiences into the final draft of his first novel.

Chapter 3

# All Tomorrow's Parties: The Route to *The Recognitions*

Now informality is one thing; but a hand reaching into one's breast pocket for a cigarette while its owner spits on the floor—as I say, am I still a Merricourt boy?

William Gaddis in Spain, 1949

In his Long Island youth and early manhood, nobody would have called Gaddis "encased," and few whom he knew well later in life would find him so "thoroughly . . . unreachable" as would Muriel Oxenburg Murphy, who lived with him in the 1980s and early nineties (*E* 95).[1] Yet Gaddis understood already, once he began a period of youthful travels mostly on his own, the effect his early worldly separation from hometown and family might have had on him, enough that he could ask of himself (in a letter to his mother, whom he knew as well as himself), if he were not to be, always, "the miserable ingrate? the shy boy with boarding-school manners and New England shyness? [. . .] am I still a Merricourt boy?"[2]

The occasion of this early reflection, a foreign man's invasion of his person, not just his privacy, might suggest what was at stake for a young man who was so keen to prove himself by getting out into the world he'd been encouraged so richly to imagine (in school, in books and children's magazines, and in movies that were seen rarely enough to make an impact, every month or two in excursions with classmates to theaters, not daily in isolation, and not with earphones cutting one off from any chance of sociality, so that in Gaddis's youthful experience the aesthetic could be assumed to be convivial, not entirely personal). Physical weakness and a "rapid pulse" in his teenage years may have limited his mobility.[3] At 5'7" and 140 pounds, Bill Gaddis was small in stature, bone-thin and only slightly

muscled, never much of a fighter though enough friends from enough different periods in his life recall a certain truculence: even in adulthood, he
might be carrying on what he thought was a friendly barroom conversation with a stranger at Clarke's on Third Avenue—and then be shocked
to hear (as word made it round to a party he'd gone to later) that the guy
had referred to him as "that queer." Harrison Kinney, Gaddis's friend at
the time (and to the end of his life) recounts that "William immediately
returned to the bar, took his place alongside the stranger, bought a drink
and threw it in his face. The bouncer grabbed him by the collar and the
seat of the pants and literally threw him on to the sidewalk."[4]

Arvid Friberg, the son of a Farmingdale High School friend of Gaddis's, recalls similar incidents—many of them also involving alcohol: "Oh
I . . . remember my father talking about going to the bars with Bill before
and after the war and that he would get some drinks and pick a fight
with the biggest guy in the shop. He would not even get a punch in and
it would be all over but he would continue to get up and try to fight.
Eventually my father would have to pick him up unconscious or not and
carry him to the car."[5] The fun and games would be no less boisterous
into the 1960s, in the bars of New York when Arvid's grandfather would
sing with Ethel Merman, then at the height of her Broadway fame. "My
Grandfather played piano for her when she was training her voice," Arvid
recalls.[6] Back home in Massapequa, when Arvid was six or seven (around
1963, he later clarified), he watched as "a drunk Bill came to the house
with a drunk Ethel. I sat on Bill's lap and smelled what I know was Scotch
as I had already sampled everything in our liquor cabinet. . . . She sang
there is no biz but show biz for a couple of stanzas. . . . Bill told me
never to be a writer of any sort. He talked about working on the Panama
Canal. I later went through the canal and took a picture of the building
he described."[7]

Gaddis's high school friend, also named Arvid, had tried heroin in his
youth and later became an addict after service in the war. The younger
Arvid would not have said that either of them, Bill or his father, was
"really wild. What do you think most kids do in high school. Taking a
couple of shots of liquor and then trying to beat up the biggest guy is
a sign of some other problem and not alcoholism or being wild." The
younger Arvid's boyhood memory rings true. Fighting among boys was
not policed then the way it is now in American high schools and neighborhoods. Drink and drugs had neither the blaring popularity of the
sixties, nor the legalistic suppression (and a heightened market-oriented
control on personal intake and social gathering) that got under way with
the Reagan administration's "war on drugs" in the 1980s. In Gaddis's

time, people could more or less work it out for themselves, their tolerance or measured participation in drinking, smoking, and harder currencies. Gaddis for his part did seem to distance himself when his friends' usage got out of hand. As Arvid Friberg recalls, "Bill probably did not hang out with my father much [in the sixties] because of my mom and my father's drug addiction suffered by heroin withdrawal during the war."[8] One's affiliations, and distances, however, had to be negotiated day by day and night by night in the bars and gathering places, and that held also for one's sexual identifications: what Gaddis was up to in the bars and backstreets of Massapequa and Farmingdale was not all that different from what Hemingway was demonstrating worldwide (arm wrestling with Castro and so forth), or what returning World War II vets (Mailer notably) would soon be doing in Manhattan parties and writing about in papers and journals with an international circulation.

The difference of course is that Gaddis didn't have the physical stature for fighting and (unlike his more media-savvy literary predecessors), he never broadcast his personal experiences—except through his character Otto, and then only indirectly in the scenes from Central America:

> He stood, stretched as though at ease, yawned a feigned yawn. Jocularly, man-to-man, he said, —Good night, Jesse. I don't want to seem to throw you out, but . . .
> —Throw me out! Why rabbit you couldn't throw me . . . you just try, if you want me to kick you from one end of this room to the other. Throw me out, rabbit, that's a good one . . ." (*R* 158)

From treatments in fiction, one would not have imagined that Gaddis himself, in life, would have tried the patience of such men, though evidently he did so. And enjoyed the novelty, and mild homosociality of encounters with working-class men on ranches and ships: "I did get a roommate in Panama," Gaddis wrote home from Los Angeles after passing through the Panama Canal:

> —his name was "Davey" Abad, a native Panamanian who was light weight (I think) boxing champion of the world! He was really quite a character—sort of genial, sloppy, tough, and paunchy, about 34, and his only faults that I think of now were really ripping nightmares he would get and bounce around in the top bunk and yell out in Spanish until I thot it might be unsafe to room with him; one night he was really going and kicked the light right off the ceiling! —I used to have to light a match when I came in at night and say, "It's me, your room

mate, Davey—" and be ready to duck. They subsided however and
we got along quite well. Then he used to come into the dining salon
patting a large tan stomach, usually exposed by a shirt with one but-
ton, and one night Ross [his traveling companion] had a miserable
time trying to eat cherries while Davey sat slapping his bare stomach
after supper.[9]

Not a word, in the letters that survive, indicates the slightest family
concern with violence, drugs, or sexual activity, though of course his
mother was close by, watching over him at home during the high school
years and few letters would have been exchanged then. When the letters do pick up (after he went up to Harvard), they are characteristically
open, congenial, and often confessional. There are also things concerning
women in his life and continued heavy drinking that are either elided or
go unmentioned, which indicates that neither he, nor Edith, put all that
much importance on his boyhood excesses.

The grave illness that caused him to miss a year of his Long Island
schooling (more on which later) had "some after effects of the 'cure'"
that continued into his college years[10]—so much so that he would interrupt his studies after less than a semester at Harvard to travel west and
take on salutary work on ranches and aboard commercial and freight
vessels. No less was his own desire to man up, and his experience boarding and working on a ranch in Cortaro, Arizona ("riding every day for
two or three hours and it is wonderful"[11]), gave him a glimpse of what
was possible. Though the Beat Generation was not yet named, he also
included in his regime "over 500 miles of hitch hiking,"[12] though his
report of the experience is sent from one of the posh Rosslyn Hotels
in downtown Los Angeles. "I 'cheated' once," he confides to his mother,
"took a bus from L.A. to Indio. I never could have gotten a ride out
of L.A."[13]

Two decades before the famed television series *Route 66*, he was often
taking road trips with his pals Ross Bryne (to Yuma) and Bill Davison
(to Mexico): that later trip, in a convertible Cord Auburn, no less, ran
aground when the "collector's car" became so battered it had to be ditched
at the Mexican border.[14] There were stints working, such as the 4 p.m.
to midnight shift on a "quarter boat [. . .] tied up here on the Mississippi
east bank across from St Louis."[15] He would even have a night when he
was arrested and held in a "calabozo" along with "a couple of cowboys in
town" for the "Frontier Days" celebration, which he confessed lightheart-
edly in a letter home.[16] But there was never a time, however many weeks
or months he would be out on his own, when he could not be assured of

support if needed, or the comforts of a well-appointed hotel such as the one in St. Louis, "with bed! and tub! and easy chair! And tonight I go out and sink my teeth into a *thick juicy red* steak—haven't had any red meat since I started! . . . And say but these dress pants feel good after a month and a half of those heavy work pants!"[17]

It was more than tourism or concerns about health that compelled his exertions in the American Midwest, as in Europe; and it was also something more than personal vanity or a fetish for commodities that drew him to some of the local products: "As for wanting anything else—well there are things down here [in Cortaro, Arizona] that make me froth just to look at them! — belts such as I never dreamed of—rings—*beautiful* silver and leather work—but I figure I don't need any of it now and will let it go until I've been around a bit more and seen more of these things that I've always known *must* exist *somewhere!*"[18] The idea that an original must exist, independently of him and (by extension) his familiar New York and Cambridge locales, had a hold on his imagination a full decade before he would make the recognition of originality the theme of his first novel—that, and the engagement with something radically *other*, what could be witnessed but never fully joined precisely because it *is* other.

His travels in the American Southwest certainly distinguished him among his Harvard classmates and, later, his Village compatriots (and just as often, the same friends would be met as European expatriates: "the perpetual RITZ, or Greenwich Village, anywhere one goes"[19]). He wasn't kidding when he wrote home about the psychic distance he felt from the land of his birth, even as he participated in the transcontinental party that prosperous Americans could enjoy among the spoils of the recent World War. After his first extended stay abroad, for example, he resolves "to keep away from America. Except for New York and Long Island, but America I have such pity for, fury at, why are Americans so awful, their voices, everything. You can't imagine Pedro Miguel, what the Americans have done in 'civilising' this strip called Canal Zone, how they have *sterilized* it."[20] Gaddis's boyhood illness, his inability to join with men of his generation in the war, and his first taste of freedom during his travel within the United States—each could keep him apart from the normal lives, and also the pretensions, of his generation. Like so much that he knew as a boy out in the Connecticut woods and farmlands, his protracted illness and his time working in the American West could be kept to himself—as experiences (and projections of possible futures) he knew few of his Harvard peers or uptown companions could have had, or could have empathized with as other than exotic, or provincial.

"—I didn't know people ran off to banana plantations any more," says Herschel in *The Recognitions*, on meeting up with Otto newly arrived from Panama:

> —No, don't go to a banana plantation, baby. It's old hat.
> —Herschel, silly. He's just come back.
> —All the more reason. What are you wearing that thing for? (174)

We can assume that Otto's blundering appearance (with a golden mustache, and an arm in a sling that everyone can tell is fake) was one that Gaddis himself would not have attempted and if he did, then kudos to Gaddis for rendering his own youthful vanity in fiction.[21] His experiments with facial hair in any case were "hopeful" at best, as he told Edith, but it is safe to assume that he learned to keep these things to himself. Or never needed to "learn" discretion since the tendency toward secrecy is also central to his formative vision of the artist, along with a spirituality that is less clear but equally present. This conflation of aesthetic secrecy and a secret conviction "that he was damned" is detailed in the account of Wyatt's boyhood growing up under the tutelage of his Aunt May, and the spiritual model of his increasingly distant and aloof Reverend father.

> He made drawings in secret, and kept them hidden, terrified with guilty amazement as forms took shape under his pencil. He wrapped some in a newspaper and buried them behind the carriage barn, more convinced, as those years passed, and his talent blossomed and flourished with the luxuriance of the green bay tree, that he was damned. Once, digging back there, he came upon the rotted remains of the bird he had killed that day he had burst into tears at Aunt May's conjectural challenge and punishment, the vivid details of the Synod of Dort: even that evening he had gone to his father's study to try to confess it, for it had, after all, been an accident (he had thrown a stone at the wren, and could not believe it when he hit it square, and picked it up dead). But when there was no answer to his first faint tapping on the study door, he retreated. (34–35)

The figure of the father "absenting himself" in all of Gaddis's novels is "akin to that talent of the Lord," and Gwyon is for his son "about as unattainable." The same is true of Liz and Billy's father in *Carpenter's Gothic*, who left their estate in total disorder; it is true of Judge Crease, father of failed author Oscar and stepfather of Christina; it is true of

Edward Bast's father James in *J R*, who throughout that novel is off in Europe accepting an award for his lifetime musical achievement, one that Bast wishes to emulate. It is no accident that Bast and Wyatt and Oscar (and Liz in her own, equally tentative efforts at creative writing), turn to the arts as a way of compensating for the paternal absence, which was no less important than his childhood illness to Gaddis's own formation. The depiction of Wyatt's sudden, unexplained, and protracted illness is at once a naturalistic portrayal, and an expansion to the medical profession of the theme of the absent, hapless authority (one that extends throughout Gaddis's work from fathers to doctors to every emerging techno-scientific profession in the United States):

> Wyatt was taken with a fever which burned him down to seventy-nine pounds. In this refined state he was exhibited to medical students in the amphitheater of a highly endowed hospital. They found it a very interesting case, and said so. In fact they said very little else. Physicians, technicians, and internes X-rayed the boy from every possible angle, injected his arms with a new disease they believed they could cure, took blood by the bottleful from one arm to investigate, and poured the blood of six other people into the other. They collected about his bed and pounded him, tapped his chest, thrust with furious hands for his liver, pumped his stomach with a lead-weighted tube, kneaded his groin, palped his spleen, and recorded the defiant beats of his heart with electric machinery. (41–42)

A photo taken during this period (around 1936) shows young Billy lying on a small hospital bed that is held aloft by two dark-suited men, against the background of a grey cloudy sky above his two-story Massapequa home. As Gaddis would recall in 1986, the two-year-long illness "of what was at last resignedly diagnosed as a 'tropical fever of unknown origin' (I'd never been in the tropics)" may have produced "the most voluminous case history in New York Hospital." He says he was "finally sent home without prospects when I demanded that my dog be brought in for a visit; after which things gradually mended with no more explanation than what it was all about in the first place. Lord, when I remember those hospital days waking bright as a penny sitting bolt upright learning/practicing Old English lettering doing Do Not Disturb signs for the nurses [. . .] and by evening a temperature of around 103° & pains generally not earned until age 80. . . ."[22]

He would practice archaic lettering and calligraphy throughout his life. The dog is shown also, at the front of the photo.

Attending Wyatt in Gaddis's narrative account of the illness is one "Dr Fell, with a scalpel in his hand and a gleam in his eye seldom permitted at large in civilized society," a gleam that recalls (to Wyatt's Reverend father) the gleam in the eyes "of a Plains Indian medicine man" (42). Composing this recollection a decade later in *The Recognitions*, Gaddis must have regarded all of the doctors in attendance then, and later at Harvard, through the rhythms and rhymes of a seventeenth-century squib by Tom Brown:

> I do not love thee, Doctor Fell.
> The reason why I cannot tell.
> But this I know, and know full well
> I do not love thee, Doctor Fell.

If the choice is between the professional doctor "of unconscionable talents and insatiable curiosity" (42) and the medicine man, Gaddis would side with the latter even if that became an absurd solution to a real cultural bifurcation, between the mythic and traditional on one side (being worked through as modern poetry by Gaddis's hero, T. S. Eliot), and, on the other, an acceleration and expansion to all professions of a managerial, progressive technological culture. Though he would over time acquaint himself with the technical details behind the contemporary rise of a corporate, cybernetic world, his sympathies throughout his Harvard years and his subsequent self-education would fall clearly with myth, and its foundational recognition that we are each of us alone in the face of death, and therefore only long-standing structures give a sense of human continuity over time and throughout the social sphere. What, then, to do when confronting death directly? Taking a leaf from Sir James George Frazer's monumental study of religion and magic, *The Golden Bough* (a page that is literally cited in *The Recognitions* [49]), the Reverend Gwyon performs a sacrifice of the Barbary ape that he'd brought back to his Connecticut household from Spain. The ritual, and the entire structure of mythic, religious, and traditional beliefs it includes, are presented in this first novel with more seriousness than absurdity, and they are anyway no more troublesome to the child Wyatt, over a stormy night, than all the endless treatments for an illness that the doctors can neither name nor cure: they are technicians and businessmen, not healers.

Yet despite his sympathy he could not quite bring himself to believe in "the myth—tradition" that had so influenced him in Frazer, Eliot, and Robert Graves:

(Lord how I miss New York!—You see what I am occupied with now is this whole business of the myth—tradition—where one belongs. And while disciplining myself to behave according as my intellect teaches me—that we *are* alone, and all of these vanities and seekings (the church, a wife, father etc.) are seeking for some myth by the use of which we can escape the truth of aloneness. Poor Bernie, he won't accept it, nor Jake that more successfully. But that is the whole idea (message) of my novel. [. . .] I am afraid my letters are getting worse, also handwriting.[23]

The closing parenthesis is missing in the original, and he did not bother to clean up his syntax or poor lettering. Whether as a result of drink or tiredness, whenever he would let his discipline on the page lapse for even a moment, he knew what was happening. Though it could of course be no more than an accidental switch of subject, we might also remark how, when the myth/science dichotomy becomes too much to resolve, Gaddis turns his attention, again, to the materiality of his own writing—just as he had calmed his childhood delirium with the practice of hand lettering. Through lettering, too, if not through personal contact with his father and namesake, he might better imagine participation in a paternity that had gone missing in his life: "P. S. How do you like the new 'G' in Gaddis in the envelope? I think it's better."[24]

The illness would not leave him entirely or allow him to participate fully in the life of the university, or publicly in the life of the nation during wartime: "Tried to get into Merchant Marine," he tells his mother: "couldn't because of albumin."[25] This was not his only try at governmental or military service, nor was it the first time that illness kept him apart from his generation. During one spell for example in the Harvard infirmary, whose doctors could define his illness no better than those in New York or Massapequa, he would sit in his hospital room listening to the cheers and cries on the radio from the game across campus: "Harvard just made a touchdown and the stands are going crazy—me too only for a different reason—because I'm not there."[26] His need was very real, to counter these early signs of mortality with a wider, sustaining social life. His joy was palpable, when he could report from Wyoming that his fellow work hands, experienced riders, had taken to calling him "an Arizona cowboy" based on his riding skills developed just weeks before.[27] His grandmother Ida, in Keokuk, Iowa, found the persona endearing enough: "Well, the Cowboy is here in boots, hat, grey slacks, &c—& looks perfectly ok. & attracting plenty of attention you may guess."[28] A school friend named Ed, who himself evidently made a visit out west, spoke of his unlikely ability "to carry on the Bill Gaddis Western Tradition," even as he thought to ask after the courses Gaddis was taking at Harvard and "by the way Bill have you met any new numbers?"[29]

Gaddis's Harvard (and lifelong) friend Mike Gladstone recalls a certain aura, a distinction and uniqueness around Gaddis's Arizona adventures. Others at the university may have been less duly impressed, although his attendance at open houses at the Harvard Dramatic Club, the Spee, the Delphic, and the Speaker's were reported home hopefully. The latter invited him "to two punches," he told his mother, "and i seem to know quite a number of the fellows (many of whom are 'Poon men), so i may make a club yet."[30]

He never would make any of them, but he could not yet know that his youthful enthusiasm would amount to a lifelong rush for second place. In his adult view, everything in these years was "just missed," as Muriel recalls him saying: "'just missed' or 'almost made.' He himself a biographical error. He 'almost' had a Harvard degree, he 'almost' made one of the final clubs at Harvard, but was not quite 'shoe' enough: he 'almost' had one successful marriage, and then another" (*E* 95). If he had no better luck at Harvard with the all-male A— D— Club, he did meet there the president of the *Harvard Lampoon* and through these connections found his place in the social-literary scene: if he could not be a proper clubman, what better way in than through an organization recognized as a forum for publishing serious essays, short stories, and poems, but devoted also to lambasting the very conventions and social and entertainment activities that otherwise were so important in the pursuit of status at Harvard?

Comedy—of a particular, knowing, halfway literary but much of the time nihilistic sort—offered Gaddis a way to be at the same time an insider to the rowdy ways of collegiate life, and an outsider unable to follow more formal routes of inclusion. In the event, Gaddis proved himself quickly at the *Lampoon*: "what with the dearth of prose writers i was called on and kept busy, as i am afraid the next issue will attest to. in fact, i even wrote the editorial!"[31] Since he also possessed a strong work ethic, which was doubtless rare among 'Poon men, he would actually see manuscripts into press and publication with some regularity. He found himself before long on the literary board ("really the right and top side of the 'poon to be on"[32]), served as president and had written over sixty columns, stories, and editorials by the time he was asked to leave the university in January 1945.

In those two glory years, his life took on an energy that could only bode (for him, and for Edith, reading his reports) a bright future that seemed to take the shape of an endless party, each evening better than the last and more to come tomorrow. In his rooms, most nights during this period, the joint was jumping: "Right now it's time to stop— Stanley Gould just came over—from "Watch Hill" in Connecticut—who practiced drums for 6 years—and my room mate—and a record named Chasin' with Chase are all going at once—so—I'd better get to work."[33] One New Year's Eve, at the Hasty Pudding dance, he was observed by Joseph Eldridge, one of the members of the *Lampoon*, "sitting bolt upright in one of the great black leather club chairs, wearing his impish beatific smile. When the lights came on again, his position was inverted. Still clutching his half-empty glass. . . ."[34]

The high jinks were intermixed with more civilizing activities. A try at fencing, "first physical ed I've had in years—and it was wild!"[35] A momentary enthusiasm for ballet, "last night" and "again tomorrow,"[36] emerged along with his fast developing attraction to one Jean Campbell, "an awfully nice girl"[37] from Radcliffe who had been with him twice a week in a short-story writing class. The attraction, quite possibly, was too quick: "as for Her, we had a little trouble last evening. heavens i wish i could fall in love like a rational person and not rush it and get involved before things have started and then miss the beat and stand and watch it sail away. you can see that i am rather in a state."[38] The cost of abandon, in love and in aesthetics, could be high when so much is at stake—and Gaddis at this time did put a lot into the relationship, as he had in the clubs, and in his appearance which was no small concern ever, not when a young man is being so carefully watched amidst the apparent freedom of hot jazz and late nights at the opera: "I do want to get a pair of shoes," he might say in a typical letter home, "and the ballet is so important—as she is."[39]

Anatole Broyard, who knew Gaddis during the Village years and shared his taste in women, recalls meeting "a pretty Radcliffe girl at a party who had gone with Willie when they were in school together. When she broke off with him, she said, he climbed into the window of her apartment and burned her clothes in the fireplace." Broyard goes on to admit, "I was impressed. It seemed a passionate thing to do. I admired people who were driven to desperation and wished I had a greater capacity for recklessness in my own life. Desperation, I thought, was the measure of authenticity, of truth."[40]

Broyard recalls that Gaddis's male friends in the Village, "at least the few I met, were androgynous Harvard boys and perhaps Willie had some anxiety there, but I saw him as masculine, even gallant." At this period, and throughout his twenties, Gaddis certainly could appreciate (and might have preferred) quieter, less emotionally stressful, less convivial entertainments mostly in the society of male friends: "A lovely evening last week," he wrote his mother from the Canal Zone in 1948, "I heard Handel's Messiah at Juancho's house—and this week am looking forward to a whole evening of Bach. How fortunate to find someone with similar musical tastes and enthusiasms!"[41] And he was not oblivious to the substantial (but also staid and leathery) educational opportunities facilitated by Harvard:

> Have been reading Nietzsche and Schopenhauer and got a book of Kant's out of the library today. Incidentally, we have the most wonderful house library in Eliot; all kinds of books, but an accent on classics and such, and big leather covered chairs etc. Gee it's all really wonderful.[42]

He goes down to Boston to see a French film of *Crime and Punishment*, and a German one of *The Brothers Karamazov*. He spends serious time at the Widener library: "I am now becoming a regular supporter . . . paying fines I mean— . . . 5 cents per day overtime!" In psychology class he watches a film of "a dog with half a brain!! boy they have everything here." And a "new discovery—the music room" at Eliot House with a "fine record player and all kinds of classics—*Afternoon of a Faun* and *The Bolero. Porgy & Bess, Sheherezade*, everything."[43]

The idea that everybody would want to know the "everything" that he was discovering, while perhaps naive was also part of a democratic disposition (in spite of his occasionally superior manners). It was an ethos handed down from his mother, who'd been celebrated as we have seen in a *New York Times* profile for her thoroughness in getting to the bottom of a job and "knowing everything it is in your power to know." The theme is mentioned also by Gaddis in a 1948 letter to one of the major short-story writers of the time, Katherine Anne Porter. At a postwar moment when everyone was reading Sartre and Kafka, the need simply to know, and to record what was happening from one day to the next appeared to Gaddis as his own, unavoidable burden of truth and authenticity: "There is such an accumulation," he sighs: "Did you have the feeling, early when you were writing a novel, say, that you must get everything in? Everything." Before he'd actually started his career, it is clear that for him the ability to grasp the significant detail, would prove him "worthy" and capable of coming into possession of what is truly "mine" and what others might then share.[44]

To be sure, his abrupt departure from Harvard was an early impulse to his lifelong outsider status, but it was not felt at the time as all that life-changing. He had, after all, entered and left the university on a semester-by-semester basis, depending on his health, and means, and mood. He'd already acquired a kind of roughshod, debonair attitude, and after two of his trips out west he'd already mentioned to his mother that he no longer cared for example about "'the right times to enter' in a regular normal way anymore—I'm way past that!"[45] At least some of his Harvard friends did recognize his western travel and work experience as a kind of distinction, as Mike Gladstone recalls. So it's not surprising that his initial impulse, as in the past, was to treat his "enforced leave of absence" (Harvard stopped short of an outright "dismissal") as just that: a chance perhaps to return to the American Southwest, among horses, property owners, and ranch hands. Being kicked out was not by itself the end of the world, for someone ready to capitalize on his Harvard connections. But it suited Gaddis better, using his *Lampoon* connections to work as a *New Yorker* fact-checker than to take up a life in business. Or later, he would work as a writer "for a magazine the State Department publishes in Iran—good enough income and I still escape the *office job*."[46] This way, too, he'd stay in touch with his literary contemporaries while at the same time superseding them in the attention he paid to facts of all kinds—that is, to the "everything" whose gradual accumulation, over the next decade, would find its way into *The Recognitions*.

S. E. Williams, Gaddis's great-grandfather, a composer and educator

Reproduced courtesy of Special Collections, Washington University Libraries, and the Estate of William Gaddis.

Savage & Pierce, WINCHESTER, IND.

Williams Family Orchestra: Ernest (with cornet), Mabel, Grace, and Jan in Wayne County, Indiana, in the 1890s. Their father and Gaddis's great-grandfather Samuel Williams founded the orchestra for the purpose of keeping the family together. A generation later, in 1922, the Ernest Williams School of Music was established at 153 Ocean Avenue in Brooklyn, New York. The school's summer band camp was set up in Saugerties, New York, deep in the Catskills.

William and Edith Gaddis, with son in carriage, circa 1923

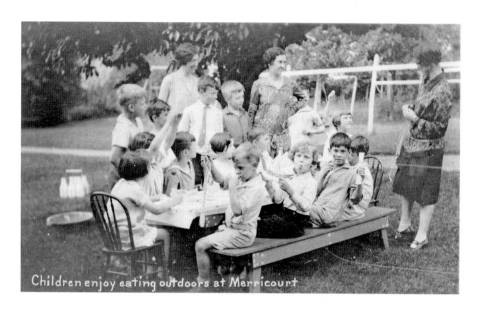

Children enjoy eating outdoors at Merricourt

Students and staff at Merricourt, circa 1928. Billy is second from left on the bench in the foreground, with a carrot in his mouth. Near the end of his life, Gaddis acknowledged Stanley Elkin's uncanny depiction (in his 1985 novel *The Magic Kingdom*) of an eight-year-old geriatric named Charles Mudd-Gaddis: "How do you do it?" he asks Elkin. "How [. . .] did you know! Staggers. [. . .] prescient my God it's I, it's me today that brief touching elegant agonizing profile believe me real age 72 is daily more infringed by that blond pageboy off to boarding school age 5 . . ." (letter of 9 November 1994).

Young William out on a limb.

JAN .

Dear    Grandaddy

This   is    the    typewriter

that    I    Told   you    about

Mother   was   with   me   some

of   time  ,

And   I   had   A   good   time  .

I   am   going   back   to

Merricourt   thursday

Igot   a   lletter   from

Uncle   John   and   some   of   it

siad   we   would   have   a

orchestra  .

*with love Billy*

Letter of 7 January 1930 to his great-grandfather, who had formed the Williams Family Orchestra four decades earlier. The "Uncle John" mentioned here is the Merricourt school director (and not related to Gaddis).

Drawings around age twelve demonstrate a tendency to imagine a multitude of people arranged at various angles, "all mentally and physically the wrong size," as Gaddis would later write in *The Recognitions* (305).

After hospitalization in New York, when William was "finally sent home" to Massapequa "without prospects" (as recalled in a letter of 13 December 1986)

Harvard *Lampoon* Board, 1944; Gaddis is seated in the center of the first row.

Photograph by Chester T. Holbrook. Reproduced courtesy of Special Collections, Washington University Libraries, and the Estate of William Gaddis.

Gaddis with Margaret Williams in Paris, 1950

Reproduced courtesy of the Estate of William Gaddis.

With Pat, pregnant with Sarah, Massapequa, Long Island, 1955

Photograph by Martin S. Dworkin. Reproduced courtesy of Special Collections, Washington University Libraries, and the Estate of William Gaddis.

Gaddis in Upstate New York, 1968

Photograph by Santi Visalli; copyright © Getty Images.

Judith Gaddis, late 1960s

Photograph by Martin S. Dworkin; property of Judith Gaddis. Reproduced courtesy of the Estate of William Gaddis.

The Piermont writing desk, in a modest closed room where manuscript
pages could expand indefinitely through marginal glosses, coded references,
and typed inserts attached with Scotch tape. Gaddis in the 1980s reflected
on the similarities of his homespun methods with current word processing
technologies. Gaddis also liked to keep the books he "referenced" close at hand
when writing a novel.

William Gass in conversation with Gaddis at the 1986 PEN party

Gaddis flanked by Donald Barthelme and Muriel Oxenberg Murphy at a party celebrating William Gass's election to the American Academy and Institute of Arts and Letters

In front of his portrait by Julian Schnabel. Scholar Peter Wolfe wrote of
Gaddis's vision of himself, as it emerges in the work: "The lines don't all
join and the colors don't all lie flat. He is a scold and an ironist, a parodist, a
cynic, and a sage, and these different selves may undermine each other."

In Cologne in 1999. As recollected by Stewart O'Nan, "He was bony by then . . .
and carried a walking stick like some down-at-heels country count . . ."

Photograph copyright © by Isolde Ohlbaum.

# Chapter 4

✦

# Anticipations of Failure in *The Recognitions*

And then suddenly realise, in the midst of all this thought, here I am 25 and my education is just beginning. Honestly, I wonder what I "studied" at Harvard.

William Gaddis in the Canal Zone, 1948

The departure from Harvard, while sudden and life-changing, was not wholly out of character, and Gaddis himself might have seen trouble coming even as he gained through his activities on the *Lampoon* a measure of confidence and, doubtless, exasperation with the Harvard mainstream. In a rare moment of pique in the letters, he cautions his mother not to "bandy that term 'free and gay' about so unadvisably. I am on probation, and have lost my room permission among other things."[1] Though he doesn't mention it in the letter, he'd violated "parietal rules," meaning he'd had a girl in his room. That occurred late in his third year at Harvard, November 1944. Less than two months later, on the evening of 8 January 1945, he and Douglas Wood were drinking in Mike Gladstone's room and later that night, another student pushed his hand through a large pane of glass. The student was taken to the infirmary, became belligerent, and Gaddis went to a neighboring shop for help. He was in a Cambridge phone booth when a cop came by to see what the trouble was. The distracted Gaddis, not to be bothered by such intrusions, uttered a dismissive expletive and was then hauled in for drunken and disorderly behavior.

Prior to the incident, he was on the dean's list for academic achievement, twenty weeks from graduation, and granted the right to appeal, and return. His appeal was accepted a few years later, on condition that he live on campus for the remaining semester. By that time, having lived on his own and traveled freely, he refused Harvard's conditions.

The next we hear of him, half a year later, Gaddis is traveling again—to Montreal, but by now "Frankly the more I move along the more I find that every city is quite like the last one. Perhaps there are sights in Montreal which I have missed (I have visited the Wax museum). But I feel little like gaping at anything."[2] To be left standing, empty and "agape," though it is just a word that came to him in a down mood, would in time become a favored expression for a spiritual desolation larger than his own. A gaping void is how Gaddis came to regard a lack of direction in American culture generally and its contrast with the ideal of Christian fellowship, *agapē*.

In Quebec, he received news that his college love interest "Je— plans to be married as soon as possible, to this fellow." Gaddis anticipates that the "thoughts that run through" his mother, reading the news, will be "similar to mine."[3] The reciprocation that went missing, with the girl, was secure between mother and son. He does not bring himself to spell out Jean Campbell's name.

What Gaddis set out to do, at first tentatively but with increasing determination, would not happen today and was barely possible (but still widely felt as an ideal) among writers of his wartime and postwar generation. As William Gass, a younger contemporary, points out in his introduction to the 1993 edition of *The Recognitions* (reprinted in 2012), its author was "romantic" in the sense that he concerned himself with creating "a masterpiece," after any number of false starts, lost manuscripts, persisting doubts, and unexpected encouragements (vii). Gaddis did none of the standard "career-enhancing things," like reviewing others' books. He didn't publish many excerpts of work in progress, to keep his name circulating. (One story that he placed in *New World Writing* was enough to attract the attention of agent Bernice Baumgarten, who in turn showed it to the editors at Harcourt, Brace.) His travels made it hard for him to finish work, even small excerpts, in time for deadlines. Like Mark Twain before him, he had no time to write short letters to publishers, and so he wrote long ones to friends and family. And he was temperamentally unsuited to working the academic circuits and publisher parties that would help prepare the way for a kind of recognition he had no interest in anyway—not if it came through mainstream media whose reviewers could not be expected to read through to the end, let alone celebrate, such an unsponsored, unusual accomplishment.

Of course, Gaddis hardly expected that it could be done, even as he was doing it. He felt for example belated and "furious," while reading a biography of Eugene O'Neill in Panama, "that one can no longer live as he did—just wandering about, one job, one ship to another. No. To travel now—and this most especially for the woeful American—one must have money, and be ready to pay at every turn."[4] Gaddis of course was doing just that, though he had the advantage of paying with dollars in postwar European and South American economies in debt to the United States. "Thank God for the Marshall Plan," recalls Ormonde de Kay, a Harvard classmate who got to know him in Paris: "Willie was working on *The Recognitions*. And he could live quite well in Paris for a hundred bucks a month,"[5] his allowance from the rent of the Massapequa home inherited by Edith.

He was also taking jobs locally, at least as often as he could sign on for stints with UNESCO and the United States Information Service in Paris and Manhattan. In the era before mass tourism, more often than not he was paying local prices, avoiding the Left Bank Bohemian life by setting himself up in a working class district across the river, on the Rue de la Chaussée d'Antin in the First Arrondissement. He preferred, as de Kay recalls, "Not to run with the crowd. The First is very businesslike."[6] In Panama and Spain, he would learn the language fundamentals, "enough to be able to struggle through meals and get directions when I get lost, which is often."[7] Some decades later a friend overheard him, as he took an expected international call at a New York gathering, speaking a halting but fluent French.[8]

That he himself could scarcely believe that he'd actually emerge with a literary work in hand on the order of O'Neill's plays is hinted in the way he would lose sole copies of his manuscripts along the way, and pay this no more mind than his character Wyatt does when his wife Esther tells him his stored paintings have been lost in a fire. Wyatt asks about a letter that arrived that morning, and his wife responds:

> —The letter? This? Yes, that warehouse, the place in New Jersey where you had your things, it burned. And here, they send you a check for a hundred and thirty dollars.
> —Really? [Wyatt replies] That's fine. (90)

Gaddis showed no more regret when he told his mother of the manuscripts lost en route to Mexico: "a touch of trouble, my leather suitcase stolen from the car last night, therewith all of my shirts, neckties, and all of the work I was taking with me."[9] Mentioned almost in passing, the lost pages are in fact "the work of the last year or two" that all this time had been the justification (to his mother, if not himself) for his avoidance of a stable, settled life. But Gaddis at this time was in "buoyant" spirits and one senses the sheer pleasure with which he coursed through Central America in particular, as when he made his plane in Costa Rica "with

7minutes to spare (one is supposed to arrive 1hour early) and of course managed to lose a notebook on a bus."[10] It was as though neither he, nor Wyatt, *wants* to move his many promising and false starts toward the finality of an original work.

Throughout his life, he would neglect to make copies of his final, irreplaceable manuscripts, in contrast to the care he devoted to each sentence over many drafts and many years, and the need to carry boxes full of drafts with him at various stages of completion in various stages of his life—from his summer house on Fire Island back to Croton, or in and out of storage at the East Eighty-Second Street apartment near Third Avenue that he shared with his Harvard friend Douglas Wood. Martin Dworkin told his friend and future memoirist Bernard Looks about the time Gaddis "brought *The Recognitions* in to his agent, Bernice Baumgarten. She made some remark indicative of her assumption that he still had a copy of the manuscript. She nearly flipped when he told her it was 'the only one' and she had it. 'That's what the book's all about,' Gaddis said."[11]

What it was about, evidently, was Gaddis's improbable belief in "the unswerving punctuality of chance," a term cited without attribution in *The Recognitions* and in each of the four succeeding books that Gaddis picked up from Thomas Wolfe's *Look Homeward, Angel* (1929): "Inevitable catharsis by the threads of chaos. Unswerving punctuality of chance. Apexical summation, from the billion deaths of possibility, of things done."

A man who was otherwise so attentive to details could hardly have been so careless in these other respects without possessing an essentially religious faith in *chance*. The affective periodic manner of Wolfe's "unswerving" predestination also captures the combination of wild abandon and detailed control that intensify Gaddis's worldview—carried over, as we shall see in the next chapter, from the historiographic work of Arnold Toynbee concerning "the solution of abandon and that of self-control"; solutions that need to be held together lest they produce either an emptying out of value when "abandon" takes over, or fascism when "control" is wielded by the few over the many.

In *A Frolic of His Own*, the attorney Harry Lutz would argue that the law is "a vehicle for imposing order on the unruly universe" (527). The legal system is another solution to the problem of abandon and control, but Harry also recognizes that the "compulsion for order ends up" in fascism (11).

The world-historical context would enrich Gaddis's literary vision and shape his lifework though it also made for some strange personal characteristics, and these too would persist to the end of his life. One can scarcely believe, even now, that an author of Gaddis's stature could be so resistant to copying even a typescript on paper. Did he feel that authenticity would be reduced somehow? That unauthorized copies would be stolen, and plagiarized? Was he so concerned that a material copy would somehow turn his own writing into one of the forgeries the book was about?

That issues of *ownership* were deeply embedded in this quite deep and certainly irrational disposition to lose the very things he himself had taken so much time to craft and create can be gathered from Gaddis's response at age twenty-five when he learned of a fire at the music school in his hometown of Massapequa. Lost to future generations, presumably, were historical manuscripts specific to his region. But for him, the loss was tied up with what he himself had lost in the process of growing up, continuous in his mind with the "billions of deaths of possibility" in all our lives: "Somehow the whole affair has been wrapped in disaster since I was 5, all of it has always seemed to me hopelessly sad" and waiting for just this devastation by fire. As for the loss of valuable manuscripts in the school library: "well that is what happens when you own *things*; and if you will own I suppose that insurance is part of responsible ownership &c. &c."[12] Ownership and all that goes with it are understood as mechanisms of control that are well avoided by a young man who has been able up to now to live and travel free of encumbrances (whether material or to do with social and professional relationships). Indeed, in the months leading up to the publication of *The Recognitions*, he would mark in himself the moment when "youth is gone indeed" as the time when he would "settle down to something with an income attached"[13]—and a wife, a family, and some property he would purchase in commuting distance of Manhattan with money earned on salaries and commissions.

Those reflections were posted at around the time Gaddis was working over the final proofs of his novel, with as much time spent sitting on his hands waiting for the editors to finish whatever "reading they appear to find necessary. All of this badly complicated by there being only one copy."[14] Gaddis never would get over this strange reluctance to photocopy the manuscripts that carried in them months of irreplaceable, final-stage labor after years of sustained attention, and so a full four decades later he nearly lost the 640-page manuscript of *A Frolic of His Own* after he'd sent his proofread and corrected copy back to his publisher by Federal Express, who misrouted it: "A week of agony. They found it minus p. 638, 3 days of recasting that, & it is now presumably in the hands of the printers."[15]

Martin Dworkin recalled a remark Gaddis made, on a visit, when he saw in Dworkin's apartment "the sculptured head of T. S. Eliot, which

had been done by Sir Jacob Epstein. [. . .] 'You mean this is the only one,'
he exclaimed."[16]

*The Recognitions* almost *was* lost for good, more than once. Gaddis's
career was in any case suspended, and could easily have ended with the
work's publication. "Following the hubble bubble of its initial reception,"
Gass continues in his introduction to the 1993 reissue, *The Recognitions*
"was left in a lurch of silence, except for those happy yet furious few
who had found this fiction . . . about the nature, meaning, and value of
'the real thing' . . . found it to be the real thing" (viii, his ellipses). The
author too may have earned for himself a Village aura of authenticity:
He had been active socially during his years working at the *New Yorker*
and living on Horatio Street, then an empty stretch of tenements but
steps away from the San Remo Bar on MacDougal and Bleecker. Lower
Manhattan, with its short blocks and uneven streets and neighborhood
restaurants, and with working-class bars whose immigrant owners were
glad to be found out by Ivy League graduates and itinerant beatniks, was
ideal for making oneself known and for keeping up. The networks func-
tioned in town and also internationally, even if the participating youths
were not yet identifiable to the general populace (as Beat, black humorist,
or countercultural), not yet captured in their postwar exuberance (not
by any novelist, though Wolfe's mystical periods anticipated Kerouac's),
and television was not much watched, nor capable yet of making serials
and situation comedies (with commercial breaks) out of city "scenes."
The generation of Ivy League–educated TV and media producers who
would recognize the market potential of social networks definitely was
a presence in the Village, as Gaddis shows in *The Recognitions*: Ellery,
the ad exec and suave womanizer ("—Now remember," he tells his nervous date on the stair, "no matter what anyone says, you just comment
on the solids in Uccello. You can say you don't like them, or say they're
divine" [175]); Herschel, the flamboyant homosexual whose fading
photo portrait is still on display in his Iowa hometown; Agnes Deigh (her
name a play on *agnus dei*, the "lamb of God"), the languorous literary
agent surrounded at parties by a curtain of trousers, who lets under-
lings read manuscripts for her; and Benny, whose high school buddy
recalls how "real serious" he had been: "—he was going to do great
things then, he was going to design the most beautiful bridges you ever
saw, and look at him now" in a double-breasted woolen suit not unlike
those Gaddis favored at the time. Benny is hiring writers for scripts, and
drinking heavily. "—Even a year ago I saw him and he was real," says
the buddy, "like the guy I used to go to school with. He isn't real any
more" (579).

There's more than a hint in the novel that the unreality of such characters comes from homosexuality in the TV, advertising, and publishing ranks—and this too may have been behind Gaddis's own, somewhat exaggerated, refusal of that world. That doesn't mean, though, that he was incapable of seeing it from the side of the execs. As in O'Neill, Gaddis leads up gradually to moments of truth-telling after long stretches of seemingly aimless dialogue, and many hours of steady, hard drinking. Here's what Benny tells the (unnamed) critic in the green sweater, who's been giving him a hard time for pretending TV's "a cultural medium," and goading him to admit he's "only in it for the money, that you've all sold out" (602):

> [Benny] was not speaking loudly, nor fast, still the cold but vehement and level tone of his voice drew several people to turn around, and listen and watch. The other sat his ground with a patient sneer. —I offered you work, and you were too good for it. We buy stuff from guys like you all the time, writing under pen names to protect names that are never going to be published anywhere else, but they keep thinking they'll make it, what they want to do, but never quite manage, and they keep on doing what they're too good for. (602)

The rant goes on for several pages, and Gaddis is clearly more sympathetic with Benny than he is with the sneering critic, though he himself (Gaddis, as author) has spent the majority of *The Recognitions* precisely demonstrating the cultural poverty of television, advertising, and commercial radio. At his best, Gaddis like all good novelists lets his characters achieve fullness and a degree of self-awareness, regardless of which side they're on in the class standoffs and culture wars. There is very little in the countercultural sixties that is not anticipated in the 1950s of Gaddis's downtown Manhattan, and even Gaddis's much bruited anticipations of black humor and postmodernism in the novel, apart from a few metafictional passages (like the one to "Willie" that I will cite momentarily), derive mainly from his scrupulous recording of all he saw there.

Nonetheless, Gaddis sometimes can be felt to be having it both ways or, worse, channeling discontent with real conditions (precisely the cultural, class, and character differences he aspired to present faithfully) into momentary private outbursts at home, or in the limited publicity of cocktail parties: "—Come on, forget that jerk. You'll be all right, Ellery said, supporting Benny. —You're making a fool of yourself." Benny's encouraged though by Mr. Feddle, the elderly guy who goes around signing books at random off the host's shelves: "—Go on. I understand you"

(605). Gaddis in *The Recognitions* is capable of speaking through the artists and writers for an as yet inchoate social and cultural transformation, through the insane (like Mr. Feddle) and the outcast (Wyatt in his clandestine work as a forger, and later on the lam in Spain), and through a character such as Benny who has arrived in the business class that he, Gaddis, had been educated for but managed till then to avoid. (There may be an avoidance also of an explicit engagement with the critic in the green sweater, who is black and referenced only, tellingly? as "The other" in the nonconversation with Benny.) The assertion of so many standpoints in the dialogue can sit uncomfortably with the detached, ironic voice of Gaddis's narrator; and in any case Gaddis himself was not at this stage making many friends among either side—certainly not with the Bennys of the world, who might have helped him toward a film contract, nor with the critics who could have given him a fair hearing in influential journals and mainstream papers.

When it came to the reception of the book itself, the fruit of seven years' labor and longing for stability, Gaddis had already prepared himself for a trashing in the press that he knew could easily send the book into oblivion: "—Good Lord Willie, you are drunk," he has someone say at a bar, midway through the novel: "—Either that or you're writing for a very small audience" (478). He fully understood the risk he was taking, though he must have hoped at least that by internalizing such self-knowledge (along with everything else he knew) in the book, he could avoid the inevitable.[17] His barroom response, at least, reveals a measure of self-confidence, if not outright superiority: "—So . . . ? how many people were there in Plato's Republic?" (478).

Those who had made their Faustian bargain with contemporary culture, and who would have been in a position to advance his career (as reviewers, publishing executives, or media agents), were not in a mood to receive the book kindly. And those who were known to him, at Harcourt, Brace for example, where they bound the masterpiece in the best cloth stamped with a self-devouring serpent and endorsed on the jacket by the most prestigious Joycean of the time, Stuart Gilbert, could do little to salvage things once it became clear that the book would not sell. As much as anything and despite the reviews (which were numerous enough at least to make the book known to potential readers), Gaddis's lukewarm reception in the end may have had to do mostly with matters of money. The production and length put the price of the book a full 50 percent above the average title of the time. Readers who might have been otherwise inclined at the stores to lug home an imposing-looking first novel by a promising new writer may have simply held on to their cash, that summer season.[18]

"Begun in 1945 without really knowing what or why, and continued in bursts from 1947" (Gass, *R* vii), pursued with intensity only in the early fifties, *The Recognitions* seemed to have itself guided Gaddis's course: The prospective author might write in letters home, half ironically, about "the great prose epic that is daily escaping from under my hand," but the unironic truth was that the work had begun to write him, not the other way around: "I have been lying awake for some time as I often do, thinking about—or rather being persecuted by this novel."[19] He has an image in his head, these late nights at this still early stage, of how the book might be presented to the public, the sort of tone he wanted to convey. He asks Edith if she knows "of a German artist-illustrator named *George Grosz*? I know this is pretty excessive—he is well known, brilliant &c. (So this is rather *between us*, if it comes to naught, as it probably will) —but I have long liked his work, serious painting and cartooning."[20] Big-bellied industrialists with bulging buttocks atop piles of money: there are several of those depictions. Society's "pillars" appear (in a work of 1926) with mugs of beer in one hand, a sword or a newspaper or a small flag of the country in the other, and heads sliced at the top to display an emerging horse, or an inverted coffee cup for a hat, or a pile of shit for brains. Those who were injured in war are presented as "Republican Automatons" (1920) with both brains and body parts replaced by mechanisms (gears and crankshafts and an occasional rolling pin; printed matter emerges from another empty head). Gaddis's idea was to try to get him to illustrate "Blague," the title of his still mostly satirical work in progress. "If only it could be done. His drawings would be exactly what I want in it—really *want* to *complete* it, as it were, besides obvious commercial advantages."

Grosz however had experienced firsthand a world war, the Spartacus uprising, and several years of activism within the Communist Party and was depicting, more often than not, military personnel among industrialists and politicians during the rise of the fascist German state. Neither the military nor a personalized fascism were to be Gaddis's subject, then (in the immediate aftermath of war) or ever—though he could not have known yet that the rise of a corporate state over decades of peace in Europe and the United States, geared more toward control through monetization than military conquest, would require more subtle satires and syntheses than Grosz's flat-out, full-on caricature.

Gaddis later admitted that not being allowed to fight, for medical reasons, had cut him off from his generation: "It was a little alienating," he told photographer-interviewer Miriam Berkley in 1985. "Everyone I knew coming back, off destroyers and in Navy whites, said 'You're not missing anything, forget it,' but you think that you *did* miss something. Well, you did, I did."[21]

During all his years abroad and in the American Southwest, and in a magazine fact-checker's obscurity, he had essentially dropped out, without knowing it or necessarily feeling himself to be eccentric or excluded—not quite. Even as he may have (without fully knowing it) alienated himself from the power brokers of his time, he had nonetheless put himself in position to win the respect of a younger contemporary such as Gass (who was studying philosophy at Cornell during this period) but also with the Beat Generation. As noted earlier, Jack Kerouac in *The Subterraneans* (written in 1953 but not published until 1958) captures an image of Gaddis in a moment of great expectations: the young novelist looking like Leslie Howard shows up at a bar flushed with the success of a first book contract, sporting a parking ticket in his coat lapel.[22]

So even as he dismissed, within the novel itself, all pretensions to fame and fortune, Gaddis might at the same time have felt entitled after all his years traveling and toiling and with the peer interest he prized that success awaited him as an American original, somehow benefiting from the state of exception he'd taken on for himself. He did tell an interviewer several decades later that after all he put into the work he "wouldn't have been terribly surprised" if he'd gotten the Nobel Prize (*PR* 58). And he might have flattered his aristocratic fantasy during the winter months when, for a small sum, he rented his gay friend Alan Ansen's house in Hewlett, Long Island. (Ansen, "formerly Auden's secretary, friend to the Beats, later a poet,"[23] appears alongside Gaddis in *The Subterraneans* under the name "Austin Bromberg.") In such digs, Gaddis was still in contact via post with the transatlantic "scene" that he now was set to document, finally and for all time, in these late-stage revisions to the copyedited manuscript. Hewlett was surely Gaddis's "most curious" residency yet, "a real suburban house with country Cadillacs squeezing past," and he could not have wished for a better library, since here one could choose from "a vast and very select collexion of books, and a battery of records and machines to play them, and by now I'm almost mad enough to be at home only in an empty house, so it should work out well, when this piece of present lunacy is done and I can contrive some means of making a cool million to support myself in the manner to which my landlord is accustomed."[24]

Ansen, for his part, was the first one to read *The Recognitions* in draft form and then, when the book was published, he sounded the first notes of monetary concern: "Does [*New York Times* reviewer] Harvey Breit have it in for you? How is your advertising budget? The *Times* [where the book had been reviewed] doesn't seem to have many ads, but that may be only the consequence of the review. De Antonio tells me you are well displayed in places like Holliday" (undated letter of 1955 from Venice, Italy; Gaddis would frequent the Holiday Bookstore at Forty-Ninth and Lexington, and Bretano's in the Village). Another friend, Barney Emmart, was more forthright about prospects in the current commercial context: "well: I hope the thing in spite of its merits surpasses Dr [Norman Vincent] Peale and Mr [Leon] Uris &c., &c., because I *should* like to have a rich friend" (12 March 1955).

A more likely expectation for Gaddis himself on the book's publication was simply that his remuneration would be in line with the work and the years he put into it. He had told Edith in 1950, for example, about "a boy" he would see in Paris "named Gordon Sager," who was signed with the same agent Gaddis was with, for a time, "and Gordon says that for a year's work [. . .] he's made 600$, or 50$ a month. Isn't this a billion-dollar country?"[25] This was all by way of justifying the more frequent demands he was making of his mother not just for sending books overseas the size and heft of Frazer's *Golden Bough*, but also for submitting manuscript stories to publishers and keeping other drafts secure at home. The book review section of the *New York Times* would arrive faithfully "every 3 or 4 weeks."[26] In effect, he was often to employ Edith as his secretary and literary agent, and this was how he managed for so long to keep his quasi-independence from the New York publishing scene:

> Now about Congdon, agents &c. I'm again sorry to put this on you, but you are a business woman, and could you talk to John about it? Frankly I don't think Congdon's much good, not much good to me at any rate. I hear him highly recommended but he's not done me nor any I know any favours. I don't know what all this rubbish about him thinking I'm terrific and expecting something any day . . . but it sounds like NY cocktail-party editor-publisher-agent-over-drinks rubbish to me.[27]

Whether a Nobel, a suburban mansion, or simply to put himself in the way of the postwar billions of dollars that were suddenly flowing in and out of his home country, Gaddis would not need to have been modest about either his literary ambitions or his expectations of worldly success. Nor would he have needed to separate the two in his mind. One needs to bear in mind that a published novelist in these years was held, in New York City and in select locales across the nation such as Kerouac's North Beach in San Francisco, in no less a regard than a film star or jazz musician, so that Brando and Dean and Miles Davis, in Alice Denham's contemporary memoir *Sleeping with Bad Boys*, would be regarded as pretty much in the same social and cultural class as the novelists and poets. "I met everybody in the literary and artistic world," Denham recalls. "The art scenes weren't separated in those days like they are now. Everybody was together—the painters, the actors, the writers, the musicians. There weren't that many people in Manhattan, and we were all, amazingly, a part of one great big general crowd. The actors hung out at Louie's tavern, the writers were at the San Remo, and the abstract artists were at the Cedar."[28]

They were all traveling in circles that a newly arrived, ambitious, hot young woman could find her way into and around; and Denham was glad at the time to meet and be seen with the writers no less than the hipsters and the stars. (She would not meet Gaddis himself until some years later, when he was between marriages and she was living in D.C. and out of the Village scene.) During his own nights out, Gaddis would have observed the actors and musicians without envy; he certainly observed the off-the-charts literary celebrity of Hemingway, and accounted for that with the effrontery of youth. We might notice for example in *The Recognitions*, at the San Remo bar (called the Viareggio in the book), a "Big Unshaven Man," probably just a BUM, who is treated to a stream of drinks by starry-eyed Villagers hoping to hobnob with Hemingway. Gaddis has this character say things like "—Damn fine music, Mozart [. . .] I tell you true" as he fills his "large pocket flask" with a pitcher of his host's martinis (632). Gaddis during his aesthetically formative Village years studied the aspirations of his contemporaries, some heartfelt but many more that were colored with falsifications and exaggerations. His ability to exhaustively represent emerging literary networks, artistic ambitions, and as yet inchoate cultural transformations depended, in no small measure, on his early and continuing refusal to promote himself outside what he knew to be the source of his support and inspiration, the small but also effective cluster of friends and family based in his native New York.

Even on Long Island, he could live out vicariously through his absentee "landlord" Ansen the cities and scenes that he'd explored himself a year or two before. During this period of self-imposed suburban isolation, Gaddis could feel a sense of camaraderie with a contemporary who, like him, was at one and the same time observing and questioning the currency of European monuments to art, philosophy, religion, love, and lust: "Here I am in Florence," a typical letter from Ansen would read, "where everybody has an IQ of 250—so I spent my first late afternoon here in a bookshop. It's a little like coming to Cambridge after New York though the likeness I prefer to confine to : :: : (you remember the sign language for mathematical ratios)."[29] The higher education that Gaddis and Ansen shared, and that they carried on independently during their improvised post-graduate search for usable, worldly knowledge, would encourage Gaddis to incorporate in the novel he was completing all that he and his small Platonic republic knew. (Ansen would close the Florence letter with a rhetorical gesture: "The Athens of the West?" That was followed by an unhesitating, "Yes, Alan"[30]) Questions of religion were foremost: "We love God," Ansen confided, "because he has permitted us to create works that remind us of our infinite littleness without his grace. Emblem: 'What is man that Thou art mindful of him?' "[31] Another letter might open with more earthbound, almost earthy news of a "turn for the better" at a hotel where Ansen is staying in Rome: "The hotel is fine: the hotel clerk (a forceful gentleman in the fifties) drinks with me, #s are allowed in the rooms, and they're very sweet about late hours. . . . And I have finally discovered the second hand books district in Rome which consists not of shops but of mobile stalls set up in the Piazza Borghese." The letters among friends are filled with shared knowledge of local resources that might be of use to a fellow writer and fellow traveler; only a hint is needed to assure the correspondent that one's manly conviviality and sexual desires are being looked after. Gender preferences, when they were mentioned at all (which is rarely), could be overlooked. Ansen writes:

> In spite of all my good resolutions I finally "turned a trick" with some local talent (I am subjecting Venice to increasingly severe tests) without at all feeling the moral hangover I felt in Rome; and I am thinking of even stranger experiments (somewhat under the influence both of yourself and—in a funny way—of Burroughs)—but more of them when and if they come off.[32]

Some days later from Munich, in response apparently to a query from Gaddis, Ansen reports in a postscript: "Going wages for the ladies: $5.00—I work like a dog for you, I'm sure I don't know why."[33] Back in Venice the rate would be "3,000 lire (about $4.80) a throw."[34]

Aside from his correspondence with Gaddis, Ansen might have at hand "a long (unanswered) letter to WH"—Auden, who employed him as a secretary in the late forties.[35] He'd regularly convey news of William Burroughs, "who is probably starving in either Seville or Tangiers—I know it will make you happy to think of him in the former."[36] So there was never a moment, during the composition of *The Recognitions*, when Gaddis would have felt disconnected from the transatlantic literary milieu that was real to him and must have given him a measure of confidence (and quasi-independence from more commercial pursuits); enough for him to work out his concerns at such length and with an intensity that he knew would be shared by the open-eyed, spiritually and sexually adventurous young men of his generation.

His Greenwich Village friend Barney Emmart, at this period living in Durham, North Carolina, would be just as free in his own account of days and nights spent pursuing a hopeless love interest, one Christi who used to accompany him on visits to the city: "Here's the $20 back," he tells Gaddis, "and many thanks for it. C. lives on such an edge of poverty that I wanted her to have a little spare clink and I needed some train fare. Borrowing from the broke to give the broke, a weird Christianity on my part."[37] Another letter to Gaddis, written when Emmart was "still half out of my mind, still not working clearly," details Emmart's arrival in New York "at 1:00 p.m. when the bars were just opening. I didn't phone you because you have had enough of my troubles in this line, and because I didn't want to be talked out of anything—the slightest touch of reason would have been poisonous."[38] So he drank through the day: "I did the rounds of the village, and saw no one. An hour of drinking just about did me in. Finally went to the Remo wondering if they were in there celebrating their reunion." He recalled how Christi, a week earlier "in that dark house in Durham," had arranged that he should run into her new boyfriend, who apparently broke the news to him. "I started down for Van Dam Street, but had to sit down for a bit, shaking with anger, fatigue and cold, on a bench in the Square. Sitting down was fatal, and I felt as weak as I have ever been, and remembered that I did, after all, love the fool girl, and what was the point of making a scene that would upset her, get her kicked out of this new job, earn her hatred for me, and madden me."

There were hundreds of stories like this one, and like one's own on any given night in the Village, and Gaddis was devising a nonlinear and mostly spoken narrative that might convey a sense of them all, their simultaneity, their private intensities nonetheless worked out partly in public, and certainly talked about, talked through, and talked to death. ("Dear Willy, Dear Diary" is how one letter from Ansen opens, a single *i* in the middle and a curvy *y* at the end joining the two words visually.[39]) The letter form for these young men and women at this time was a way not just to vent but also to *communicate*, materially, experiences that one trusted were not unknown to the listener, as the Beats' voluminous published correspondence demonstrates. Emmart for example might feel himself "a miserable son of a bitch amusing myself by writing a letter" to Gaddis. But he'll "post it however, even though it may distress you, because since I cannot write to her I would like you to read it her if she phones you, or at least tell her. Or maybe not; I don't really know."[40] The intimacy of a lost love could thus be transferred, in part, to the mutual understanding of two young men, each with the knowledge that the other would process this knowledge (in literature, on Gaddis's part, and in Emmart's current position as an honorary fellow of the "Institute for Parapsychology" at Duke University).

In the background, always, were economic concerns that became ever more pressing every year for the men, and also for an increasing number of women whose increasing freedom from the need to marry and raise children opened them, in their private lives more directly, to market pressures. These concerns were ever present, for Denham in her modeling career, for Ansen hoping to make a Village and transnational career in poetry and poetics, for Emmart in his experimental psychiatric program at Duke University, and for Gaddis during his recent years on contract to the State Department (and in the career of corporate writing that he must have known awaited him, if the first novel didn't sell). That looming reality was felt by Emmart distinctly that particular afternoon, on the bench in Washington Square: "By this time I was fairly calm with fatigue, and made a clear statement of what is really troubling me: that at thirty I am still living in a furnished room, fearing to buy books, say, because I will be moving from one temporary toy job, to another."[41]

The idea that these private networks among family and friends could somehow sustain the artist indefinitely, that they'd protect those who knew the right bars and the right people, may have been reinforced after the appearance of *The Recognitions* when Gaddis received through his publisher a monthly remittance from an anonymous lady donor. At $200 (worth around $1,700 in 2015), the "patroness' largess"[42] must have eased the recently married author's transition into family and eventually corporate life, though in retrospect the patronage, like much in and around *The Recognitions*, was a gesture that could only echo an earlier, commercialized yet not so fully corporatized era of literary life and fortunes—as when Harriet Shaw Weaver for example supported James Joyce, Nora, and their children in Paris through many, many years and the creation of *Ulysses* and *Finnegans Wake*.

Gaddis's self-conscious refusal to aggrandize family and friendships (and least of all, the arts) into corporate programs would come later—two decades later in *J R*, after he'd experienced firsthand precisely the kind of uncreative office work he'd given to Wyatt in *The Recognitions*, while also doing his share of the ghostwriting and flack work that keeps afloat many of the writers in the novel. When working on *The Recognitions*, Gaddis had not yet started a family of his own, nor would he have thought it necessary to formulate his personal experience in opposition to corporate programs. That an increasingly programmatic sociality and aesthetic were in fact where America was heading was not at all obvious or understood at the time, even though Gaddis's catalogue of social artifice and cultural, artistic, and religious searching could well be understood, in retrospect, in this context. Critiques and (more often) send-ups of the "company man" might have convinced those having the leisure and education needed to read and appreciate such works that the corporate model, as applied to society and aesthetics at least, could never last. The conviction would have been mistaken. Richard Yates, in *Revolutionary Road* (1961), was perhaps the one novelist among Gaddis's contemporaries who best understood that the Company would patiently, over the course of a young man's career into a compliant middle age, overcome all revolutionary dreams—including (and especially) the personalized, privileged, postwar dream of living abroad and creating art. (Yates himself, like Gaddis and many, many others, would later find refuge in academic employment; later still, when his revolutionary dreamers were safely situated in a black-and-white past, Yates would see his book made into a Hollywood film. That was an economic escape for Yates, and an order of magnitude enhancement of his audience that Gaddis himself desired but did not attain.)

If one were inclined toward literature in the forties and fifties, a way out (in the wake of the New Criticism and close reading practices taught at Harvard and throughout higher education in the United States) was to look back systematically to "tradition" for living alternatives to the present. For some, such as Frazer and Graves, tradition would extend even past the introduction of print, toward pastoral, pre-Christian, prehumanist poetic practices that determinedly placed the natural world over the not yet ubiquitous city. A *layering* of pagan and Christian motifs in *The Recognitions* is systematic and consistent with Frazer's influential study that posits Christianity not as something new and original and revealed, but a pale copy of earlier pagan traditions, as can be seen for example in the construction of the Saint Clement Basilica directly over a Mithraic temple. Mark C. Taylor, a historian of religion and a practicing artist, finds in this overlay, not a simple dichotomy of original or copy, but a thoroughgoing reflection in Gaddis of the multiplicity of diverse religious forms in the world throughout history. Taylor notices how the Reverend Gwyon's apostasy does not even ground itself in paganism, since, perhaps, "neither Mithraism nor Christianity is original but both are copies of the even more ancient myth of 'the sacrifice of the king's son.'" If Gwyon's "suspicion were proven correct, Christianity would be a copy of a copy or, even worse, a counterfeit of a counterfeit."[43]

In rural Connecticut between 1920 and 1950, Reverend Gwyon belonged to the last era when religion, however deeply it might be doubted, was still widely practiced and belief was the norm. His son Wyatt's (and Gaddis's) generation was living through the start of a transformation of belief enacted through global technologies and media of communication. If the First World War had brought in technologies of human destruction on a scale hitherto unimaginable, and a realized revolution in Russia (unlike any projected by European Marxism), the Second World War brought different, systematic, and potentially lasting transformations (having reduced to rubble, or pockets for later tourism, what was left of Europe's old world urban infrastructure). A "Waste Land Part 2," which Gaddis seemed to be writing, could still look back on tradition but only ironically, not as a way to "shore up our ruins" (as Eliot had written in 1922; Gaddis not only quotes that poem often but at one point in the composition intended to weave each line of *Four Quartets* into the text of his novel, such was his affiliation with Eliot's vision and ethos). For all their temperamental and cultural affinities, Gaddis cast a far more skeptical eye than Eliot on the religious roots of the premodern literary tradition in Europe, without which there was scarcely any way to discern the authenticity of artistic inspiration. And Gaddis knew already, in *The Recognitions*, that a people without the authority of religion, and without moral absolutes, could easily be overwhelmed by a corporate culture where all differences become relative, all human relations negotiable, all "others" just like us and hence reducible to exchange according to market value.

Here is the closest Gaddis, or his voice-over narrator in *The Recognitions*, could allow himself to come to an unironic expression of the problem of living in a world without absolutes, where actions and personal interactions were felt to be shorn of consequence:

> Tragedy was foresworn, in ritual denial of the ripe knowledge that we are drawing away from one another, that we share only one thing, share the fear of belonging to one another, or to others, or to God; love or money, tender equated in advertising and the world, where only money is currency, and under dead trees and brittle ornaments prehensile hands exchange forgeries of what the heart dare not surrender. (103)

That passage appears relatively early in *The Recognitions*, amidst scenes of half-hearted celebrations of the Christmas season in the bars, apartments, and snow-covered streets of Manhattan circa 1950.[44] A year,

and six hundred pages, later it is again Christmastime, but this time, at
what is also a later stage in the composition, Gaddis seems to have recognized that tragedy wasn't all that had to be foresworn. So must the
elegiac, aloof tone of his own narrator be held back, modulated, and
guided by voices, not authorities:

> —That's all it is, Benny went on. —What's tragedy to you is an
> anecdote to everybody else. We're comic. We're all comics. We live
> in a comic time. And the worse it gets the more comic we are. [. . .]
> —Benny, relax, forget it, look, that church gimmick, you're in,
> you're made Benny . . . Ellery was supporting him, but he wrenched
> away when he saw Mr. Feddle who had just finished inscribing the
> book he held, *with best wishes from Benedict Arnold.* (640)

The passage restates the fall from "foresworn" tragedy in a different register, as the party going at this late stage in the novel overtakes the narrative
action and voice-over commentary. (Not that the comedy diminishes for
one moment the pervasive sadness of the final third of the novel, where
each major character either dies, commits murder, or separates in some
way from the society that he or she might have influenced.)

Whether or not Gaddis resolves the aesthetic issues he poses in the
novel, at this stage in his career he still openly embraced tradition and
could still imagine the arts as a secular alternative if only the artist could
see through all the fakes. And he *would* present *all* the fakes, here and
throughout his work, in every activity in each cultural and linguistic register, with an authorial commitment that rivals (without ever presuming
to displace) the religious commitment that marks the character Stanley. At
this stage, Gaddis was more or less following Eliot's conservative dictum
against putting "personality" before "tradition," but he also anticipated
Pynchon's more programmatic refusal of publicity as the machines of
corporate media geared up. Gaddis's party scenes in particular anticipated Pynchon's depiction a decade later in *V.* of "the Whole Sick Crew,"
who similarly range from sailors to ad executives to psychoanalysts
to dentists (who doubled as psychoanalysts) who could all still, at this
time, be brought together in the same Village lofts. There, an upwardly
mobile generation of "people all mentally and physically the wrong size"
(*R* 305) and a concentration of publishers willing to subsidize literary
fiction could give legs to what now looks like the last avant-garde literary aesthetic to reach a sizable U.S. and international audience. The
same impulses that sent Gaddis and his younger contemporaries "on the
road" can be found in a postwar generation that could at best manage,

most of them for most of their lives, to commute between downtown Manhattan and the uptown Avenues. Some of them, better connected or with family support, would instead voyage by ship to the older, suddenly more available cultural centers throughout Europe and in North Africa (as described by Paul and Jane Bowles, and by Gaddis in a late section of *The Recognitions* [877–79] based on a month in 1951 when he stayed in Algiers). But even the old European centers, to the surprise of those who inhabited the downtown scene, would be supplanted by commercially powerful art centers in postwar America; and once travelers could take flight, rather than ship out, the transatlantic journey would itself take on the spirit of a commute, attaining—as Gaddis wrote to a British friend while crossing the Atlantic—"that peak of sophistication where movement across water is simply a matter of adjusting one's watch, where crossing the Atlantic ocean is as significant as a busride to Battersea."[46] "—And I mean Chrahst," says the feckless Harvard graduate Ed Feasley, "everybody's leaving, everybody's going abroad. [. . .] I mean to Saint Germain des Prés where they're imitating Greenwich Village and here we are in Greenwich Village still imitating Montmartre . . ." (R 746).

This transatlantic power shift was in fact the context for what seemed at the time to be an endless stream of parties that felt to Gaddis like the same encounters with the same people living the same, empty lives; writing to his mother from Spain in 1948, Gaddis said, "These fellow creatures of mine who have made Europe into one large mad-house, each capital a room, and they running from room-to-room, screaming & giggling (to use a phrase of Barney's) . . . well it is all beyond me."[47] Yet it was not beyond his representational abilities. That ennui and directionless movement back and forth are conveyed, by Gaddis, in the sheer repetition of one thirty-plus-page scene at a bar, then a longer one at a Village apartment, then a still longer one that over time can reproduce in readers Gaddis's experience, and the experience of so many downtown artists and writers in the fifties. Arguably, the long-standing repressions and sporadic outbursts and self-immolations in the novel can be read as a prelude to more public revolts and reactions of the sixties. But nothing so public, or so collective in spirit, was viable as of yet. And at the end of one of these nights, what has transpired? The kitten that all the adults seem to play with at the cocktail party? Agnes Deigh finds it on the seat after she's sat on it, and stuffs the corpse into her purse. The little girl, the mother's little helper from downstairs, who asks the hostess, then each of the women present, for sleeping tablets? Enough were gathered for mommy's attempt at suicide. Ed Feasley, who's been cut off from his father until he can sell one of the family company's battleships? We've heard him complain about this night after night through the course of the novel—until this particular night when he runs into the Argentine Ambassador of Trade who showed up at the wrong party. The Ambassador (to Feasley's astonishment) offers to buy the ship:

> —And Pablov had this kitten . . .
> —But Carruthers had a mare . . .
> —Well she says she got pregnant by taking a bath right after her father, but I say . . .
> —Omychrahst, I mean, youmeanyoureallywanttobuyone?
> —Cómo? qué dice . . . ?
> — You. Really. Want. To. Buy. One.? (631)

Of course, any of these and many, many more such connecting threads could easily be missed on a single reading, amid so much intentional noise and redundancy. Reviewers, who missed more than a few connections, were wont to write off the whole endeavor as a symptom instead of a synthesis of a culture or movement not yet formed. Generations would not produce more patience, or closer attentiveness, in our powerful mainstream reviewers in the United States: "there is no headache like the headache you get from working harder on deciphering a text than the author, by all appearances, has worked on assembling it."[48] If one reads without listening for resonances, without noticing significant variations in the repetitions, without discerning signals in the noise, one might well assume that much of Gaddis's writing is nothing more than a straight transcription of recorded talk. But it is demonstrable, empirically demonstrable in close readings published over the years in print and online, that each thread has been gathered up by the author and developed toward a conclusion, even if it's simply the punch line to a joke about Carruthers and his horse (A mare, not a stallion: "Nothing queer about Carruthers"); and even if we need to read around to recall that Pavlov's experiments were on a dog, not a kitten—the correct reference, and correct spelling of the scientist's name, is there in *The Recognitions*. The difficulty, though undeniable, is not unsurpassable by readers who come to the novel with an open mind, a sense of humor, and a touch of generosity.

That we have so extensive a record in Gaddis's first novel of what writers, artists, and business people of the day were saying to (and past) one another during a cultural downtime, a period of social and aesthetic incubation, is itself a testament to the author's concentration through it all. The work of synthesis, nonetheless, is no less real, or entertaining, for an ordinary reader who is ready to join Gaddis in his long day's journey into night. The journey is no less enjoyable if its outcome is unclear, as it must be to Stanley in his music, to Wyatt in his painting, and to Gaddis himself over the course of the book's composition when they ask themselves if their years of work can ever coalesce into the "one whole" that they seek:

> —But Stanley, couldn't you just . . . I don't know what a palimsest [*sic*] is, but couldn't you just finish off this thing you're working on now, and then go on and write another? She ran her hand over his, resting on the chair arm there: and Stanley called her by her Christian name for the first time. —No that's . . . you see, that's the trouble, Agnes, he said. —It's as though this one thing must contain it all, all in one piece of work, because, well it's as though finishing it strikes it dead, do you understand? [. . .] you feel it all the time you're working and that's why the palimpsests pile up, because you can still make changes and the possibility of perfection is still there, but the first note that goes on the final score is . . . well that's what Nietzsche . . . (599)

It's what Nietzsche called "the melancholia of things completed," which would rather "rest in the hiding places and abysses of perfection."[49]

Stanley does eventually complete his masterwork. Is it a tragedy, then, or one more comic irony, or plain sadness when the cathedral crashes down around him the first time he performs the work on the organ at the ancient church at Fenestrula, Italy? It's a beautiful way to end a novel, but the ending is also tonally in keeping with the book's irresolution and its cultural and aesthetic ambitions toward a wholeness that few in this society would know had gone missing, in any case.

# Chapter 5

✦

# Gwion's Riddle and Toynbee's Solution

(Item) With hands shaking in anticipation, I received the book by Robert Graves. It has proved to be 4 times as wonderful, and 40 times as difficult, as I had expected. But with the marvelous opportunity I have enjoyed in other lands, what with my lack of the reading I need, has proved as I hoped-against-hope to be exactly referent to the web of questions in my mind at present—as the Toynbee did when I was happily marooned on Caribbean shores. If I put down here on paper all the things I want to I would not send the letter, because that would amount to making the notes on these ideas which I am trying to make for my own nefarious purposes.

William Gaddis in Spain, 1949

Though Gaddis made the most of his years abroad and knew that his real higher education had begun the moment he left Harvard, he still must have known all along that the time would come when he would have to settle down, like his partial self-projection Wyatt in *The Recognitions*, to office work and domestic obligations, which he took seriously—even as he and his friends might have worried that these obligations held him back from his creative work, and even as he understood that he could "do more" than what others had done and (what he really cared about) more than he himself could manage while moving around so much. "The self who could do more" is indeed the defining characteristic of Wyatt. (The phrase is drawn from *Redemption*, a lesser known work by Tolstoy cited by no less a personage in the novel than Mr. Feddle, the elderly unpublished writer who signs other people's books off the shelves at parties—books that he, too, might have written if only. . . .)

Gaddis set out his earliest conception for the novel for his Harvard friend Charles Socarides and doubtless for himself also in a letter of 1948 (character identifications inserted in italics):

It is a good novel, terrific, the whole thread of the story, the hap-
penings, the franticness. The man [*Wyatt*] who (metaphorically)
sells himself to the devil [*Brown*], the young man [*Otto*] hunting so
for father figure, chasing the older to his (younger's) death. And the
"girl" [*Esme*]—who finally compleatly loses her identity, she who has
tried to make an original myth is lost because her last witness (a fellow who takes heroin [*Chaby*]) is sent to jail—the young man ('hero')
the informer.[1]

All of which may have struck Socarides as extravagant when he received
this letter from his old *Lampoon* friend. But Gaddis already anticipates
any rolling of the eyes, in Socarides and perhaps in his eventual readers,
with an appeal to verity: "Here the frantic point: that it all *happened*.
Not really, maybe, but with the facts in recent life and my running, it
*happened*."

A memorable event in the opening chapter of *The Recognitions* did
happen to the British couple John and Pauline Napper, whose home life
and dual career in the arts impressed Gaddis as a model for how to live.
Wyatt's mother Camilla, newly married, is shown Byzantine gold earrings by an architect (he was an antique dealer, in Pauline's case). When
told she can have them if she can wear them, she rushed to the washroom and returned bloodied because it is the first time she has worn
any earrings since she tried her own hand at piercing her ears ("done
with needle and cork years before" [14], the kind of detail that perme-
ates Gaddis's work). The story was conveyed to Gaddis on a visit to the
couple's Sussex home over the Christmas holiday of 1950. In the novel,
Wyatt's Congregational upbringing under the tutelage of Aunt May con-
flates Gaddis's boarding school regime with the Quaker aunts that he
must have heard about from his mother. Wyatt's father, Reverend Gwyon,
was based directly on the author Robert Graves, and the inability of
father and son to communicate also has its parallel in Gaddis's meeting
with Graves in Majorca in 1950. As Gaddis wrote John Napper from
Deya:

> I've found Robert Graves, who proves to be extremely pleasant,
> though a very nervous man, especially when one gets on a topic
> which interests him, so that I find it difficult to talk with him about
> White Goddesses, Recognitions, crucifixions, incarnations, saints,
> what-have-you—easier to go swimming, though I haven't seen a real
> (Palamós) beach on Mallorca, all sheer drops to the sea, and small
> openings where you can descend to the water.[2]

His visit, he recalled many years later, was "the only time I have ever looked up what I thought [was] a famous, a great writer." Gaddis's intention was to fill out some material he needed for the novel: "The essential question was, if an elderly Protestant minister were despairing of his entire congregation and his mission and thought they were not behaving like Christians at all in real life, and gradually is losing his faculties and going backwards into some early, pre-Christian religion, what might he choose in the way of primitive religions." Generous though he found Graves to be (and the celebrated poet, mythographer, and memoirist would over the years welcome to his home in Majorca supplicants diverse as Ava Gardner, Robert Wyatt, and Jorge Luis Borges), Gaddis at this time "never got this information from him," but he did over much time spent with him get "very much a picture of who this reverend was," who he was imagining as the God-like, distracted, and self-absenting father in *The Recognitions*: "a towering man with kind of wild, gray hair and blazing eyes, so that when I went on for the next couple of years working on *The Recognitions* and Reverend Gwyon was in the background, he always came out looking [*laughing*] just like Robert Graves. So that was a case where I really saw the person, modeled on the *looks* of the person, not on Graves himself."[3]

The parsonage in Connecticut where Wyatt grows up would be just the place for Gaddis's desired reflections on crucifixions, incarnations, saints, sacrifices of Barbary apes, and such like. The goddesses he would find elsewhere, eventually. Inhabitants of the European and downtown Manhattan settings that Gaddis frequented during a decade of exploration would populate the novel. The vanities he'd treated playfully at Harvard would extend to all aspects of Western art and production as the novel grew steadily in length and its central theme—forgery—developed far beyond Wyatt's own career and came to embrace each of the men and women he got to know, at every social and economic level during these years, from the drug addict Chaby Sinisterra (an acquaintance of Sheri/Esme) to the downtown New York intellectuals (Anselm, Stanley, and Wyatt, whose collective knowledge expanded after each time Gaddis talked with Martin Dworkin), to the literary agents, ad men, and bourgeois uptown couples (such as Maude and Arny Munk, whose cocktail hour starts early).

The meeting with Graves is the first mention of "Recognitions" as a way into the book's theme. In letters to Socarides and Katherine Anne Porter, Gaddis was calling the novel "Some people who were naked."[4] It is to be a novel of desperation, which he understands "cannot be written in desperation" (as he said to his mother in another letter around this formative period in 1948[5]); a novel depicting deadly enthusiasms when "it is *enthusiasm* that I mistrust," as he told Porter;[6] and not least, though he doesn't say so explicitly in the letter, the religious enthusiasm that influences so many of his characters, what Catholic apologist Denis de Rougemont (and also as we shall see momentarily, the world historian Arnold Toynbee) described as a "kind of frenzy or delirium which is neither conceived nor born in a man's soul except by the inspiration of heaven. It is alien to us, its spell is wrought from without; it is a transport, an infinite rapture away from reason and natural sense."[7] The mistrust, then, of enthusiasm has to do with a deflection from Platonic love of another (which can be confirmed through intellectual interchange in the here and now) and the religious rapture that is unreasonable and asocial.

Wyatt himself is both an idealized and a deeply flawed artist, a figure of respect and some mystery who stands somewhat apart from the Village scene—which Esther inhabits intensely, as does young Otto, newly arrived after a stint in Central America with a manuscript of his own to show around to agents (who don't bother reading it) and authors in town (who crib from it, as happens to every naive or generous author in every Gaddis novel even as he himself throughout his life was accordingly strict about not sharing unpublished work). Wyatt gives Otto a book to read off their shelves, *Adolphe* (1815) by Benjamin Constant: a kind of assignment. "You read it," he tells Otto simply (133).[8] Consistent with this postwar era of (as yet) quiet exploration into possible gender roles, we have Wyatt's and Esther's domestic arrangement, where each is free to cultivate aesthetic and philosophical passions (in Wyatt's case), and the social connections necessary for success and sexual fulfillment (Esther's main concern, and Otto's as he gets to know the couple and their Village circles).

In the depiction of Wyatt and Esther, Gaddis could bring to bear his own experiences living in Manhattan with Helen Parker, a slightly older woman (with two boys) who, like Esther, had literary aspirations. He would not himself marry until he had finished writing *The Recognitions*. But that would be, in its early years at least, a more settled marriage than the one he projects in his first novel from his earlier experiences with women on their way to careers, to more settled lives than Gaddis seemed ready to offer and (in Sheri Martinelli's case) toward a deeper engagement in poetry and the arts. Somewhere other than with him, in any case.

In the novel, however, it is Wyatt who refuses the attention of the women in his life. As often as his comment about the artist as a "shambles" is cited, no commentator I know of has pointed to its domestic circumstance, or its defensiveness. *What is it they want from a man?*

> —What do they expect? What is there left of him when he's done
> his work? What's any artist, but the dregs of his work? the human
> shambles that follows it around? What's left of the man when the
> work's done but a shambles of apology. (95–96)

He and Esther had been listening to a favorite poet on the radio, and
Esther asked if he knew that the poet was homosexual. She has been
feeling neglected by Wyatt, and his indifference eventually pushes her
into suggesting that he too could possesses homosexual tendencies. She
is also acutely aware of unresolved spiritual conflicts from when Wyatt
left his studies for the ministry, where he was intended to follow in his
father's footsteps. Taken in this context, Wyatt's question "What is it they
want?" projects an unknown artist's private situation onto a justified concern about his wider reception. The question is posed in opposition to
a peculiarly American attitude toward the production of art as a kind
of personal performance, or an attempt to satisfy expectations in readers, to enter a kind of contractual relation with them consistent with
everything else in a commercial culture. But even as Wyatt asserts his
position, the woman he's speaking to has questions of her own. What
is it *he* wants from a woman? And does he want a woman, really, in his
own uncompromising search for recognitions that come about only seven
times in a lifetime (92)? Or is such seeking only recognizable by men who
share his seeking: by those who are secure enough in a male-dominated
order to eschew publicity; by the "few minds, ever the same," who devote
themselves, priestlike, to literary creation (in the line from Flaubert that
Gaddis would cite in his final fiction, *Agapē Agape*).

Esther is presented as an answer to Freud's famous exasperation when
after years of experience the analyst could still find no answer to the
question "What does a woman *want?*" In *The Recognitions*, Esther is
generally depicted, in an avoidance of domestic conflict typical of Gaddis,
not as wanting this or that but as wanting *more*. She certainly wants more
from Wyatt. She wants to give him a manicure (92); wants him to stop
wasting his time at his drafting job "copying lines, copying plans, one
bridge after another" when he and everyone who knows him, knows he
could "do better, . . . do more" (84). She wants him to finish the portrait
of his mother that he drafted as a child, so that he can rid himself of "the
need to pretend, . . . this secrecy . . ." that is a part of his New England
upbringing. ("—Aunt May," Wyatt recalls, "when she made things, even
her baking, she kept the blinds closed in the butler's pantry when she
frosted a cake, nobody ever saw anything of hers until it was done" [88].)
Esther wants to know, if it isn't a secret, what happened the night he

was snowed in with the Bavarian Han in Interlaken while they "worked together, and drank together and traveled together," the uniformed German "pounding his finger with a beer stein" (93, 95). Her curiosity might have been answered by passages Gaddis cut in revision, in which Wyatt is seen to have murdered Han! But such a resolution is out of keeping with Wyatt's character and the tone of the book, and perhaps it was too close to Gaddis's own boyhood habit in Farmingdale and Massapequa of picking fights with the biggest guy in the bar. The cut was well advised.

In any case, the scene with Han would have been redundant considering the assault Wyatt does commit—against the art critic Basil Valentine, the Hungarian spymaster who provokes Wyatt's denunciation of critics who can only compare a finished work, with all its flaws, to the flawless because unaccomplished notion "if I'd done it myself" (335). When Valentine does attempt, in secret of course, the retouching of one of Wyatt's forgeries, at its presentation he will hear suspicion and outright ridicule from the guests from France and the British Royal Academy: they see immediately the obviousness of the forgery (a restoration of the Virgin's face in a reconceived Van der Goes that Wyatt—after doing it right—had reluctantly damaged to make it look more authentic). The European critics also notice the restored face's "vulgarity," so out of keeping with the rest of the painting. Valentine's final, sexual offer to Wyatt, later that evening when all the guests have left, is that "it won't be vulgar . . ." (691–92). Instead of yielding, Wyatt stabs Valentine several times with a penknife, then hires a cab to go in search of the one woman he finally, belatedly, recognizes can save him—namely Esme, the heroin user and habitué of the Village arts scene, modeled on Gaddis's own unrequited love interest, Sheri Martinelli. But before Wyatt realizes (after years of neglecting both Esther and Esme) that his salvation lies in Esme's irrational though committed life-aesthetic, she has already left for Europe. (In life, Gaddis is the one who leaves for Panama on the night he'd intended to discuss with Sheri "some permanent arrangement at her decision"; she avoided meeting Gaddis with a telegram, "sister Judith is in town."[9])

With Broyard, during sex Sheri would sometimes scream out, a soft scream that seemed to him staged and was never explained; she would also show up unexpectedly once at Broyard's parents' home in Brooklyn; after their breakup, she sent a cop to Broyard's apartment to collect a painting of hers she claimed he'd stolen (*Kafka Was the Rage*). The girl was a connoisseur of the unexpected, an experimentalist in love and in the arts, and Gaddis knew how to read her. The lessons of his own encounters with Sheri ran deep, and at no time did he feel resentment about her avoidance of a meeting that one night; to the contrary, he considered himself in Sheri's debt—for what she had taught him about love. One can see how, at the time, he channeled his emotions for Sheri through his work when he ventures a metaphor for their relations (in an undated letter draft): "Do you remember, that I said on the phone, how difficult it is for the debtor whose creditor refuses to acknowledge the debt—since it is the exact reverse of the grounds for litigation in our society, reversing the law, the law being theoreticly [*sic*] (and sociologically theory is practice) the will of the people. . . ." He can grasp the theoretical "down to a banking-material basis" but the reason their exchange of values and shared intimacies stand outside (and can overturn) social and financial construction is that they undermine a structure of conventional beliefs. The reason he was indebted to Sheri is that an unsentimental, even "indifferent morality" on her part may have helped him to see through so much false moralizing, no less than the many counterfeits and cheats and self-deceptions (not least in love) that he would document in *The Recognitions*: "You see Sheri you have made it impossible for me to believe so many lies. I could have been an awful fool if I had never met you."

Sheri became for him a model of the kind of being he'd described to Katherine Anne Porter, for the need to protect oneself against *enthusiasm*—not least against all the false promises made in the name of love.

No less dangerous is the enthusiasm that comes from sheer greed and the desire for worldly advancement—against which Gaddis, arguably, protests too much. "I am trying to be honest with you," he writes in one of the letters to Porter, inadvertently echoing T. S. Eliot ("I would meet you on this honestly"), though the echo is obvious coming after his direct citation for Porter of two lines from "The Love Song of J. Alfred Prufrock." The letter from the twenty-five-year-old aspiring author is notable, as much for its fandom as its awkward attempts at suppressing this. Here we find a rare example of the way Gaddis could sometimes open himself to an older contemporary and habitué of New York publishing circles. And it's one of the few occasions when we can observe in him a character trait noticed by his youthful peers and Village acquaintances, a trait entirely consistent with his motivating tension between an internalized control and what Anatole Broyard called a "capacity for recklessness," between secrecy about what he was working on and the desire to make known all that really was happening to him and his contemporaries: "like many of us," Broyard recalls, "Willie was a closet writer and his conversation was warped or deformed by this hidden ambition, which was either repressed in a way that almost disarticulated him or there would be sudden uncontrollable bursts of literature in his talk that had broken out of his notebooks or journals."[10] It might have been that Gaddis simply "didn't trust" Broyard, but if that is so, a tendency to hide materials he had under way was noticed not least by Broyard himself, who became a model for the smooth sailing Max in *The Recognitions* and who in life, as we will see, was a competitor for the affections of Helen Parker. But the same attitudes in Gaddis would be noticed also by Parker, who never saw the portrait of herself (as the character Esther) that Gaddis was producing when the two were living together in the Village in the late forties.

He mistrusts enthusiasm not least *in himself*, as he represents himself here for the first time at age twenty-five, to the first established writer (Porter) with whom he'd initiated formal contact. He distinguishes himself from what he regards as the (very American, typically New York City) "vanity of letter writing, of shouting out for witness." He would see still more distasteful forms of this behavior in Americans abroad:

> with the camera everywhere, that filthy silent witness; and to jump off of the aeroplane when it lands in one country after another: no time to look at the volcano or feel the air except to say to another how hot it is, but (because the 'plane will only be in Guatemala, in Nicaragua, in Costa Rica, for fifteen minutes) that one must get to the counter and send off postal cards with a picture of the volcano he did not see, to witness.[11]

That he was writing to Porter (whom he'd not met) from the Canal Zone, where he was employed at the time, should have suggested his separateness from the postwar transnational tourist classes. He may have been less convincing about his disdain for the necessary arts of professional networking, especially when he admits in his letters how much he could value a kind of witness achieved among equals, those whose companionship and good report one desires. At this early stage in the conceptualization of his novel, he was also capable unselfconsciously of paraphrasing (chapter, verse) his current reading of the New Testament, when Jesus ("in Matthew 9:30, 31") after healing the blind man told all observers, "See that no man know it. But they, when they departed, spread abroad his fame in all that country."[12]

Porter, for her part, could impart to Gaddis a confidence in his own affective response to current writing that was being celebrated: He had read her analysis of Gertrude Stein in *Harper's*; the editor of that magazine had given him Porter's address. She wrote back, probably because of the boy's Harvard cachet and his position, however lowly and brief, at the *New Yorker*, where she never had a story accepted. (*Harper's* and the *Atlantic* were her most important venues.[13]) Porter knew the stakes and the need to stay in touch with the generations. But there was something more that she was able to give to the correspondence. Her taste in literature was no less visceral than his; in the editorial headnote to her essay, Porter admitted Stein "has had a horrid fascination for me, really horrid, for I have a horror of her kind of mind and being; she was one of the blights and symptoms of her very sick times" (quoted in *L* 85n). The lack of such feeling in Stein, as far as Gaddis was concerned, was connected with the "nihilism" and "absolute denial of responsibility" that he rejects in a more intellectual way.[14] Indeed, Porter's ability to combine affect and intellect separates her work from the writing by women that Wyatt complains about in *The Recognitions*, when it "—seems to get sort of . . . Sharp, eager faces; acid, unpleasant odor . . ."(82); or Esther's attempts that seem to him "partial to the word 'atavistic' " (113). What purpose could such close observation serve when nothing of consequence was being *witnessed*?

Gaddis was not alone in his admiration, and collegial pursuit, of Porter. Alice Denham a decade later, when she spent a week in Lower Manhattan with Gaddis, had come to regard Porter and Flannery O'Conner as the two best short-story writers of the era; Porter won a National Book Award for her *Collected Stories* in 1965 although she would not have "enough money to write full time" until the age of seventy-two, after a Hollywood film had been made of her one novel, *Ship of Fools*. In an interview with Denham, after a few drinks Porter shared her thoughts on a number of notables besides Gertrude Stein:

> On Bellow—"All that pity, pity, pity me."
> On Mailer—"A smutty little boy."
> On Simone and Sartre—"To be born is to become responsible.
> They didn't discover the principle." (*SBB* 250)

To hear such strains from one so celebrated in Village circles as Porter, who had published nothing herself before the age of forty, might have conveyed to aspirants a sense that the literary field was still open to newcomers and ripe for revaluation. Gaddis at age twenty-five was able to participate through direct contact with a published author in a small but persisting community of like-minded though aesthetically varied writers whose opinions for him carried more weight than the journalistic or academic consensus of the day. Here was a woman who in her reply had "offer[ed] in some fifteen words" what Gaddis himself had realized ("with such triumph!"[15]) just a few months earlier, in pages and pages of his own working drafts: namely, the distinction between loneliness and solitude and the "incumbent responsibility" on the writer who takes seriously his aloneness. Like Denham, Gaddis mentions Sartre as a point of reference. That lived, existential dimension is what he felt went missing in Stein. Before reading Porter's essay, he'd "come on so many acclamations of [Stein's] work, read and been excited and cons[t]ernated, and not realized that emptiness until you told me about it."[16]

Denham, for her part, after borrowing a rare copy of *The Recognitions* from David Markson, would find Gaddis's main character Wyatt—like so many projections of alienation in this postwar period—to be "the height of male literary chic. A refusal to reach out, disguised as inescapable human frailty. Each in his own cell, in solitary." Much as Denham "marveled at Gaddis's symphonic, erudite slangy style," she would resist the main character's "megalomania, suffocating self-love." What she found in Porter's writing, by contrast, and aspired to in her own work, was how to represent the ways that "ordinary men and women did manage to get close, to know and touch and relate" (*SBB* 100).

Denham wasn't the only one, by the way, to benefit from Markson's active, unstinting promotion of Gaddis in and around the Village in the late 1950s: partly thanks to him, Gaddis's book, she recalls, "became the underground cult novel of our day. The too few copies in print were passed from one devotee to the next" (100).

There really existed, and thrived, informal networks among aspirants who would be encountering one another in the Village, so different from what one would find in the mainstream literary venues at the time or in the same geographical regions after they'd been "gentrified" or later (least of all) in the so-called social networks online. A sense of participation and even selflessness, so well embodied in the eventual efforts on Gaddis's behalf by younger contemporaries such as Markson and Jack Green, must have helped sustain a sense that an audience of writers, writing for other aspiring writers and on the lookout for vital signs, could be reached semi-independently by word of mouth if not through official channels. Green advocated on behalf of *The Recognitions* in his self-published, hand-mimeographed *newspaper*; Markson went so far as to devise a scene in one of the potboilers he was writing to support himself at the time, *Epitaph for a Dead Beat* (1961). Markson's fictive private eye, Harry Fanin, enters the empty apartment of a key witness in the case—a student from Columbia, Markson's alma mater, as it happens—and finds the following passage from a course paper recently knocked out on the typewriter: "And thus it is my conclusion that *The Recognitions* by William Gaddis is not merely the best American novel of our time, but perhaps the most significant single volume in all American fiction since *Moby-Dick*, a book so broad in scope, so rich in comedy and so profound in symbolic inference. . . ."

Restricted to highbrow pulp fiction fans until Green quoted it a year later in his *newspaper*, that passage in Markson would stand as the first substantive critical revaluation of Gaddis's first novel. Literary scholarship, for its part, would not venture such comparisons until *The Recognitions* was reissued as a mass-market paperback in 1974, when the Cambridge literary scholar Tony Tanner took that opportunity, in a review in the *New York Times Book Review*, to rank Gaddis alongside Thomas Pynchon. "In its scope, its witty-serious use of erudition, its endless exploitation of the resources available to a modern text, its brilliant use of language, and, not least, its marvelous humor and range of tone," *The Recognitions* seemed to Tanner scarcely less of an accomplishment than it had to Markson and Green: it was for Tanner "one of the most important American novels written since the last war."[17]

How different in tone the work of Gaddis's peers and younger contemporaries now seems from that of the literary establishment in the 1940s and 1950s, from Mailer, James Jones, and Herman Wouk. And how different Tanner in the 1970s must have seemed from the reigning British establishment, which was slow to include postwar American writers in the Oxbridge curriculum. Where the reigning English novelist Somerset Maugham might have analyzed and explained an artist away for readers of middlebrow journals like the *Atlantic*, Porter had taken Stein's approach to heart and had communicated to Gaddis, in turn, a critical sense of "how far can a writers' writer go." If Gaddis would be himself regarded as a "writer's writer" by mainstream reviewers and a small but steady stream of graduate and professorial admirers, his own "defeat" would not be, like Stein's, an emptiness that comes from an avoidance of the lives he'd encountered up close, of "some people who are naked" as he was calling the novel at the time. Through all the book's transformations, a dedication to a lived, learned, legislated, and litigated reality in Gaddis's writing would be no less a cause of excitement among a stream of admiring graduate students, professors, and professionals; it would also be a source of consternation for reviewers. But in either case his writing would be grounded in realities that he himself had *seen*, in his travels and professional labor and his loves no less than his wordcraft.

As Gaddis's reading from 1948 onward deepened and branched out, the biblical conception of witnessing would converge with another, broader concept—that of *recognition*, evoking the title of a third- or fourth-century Christian novel (formerly misattributed to Pope Clement, hence sometimes called the Clementine *Recognitions*) that Gaddis first encountered in Graves's *White Goddess*.[18] At the same time, he could anticipate that his own seeking was destined to go underground and largely *unrecognized*. Yet the multiple quests undertaken by his contemporaries in Lower Manhattan and abroad—these would not go unrecorded in their varying degrees of worthiness. Indeed, that was the insight on which he staked his claim to notability, even as he sought to overcome failure in the arts through its literary representation.

No resolution is possible with or between two imaginations as wrought as Wyatt's and Esme's, and Gaddis does not seek any. As happens so often with what might be serious quests in his characters, instead of lighting out for territories (the habitable earth was by then already settled) or setting a direction for oneself in connection with one's contemporaries (social, sexual, intellectual, or professional), characters are set adrift within a society in disintegration. Here is the context in which the search for Esme takes its frantic, even comic turn when both Wyatt (leaving Valentine for dead) and Otto (fleeing with his counterfeit money) search for Esme, going from Bellevue Hospital to Horatio Street, and finally confronting each other in front of Esme's Jones Street apartment house (694–99), the address where Gaddis's real-life competitor, Anatole Broyard, would stay for some months with Sheri Martinelli. (The second-floor walk-up is described in Broyard's memoir, *Kafka Was the Rage*.) The fictional Otto's abandonment and Wyatt's self-control converge, although the object of their respective quests eludes both. Esme has already left for Europe and we won't see her or Wyatt together from this point on, and neither one will be referenced by name. (Wyatt later, in Spain, takes on the name "Stephen," which his mother had initially intended for him.)

By contrast with the elusive Esme, Wyatt's wife Esther (who is based on a woman Gaddis did actually live with) is given enough space in the novel to articulate a personality and a perspective that might counterbalance Wyatt's. There is of course a real tendency in Esther's thinking that Gaddis, like Wyatt, wants to resist. The sources of creativity, for Esther, are indistinguishable from the person of the artist—in particular the sexual identity of a man that she can know directly, even bodily through strengths and weaknesses that might be unknown to him. Wyatt dismisses such knowledge as a distraction, another way of not seeing the work for what it is, on its own terms.[19] He recounts for example seeing a painting by Picasso (at a showing where he had *not* seen Esther, though he passed right by her and her critic friend, the improbably named Don Bildow[20]):

> —Look, I didn't see you. Listen, that painting, I was looking at the painting. Do you see what this was like, Esther? seeing it?
> —I saw it.

—Yes but, when I saw it, it was one of those moments of reality, of near-recognition of reality. I'd been . . . I've been worn out in this piece of work, and when I finished it I was free, free all of a sudden out in the world. In the street everything was unfamiliar, everything and everyone I saw was unreal. I felt like I was going to lose my balance out there, this feeling was getting all knotted up inside me and I went in there just to stop for a minute. And then I saw this thing. When I saw it all of a sudden everything was freed into one recognition, really freed into reality that we never see, you never see it. You don't see it in paintings because most of the time you can't see beyond a painting. Most paintings, the instant you see them they become familiar, and then it's too late. Listen, do you see what I mean? (91–92)

Gaddis himself, when he was deep in thought or distraction, may have been guilty of similarly misrecognizing even those he was closest to. His daughter Sarah, in her novel based in part on her parents' marriage, has the mother experience something eerily similar to what happens between Esther and Wyatt in the reception at the gallery. Lad is the character based on Gaddis; Sally Ann, his wife:

One afternoon she had found herself near his window. She had watered the garden, and she was near enough to see the paint peeling on the windowsill and hear him clear his throat. She took a step, and there he was in the open window. He was muttering and he looked up and they both jumped. Sally Ann turned away quickly, but not before his expression froze in her mind. His lack of expression—he hadn't recognized her.[21]

Readers inclined to join Wyatt and Gaddis in glorifying the liberating power of "recognition" in literature and the arts would do well to bear in mind the author's own necessary blind spots, in life and in his fictional creations.

Gaddis's orientation at this point in his career is unmistakably with Wyatt and the modernists, even if his characters' romanticism only left them adrift. But his presentation of Esther is no less detailed than that of her husband, and if she is as yet unable to articulate her positions, that is not so much an expression of their wrongness as of the hesitancies with which the more personalized approach to creativity were being voiced by women in mid-fifties America. More of them each year and each decade would come into positions of recognition, and gradual increasing preference in the newly rationalized, corporate culture. The creative writing program in particular, while in some sense a refuge from commercialization and mass production in the arts, would become none-theless a laboratory for these emergent expressions of diverse identities and unending desires (the better to satisfy the need for ever-renewing markets). A personalized definition of cultural diversity, sincerely felt (and Esther is nothing if not sincere), would become the way for artists and writers to legitimize themselves in the new cultural order.

"(Esther admired Henry James, but she trusted D. H. Lawrence)"; she listens with Wyatt to *Tosca* on the radio, "(preferring *Don Giovanni*)" (82, 92). Esther's perceptions, though here parenthetical and secondary to Wyatt's, are nonetheless registered, and recognized as components of a cor-poratist culture. Aesthetic tastes and emotional, sensual affects are worked into the narrative, bringing to life the often technique-centered discussions on the arts that enter their quiet apartment by way of Wyatt's drafting work, by way of the radio, and through visitors such as Otto whose youth and naïveté contrast so starkly with Wyatt's premature gravitas. Otto and Esther, for all their comparative vanity (Otto's play is titled *The Vanity of Time*), are pretty much moving in synch with the empty prosperity that would await the next several generations of upwardly mobile "creative" types: writers, artists, promoters. Wyatt for his part prefers immersion in past literatures and arts and a past life he rarely talks about when, subsi-dized by a counterfeit he'd sold of the Hieronymus Bosch painting in his childhood home, he was free to leave behind his seminary studies (as Gad-dis had left Harvard behind, to work and to roam).

Contrary to all talk of encyclopedism, erudition, and conceptual diffi-culty in Gaddis, it is arguably this affective and unapologetically didactic dimension of the novel's discourse on the arts that accounts for the con-tinuing attraction of Gaddis's first novel over several literary generations. Having been written before these personal qualities were channeled by American higher education into the burgeoning field of creative writing, the novel allows readers to inhabit a time when one's own positions, one's tastes, proclivities, and unscripted "near-recognition of reality" (*R* 92) were not yet expected to be presented so often or so stridently in the public sphere. Instead, the ways of articulating these things were being worked out in more circumscribed areas, one cocktail party at a time, one lover at a time, with a youthful intensity that could make it seem as if such things were being said and felt for the first time—in the lofts and bedrooms and studios of lower Manhattan, on the Left Bank of Paris (though not in the south of Spain, which Gaddis preferred and where Wyatt ends up: "I'm really a small-town boy," Gaddis wrote from Paris, "Seville is more my size"[22]). What Gaddis brought to the surface, with frankness and at a length rarely seen in fiction at the time, was more likely to be tolerated when readers could not find these things said daily in papers, or updated hourly online even as they are happening.

He was less subtle perhaps in his anticipations of the academic rise of cultural studies, and neither he nor his first readers ever would have imagined how quickly some of his made-up projects by nameless partygoers would start to sound plausible: "Someone else was saying, —When I finish this psychoanalytic critique of Mother Goose I'm going right on to the Revelation of Saint John the Divine" (*R* 584).

Gaddis himself was committed to exploring every dimension of the pretensions that surrounded him no less than his own identity, but only insofar as each aspect could devolve into a literary persona. In some ways, such self-projections may have satisfied the secretive nature that was at the heart of his conception of the artists in the novel, though the secret is easily enough revealed even to those who know little about Gaddis—that he is Wyatt Gwyon, who shares his initials, or Jack Gibbs in *J R*, who (less directly) derives from that other great American explorer of entropy, J Willard Gibbs. He is Eigen in *J R* (German for *one's own*); he shares his ambitions for a layered, accumulative world vision with Stanley the devout composer; he is Otto obviously (*auto*): the young author newly arrived from Central America with a manuscript and notions of authorial greatness. This is Gaddis in nearly every outward aspect, down to the white linen suit that Otto is wearing. *Except*, there was also a real-life Otto, the "simple minded" son of a woman Gaddis had boarded with in Arizona: "You see this woman is hard of hearing," he wrote home to Edith, "and her son Otto, who's about 23—is sort of—simple. He went thru college—then started in at Harvard (!) and then cracked up it seems."[23] The slow crack-up of Otto in *The Recognitions*, a subplot that could have been an entire novel in itself, is clearly in this case (and in every case) an admixture of Gaddis himself and those he knew, the kind of human palimpsest that Stanley, like Gaddis, sought for his art, and what made such a large canvas entirely necessary.

The character of Wyatt Gwyon, identical in so many ways to Gaddis in boyhood and in the women he lived with later, in some ways exemplifies this tendency to *distribute* aspects of oneself among many. That a single authentic poet, Gwion, would take on multiple names is summarized by Graves: "for nine months almost I was in Cerridwen's belly. At length I became Taliesin, 'Joannes' I was called, and Merlin the Diviner, and Elias, but at length every King shall call me Taliesin. I am able to instruct the whole Universe" (*WG* 119–20). And so William Thomas Gaddis, who in his university years took to signing his full name as William Tithonus Gaddis, would himself take over the multiple identities of the ancient

Welsh poetic tradition, by projecting himself into his many male characters in fiction, most with his own alphabetic identifier (on the model of
W G). This was the powerful and distinctly premodernist alternative that
Gaddis discovered in *The White Goddess*—an alternative precisely to the
proliferation of singular identities that Esther, in her rationalist regime,
assigns to the men in her life. But that does not itself stand as a rejection
of Esther, since Gaddis could find aspects of the Goddess in her, as in
all his female characters. From his own lived experience, as much as by
reading Graves, he had learned that "the real, perpetually obsessed Muse-
poet," who himself takes on a number of personae, would not find the
Goddess in any one woman: he rather "distinguishes between the Goddess as manifest in the supreme power, glory, wisdom and love of woman,
and the individual woman whom the Goddess may make her instrument
for a month, a year, seven years, or even more" (490). The women in Gaddis's life, however briefly or long they were with him, would become in
his fictions partial embodiments of the feminine power that could stand
as an alternative to the commercial, patriarchal, and progressive power
that was overtaking his life-world (and has reached its apotheosis in ours,
with gender-neutral oligarchs in place of the older patriarchy).

The assignment of various attributes from various people Gaddis knew
was similarly distributed among his characters. Graves himself as we
have seen was the physical model for the Reverend Gwyon; his son Wyatt
was modeled physically on photographer Walker Evans, who enjoyed a
mostly underground fame at the time Gaddis knew him in the late forties.
(*Let Us Now Praise Famous Men*, its text by James Agee and photo-
graphs by Evans, had been published in 1941.) Toward the end of Wyatt's
own prolonged crack-up, in which however he might emerge stronger, we
see Wyatt, like Evans and Agee, working in the vein of the American tran-
scendentalists and transferring the political innovations of the Roosevelt
New Deal and Public Works Administration into a call for literary innovation. That innovative aspect of modernity was one that Gaddis could
intermix (as had Eliot and Graves before him) with the transmogrifying
imagination of an ancient Welsh and Irish poetic lore.[24]

For Gaddis, the pursuit of women in his early manhood was bound up
in the conception of feminine power articulated in Graves's *White Goddess* and the "web of questions" that magnum opus formed in his mind.
The concept from the start suggested a unity in multiplicity, as the names
Esme and Esther suggest—for "me" and for "her." This multiplication
(and in Esme's case, dissolution) of identities would be indicated as we
have seen in the variety of names given to his main male character, Wyatt
Gwyon. In Graves's book Gaddis would read about the poet Taliesin's

grand conundrum, elaborations of the more human-scale "riddle" posed in one's youth by Little Gwion, the adept who "accidentally alighted on ancient mysteries" (75) such as the following:

> "I was the tower of the work of which Nimrod was the overseer. . . ."
> "I was in the firmament on the Galaxy when Rome was built. . . ."
> "I was loquacious before I was given speech; I am Alpha Tetragrammaton."
> "I was with my King in the manger of the Ass. . . ."
> "I am a wonder whose origin is not known. I shall remain until the Day of Doom upon the face of the earth." (119–20)

Graves solves the riddle by way of an elaborate alphabetic scheme that is impossible to summarize though a pleasure to read as the twentieth-century poet inhabits the unstable spellings and fluid identities he discovered in early Welsh and "contemporary Irish bardic lore" (122). For present purposes, it will be enough to note that young "Gwion with his Dog, Roebuck and Lapwing would never have gone to such extravagant lengths in confusing the elements of their conundrum unless the answer had been something really secret, something of immensely greater importance than a mere A.B.C." (121). That importance, "proof of Gwion's acquaintance" with his poetic tradition, was at once "a secret religious formula," a ritual performance, and (most important) a gift brought to the White Goddess—whose approval could not be known in advance, though the giver could be sure that the logics and commercial exchanges of a patriarchal order were not likely to please her.

Needless to say, Gaddis would have recognized something of his own heritage, of "immensely greater" than alphabetical importance in his Welsh name, with that *dd* in place of the *eth*.[25] We have observed how Gaddis in his boyhood yearned not so much for the person of his father, the failed businessman William Thomas Gaddis, as for a *paternity*. In Graves, he'd found what he was dreaming of—particularly in the elder author's mythic, linguistic, and literary ambition that Gaddis himself now determined to live up to.

The "nervousness" Gaddis had observed in Graves during their one meeting in Majorca,[26] especially when Graves would talk about things that interested him, is clearly portrayed through the character of Wyatt's father in Gaddis's opening chapter, easily among the most memorable depictions in the novel (as much so as Esme or Otto or Wyatt himself). We can observe the man alone in his library, lost in contemplation as his young son knocks tentatively at the door,[27] the boy hoping to confess his mistakenly killing a bird (but then hurrying away when there's no answer). We see Gwyon sacrifice a Barbary ape as a way to cure his son's early, unexplained illness. And we watch him descend through drink and abstruse religious study into a kind of delirium, just as we will later watch Wyatt do likewise in what must be the most obscure section of *The Recognitions*, which has been nonetheless described appreciatively by Gaddis's former Bard student, George Hunka, in a 2013 post.[28]

That same nervousness was writ large in the world vision of Arnold J. Toynbee, the other major influence Edith had heard much about after she had obtained for her son the recently published *A Study of History* (1947), abridged from what had been six volumes to a single one. Toynbee spoke not only to the world-historical dimensions of an authentic literary vision, but to Gaddis's own "wandering, this 'sense of drift' Mr Toynbee calls it."[29] Through Toynbee, what might have seemed to Gaddis a merely personal attribute of his own could be generalized as a feature of the times, indicating the inability of any one individual or group to join their wanderings or yearnings to a larger social or cultural development.

As grand theories go, few could have projected a young man's sexual ambivalence so well as Toynbee's, as one might drift from girl to girl, occasionally take up with a prostitute[30] or exert (or fail to exert, or more likely overdo) the self-control necessary for more permanent relationships. For a man in his mid-twenties, already tired of the empty prosperity of his own national culture and observing a Europe that would still be a long time emerging from the devastation of a world war, Toynbee's summary of the final stage of civilization must have seemed particularly compelling. Gaddis was writing from Central America in 1948 when he summed up Toynbee's theory:

> In this time of social disintegration there is the solution of abandon and that of self-control; of drifting, truancy, and of reason and contribution. All of this time I am between the two: drifting and trying to contribute; living a truant life and coldly insisting that the only thing that will save us from the crushing results of our current vulgarity and abandon is the rational realisation of freedom and its very essence as self-control. And so I still am unsure, for myself, how long the drift will continue.[31]

Without a transition Gaddis switches from his own truancy to America's in 1948, and back: "Only I feel that it must end for others, that USA must quit its truancy—all of this with the shadow of a war ahead so horrible and so final. But even that war, like death, is only a possibility and not a fact."[32]

As with Graves, the literary encounter with Toynbee served to push Gaddis toward a higher ambition in his own writing, a seriousness of purpose and an emerging self-confidence (or, more accurately, a confidence that his own wanderings and his own searching might reflect something larger than himself): "I have finally finished [reading] the abridgment [of Toynbee's six-volume history]," he wrote to his mother a week later, "which I think is magnificent, and am wondering if I have the nerve to start the original work, or rather to start and finish it."[33]

He had made many starts before and "the original work" had been derailed by many events, and not just the enjoyments and daily demands of living. As he later notes (again in passing, at the age of twenty-six) more than a year had passed without work on the manuscript, since the time he met up with Margaret Williams in Paris, a Vassar graduate (Jean Campbell half a decade earlier was at Radcliffe) and "a really live-wire, wonderful, very pretty American girl, very bright," as recalled by a close friend of Gaddis's from these years, Ormonde de Kay. "Margaret was his great love, at that time anyway."[34] What Gaddis experienced at the time, remarkably, was expressed by him in precisely the terms of his ongoing studies in interwar literature: against Eliot's "distraction from distraction by distraction," Gaddis felt with Margaret a "sense of concert," and some of those rare "moments we have waited for, and paid for before and after, passionless and un-looked-for."[35] Together they would meet for lunch in a café garden, or take supper at a student restaurant, or walk over the Seine (which sounds however less like a romantic excursion than a stroll with Eliot, Toynbee, and Graves "in the forest over dead leaves where they crush under quick steps refuse of nature, used, old junk, dust returning, back to the button-moulder, helpless before life"[36]). A night at the Paris opera, enjoyable and even inspiring as it must have been in life, in Gaddis's report turns into a denunciation of the bravos shouted by some of the Americans in the audience, and how his benighted countrymen "need spectacles, because the only ones who afford the grand gesture today usually end up in the prison or the asylum, so well-conducted is our sterility, so well-rewarded our antisepsis."[37]

Margaret's own transnational itinerary meant that the couple would be separated more often than not. With her, too, Gaddis would seek to share (via Edith) the books that might have brought him to the "verge of fatal enthusiasm":[38]

Item) Among the books I have brought is the incomparable *South Wind*; and in the usual spirit, I should like so to give a copy to Miss Williams, who plans to sail for Italy I think on the 12th or the 20th

[of January 1949]. Could you get her a nice copy, have it sent to her
before departure, such a splendid book for the boring days of ocean-
travel. I wrote & told her I would try to get a copy to her. It is Miss
Margaret Williams/ 439 East 86th/ NYC28. Holiday Bookstore at
49th & Lex I think had a nice copy. Would it be a good idea to call
her, to see if she is still in town by the time this letter reaches you? It is
TR6-4739. I should appreciate this immensely if it can be managed.[39]

Would it be a good idea? In the event, Edith did meet on occasion with
Margaret after she returned to the States, but the mother would be less
successful in her role as marriage counselor than in her many other desig-
nations. Young William, even as he half consciously (but with his whole
heart) set out to create a literary masterpiece, began slowly to recognize
that the freedom he'd enjoyed up to then had left him powerless to pursue
his heart's desire with Miss Williams. At the most basic level, there was
the not-uncommon awkwardness of a long-distance relationship, which
he expressed to his mother: "Lord, how far away from it I feel here; and
I suppose I envy you all some of these next weeks you're going to pass
together. Is it a strong mark in my disfavour, that I'm not on the spot
asking [Margaret's] mother for daughter's hand? I suppose; but I really
couldn't see any better way to manage it."[40]
    There was also the awkward mediation between parent and fiancée:

> I suppose funniest in this whole thing really is the round of letters we
> are exchanging, you & I & Margaret: you writing me not to be angry,
> disappointed; I writing you not to be disappointed if she can't visit
> Massapequa immediately, and saying I hope she can see and talk with
> you honestly & freely, you writing me and saying how glad you are
> that she can talk with you honestly & freely, she writing me that she
> hopes it's all right if she talks with you openly when I've just written
> her that I hope she will . . . well, with such support on all sides we
> should come through.[41]

Except that, of course, openness and honesty and support on all sides are
the excellent values one invokes when love is gone, or never was present,
on one side.
    Gaddis's first thought was to flee further, back to Spain. It is the same
internal consideration that had taken him traveling to the American
Southwest in the Harvard years; had taken him to New York's Greenwich
Village and an entry-level position at the *New Yorker* (in direct defiance of
his dean at Harvard's suggestion on his expulsion, to avoid journalism),

and had taken him ultimately to Central America and Europe and North Africa. Ever to flee: away from the one world city that refused him entry on terms that he could live with. Spain at least gave him a "feeling of permanence" (L 134), down to the plates of boiled potatoes and string beans that were served at lunch daily, and much else that carried on in the countryside "with unimaginative variety." But he recognized by now that this particular line of flight would soon be closed to him: "Sometimes it looks as though just putting everything into one bag that would fit and going back to Spain would be the easiest and by far the most sensible thing. But too late now for such vagabonding notions."[42]

Vagabondage, "the solution of abandon" in the scheme of civilizations, was never simply opposed by Toynbee to "that of self control." The abandoned and the controlling spirit, like the vagabond moving from subsistence job to job and the tourist managing a bank account across national borders, could be held in tension mentally, and this is the ideal that Gaddis sought—in reality. If he could not (but how many men could?) achieve this balance with the women in his life, the world-historical tension could be observed nonetheless through the petty conflicts and unfulfilled intimacies that he would represent so well, if also ruthlessly, in his novels. His imagination of woman and the feminine was given form in fiction, and transformative power in the world. Already he could feel, in his young manhood, "the slowly transmogrifying products of [. . .] imagination, whether consummately pagan products or not, [. . .] being articulated and validified" (L 133) not in marriage nor in travel, but in the literary work he was finally committing himself to finishing, whether or not he would be able to continue writing as a career, and whether or not he would find happiness in marriage.

His mature loves at this stage, Helen Parker and Sheri Martinelli, embodied for him both sides of the opposition. Both women, in their sensual, aesthetic, social, and professional lives, were as exploratory as their sometime boyfriend; both were a few years older, Sheri had a five-year-old boy and Helen two young sons; all three adults had numerous lovers and neither Helen, Sheri, nor young Willie would have survived for long in the Village without a measure of self-control. The men in Gaddis's novels tend gradually to lose control over the course of a long, stressed-out trial (it is as much a reason for his books' length as the need to get everything *in*, to do justice to his world-historical themes and to the vast majority of ordinary Americans who wouldn't know or care about those themes). By contrast, the women steadily, and quietly, acquire control over their own lives and (in *J R* especially) over business concerns that the men are too distracted to follow. Gaddis in his heart may have idealized the women he knew and he pursued in his life;[43] he never did so in fiction, although he may have indulged himself by having the fictive counterparts of both women suffer through an unrequited love for Wyatt. But it is the women who embody life-giving alternatives to the tensions that paralyze Wyatt to the end, even as it is Amy Joubert and Stella Bast in *J R* who gain control of substantial business assets, while the men in their lives—Bast, Gibbs, and Eigen—are variously sidelined.

In some ways, Gaddis's "sort of parapatetic [*sic*] life"[44] encouraged the solution of abandon, a resistance to bondage be it social, statist, or "the bondage of respectable employment."[45] It also enabled a level of self-control by keeping the women in his life at a safe distance. Instead of resolving conflicts, there was also always the opportunity for him (or them) simply to move on, and away: "And kind Helen," he writes at age twenty-six from the Canal Zone, "she has sent cards, and a handsome necktie, and a lovely letter (though I will admit one which, for all its love, makes me feel safer at 9000 miles from NY!)."[46] With her, as with Margaret and all women he knew while the first novel was in progress, the prospect of domestic intimacy was held at a distance, much as was the prospect of abandon on a world-historical scale: "And if [Margaret] is not on her way" to London to see him? He would "come back to Spain and keep on working as I am doing now. I think it's going well . . . But heaven knows worth staying with until something positive appears, like a marriage or a war you know."[47] The novel itself, composed while "sitting over this machine working in a small room" was for him a clear alternative, a more controlled process than either marriage or war could have been.

Sheri Martinelli, who appears very much as herself as Esme in *The Recognitions*, would admit (in retrospect) to a spiritual emptiness during those Village years until she, similar in this respect to Gaddis, found refuge in high modernist art: as Gaddis remained true all his life to his college reading of Eliot, his Christmas with the Nappers in Sussex, and his meeting in Majorca with Robert Graves, Sheri placed herself directly under the tutelage of Ezra Pound during the years when he was incarcerated at Saint Elizabeths.[48] In art and in life, it was a time of seeking amidst deep discontent with transformations that would remain, for a long time, underground, subterranean. Gaddis himself eventually came to doubt that any future biographer could capture the "under current" of those times. Here is an unsent letter on the publication of what Gaddis called Steven Moore's "version of Sheri":

> The under current of the drug ambience, Stanley Gould, Anton Rosenberg (dead a few weeks ago), Edie Shu the heavy drug connexion,

hardly the 'rival' you imply [in the published essay]. No, no you had to be there, hardly 'indifference' [Sheri's for Gaddis] but life & book were Sheri being celebrated, that winter of '47 I was perhaps unwisely contemplating some sort of permanent arrangement at her decision, instead a telegram among my papers signaling her nonappearance with 'sister Judith is in town' & I left that night for Panama, to Spain as you note the year following. No, those were youthful grand and often wild times. You had to be there.[49]

As we left Wyatt earlier in this chapter with his belated and hapless decision to pursue Esme, we can follow Gaddis's hopes for "some sort of permanent arrangement" only so far. The "under current" however can be followed, and in essence that's what the novel *is*—and what the archive can substantiate, with the urgent or evasive telegrams Gaddis saved no less than the everyday correspondence, the minutiae, the clippings from daily papers that may or may not have found their way into the fictions. Alice Denham, who *was* there, puts it this way: "Like the Beats, some of us lived the sixties in the fifties" (*SBB* 75). Anatole Broyard, who lived with Martinelli for a few months before Gaddis met her, found the "sexual atmosphere of 1947 almost impossible to describe [t]o someone who hasn't lived through it," not if we haven't internalized the specific inhibitions that upper- and middle-class young men and women of the time brought with them to their Village lives: "Before sex was explained to us in the sixties we had to explain it to ourselves."[50] The Bohemian fifties produced the road maps and cultivated sensibilities for the radical sixties. And the road maps can be read, retrospectively, in memoirs such as Denham's and Broyard's and precisely in Gaddis's first novel. It was a transnational sensibility that inaugurated (for example) a massive, decades-long transfer in the arts from Paris to New York City, and then from New York to the rest of the country (a process mapped, through Gaddis, by the scholar Lisa Siraganian, *LS* 101–14). And "sex too was foreign" and "was a modern art,"[51] as Broyard says, for men of his and Gaddis's generation, and for women of Sheri's and Helen Parker's inclinations: the sexual and the literary life each happened as part of a single exploration, and they happened only in the context of going to see foreign films, appreciating modern art, and observing the way that one's own American inhibitions were being questioned there, in the films and the arts and not least in the books one was reading. The larger cultural shifts might not have been experienced as such a big deal by those who were already moving from one set of parties to the same set at a transatlantic address, "to Saint Germain des Prés where they're imitating Greenwich

Village and here we are in Greenwich Village still imitating Montmartre . . ." as we've heard the character Ed Feasley remark (*R* 746).[52] But
this sea change in the arts and in cultural sensibilities would have encouraged, if only half consciously, the kind of dedication to literature and the
arts and one's own combination of sensual and philosophical exploration
that young men and women of Gaddis's and Sheri's talents would have
undertaken.

Helen Parker, whose days and nights with Gaddis are the basis of
Wyatt's marriage, would have shared Esther's worldliness in *The Recognitions* and would have moved as easily among men in the business
and publishing world, depending on where her career took her at a given
stage in her life. Depending on her career, or her whims: "a tall, stun-
ningly attractive redhead," Parker in the company of Tom Heggen is said
to have flirted outrageously with novelist John Dos Passos when the three
had "barely met" in Cuba. Heggen's *Mister Roberts* had just opened on
Broadway in 1948 and Heggen had thought of the Cuban vacation as a
kind of pre-honeymoon. He was "[f]iercely jealous of Helen's behavior
with other men"; in Cuba he "goaded her for being a 'literary nympho-
maniac.'" Parker broke with Heggen; she met up again in Cuba and in
Manhattan with Dos Passos, twenty years her elder, whose wife of twenty
years had recently died. "Dos" was as much "intrigued" by her literary
knowledge as by her beauty, this former editor at the sensational illustrated magazine *Liberty* who was able to speak knowledgeably about his
own work.[53]

Gaddis, for his part, also competed for Helen's attention, even as he
is recalled to have vied with Heggen and the Village "champion womanizer,"[54] Anatole Broyard. So if Gaddis could never be secure with Helen or
with any of the women he would encounter in the Village or Montmartre
during this era, he also tended to make light of Helen's own tentative
moves toward independence and professional ambition. These found
expression at this moment in her life as she moved from man to man,
most of them writers. *Mister Roberts* was already a huge success as a
first novel when she took up with Heggen in the fall of 1946. As Parker
recalls, she was corralled one evening and taken to dinner by Heggen and
his friend Max Shulman (a future best-selling author). Not for nothing
was this particular concentration of bars and restaurants and upwardly
mobile artists, post-grads, returning war veterans, and professionals
called a "village." Gaddis heard about what was going on, showed up in
the restaurant, drunk, and went on to insult Heggen. Shulman distracted
Gaddis, who somehow confused him with Bud Schulberg and told him
how much he had enjoyed *What Makes Sammy Run?* Later, Tom and

Helen left for her nearby apartment only to find Gaddis there, waiting for them.

Broyard recalls this story Helen once told about Gaddis:

> Before I knew her, she had been sick with a bad case of the flu. She called up Milton Klonsky, an old friend of hers, and said, "I'm sick and my refrigerator's empty—how about bringing me a ham sandwich?"
>
> As literal-minded as only a self-absorbed poet can be, or as careless as most men when they're not in love, Klonsky took her at her word and brought her a ham sandwich. Two slices of bread and ham with a bit of mayonnaise.
>
> She made the same call to Willie and he arrived with a large wicker basket covered with a red-checked cloth. It was filled with wine, cognac, smoke-cured ham, brandied peaches, French bread. As I said, Willie was gallant. He was like a lover in an English novel.[55]

Most of Parker's letters have disappeared, but in the 1970s she was interviewed by John Leggett for a dual biography of Heggen and Ross Lockridge Jr., author of another enormously successful first novel, *Raintree County* (1948), which is even longer than *The Recognitions*. The connecting theme of Leggett's book is that Heggen and Lockridge, after their successes, both committed suicide without producing a follow-up. Helen Parker figures prominently in the "Tom" section of Legget's biography (see especially 330–34 for her relationship to Gaddis) and was later the topic of an investigation by author Mark Lewis, who contacted Parker's sons after her death in 1993 but unfortunately came up with mostly negative results: "No one knows," Lewis writes in an e-mail, "whether she burned her papers at some point before she died, or threw them in the trash or what. But nothing was found. Gaddis, Tom Heggen, Dos Passos, Ginsberg, Kerouac, Frank O'Hara, Alan Ansen—she must have had an archive of enormous value at some point. I bet she made a bonfire of it all. But who knows."[56]

Helen's pragmatism is given directly to Esther in *The Recognitions*. Taking up with Otto, and then with the ad man Ellery ("—It does me good to be seen in successful company" [151]), Esther may pine for Wyatt and hope for his return. She might lack his talents and his experience and referential range, but ultimately it is her personalized, pragmatic, and identitarian approach that finds purchase in the emerging art culture of the late 1940s and 1950s, the culture that anticipates (as we have seen) the channeling of unruly aesthetic and sensual engagements, the lifeblood of *The Recognitions*, into creative writing and visual arts programs where such readily abandoned desires could be more systematically cultivated and, yes, controlled.

Though Gaddis was at work on *The Recognitions* at the time he knew Helen Parker, he kept the manuscript from her and never told her that she would be the basis for one of the book's key characters: "A bit childish," it seemed to her after the fact, "since he certainly intended to publish."[57]

The theme of distrust would be voiced by others who knew Gaddis intimately. Alice Denham, for example, who knew Gaddis when he was between marriages, recalls showing him a letter she'd received from a Mexican lover of hers. Gaddis "gasped" when he read it, and marveled: "why, you must have trusted one another completely" (*SBB* 242). For Denham, such trust was normal but she had the distinct feeling that Gaddis himself had never extended, or felt, that level of confidence in his own relationships with women.[58] She wrote in her memoir, after Gaddis (then in his early forties) moved in with her for a week in an apartment overlooking Gramercy Park, that his touch may have been "sure and strong and his skin very warm" and he seemed to her (after the decade of his first marriage) "accustomed to calm sex, to expect it as the natural culmination of being together" (241). But then "it never occurred to either" of them "to fall in love" (245). And it never seemed to Denham that Gaddis, or any of the writers of his generation whose parties she attended and whose company she kept, understood women.[59]

Muriel Murphy, with whom Gaddis shared an apartment and travel over a period of sixteen years, connected the pervasive distrust with his inclination, instilled as we have seen in childhood, toward secrecy. "There's no reaching someone so thoroughly encased, as was Gaddis," she would write in her posthumously published *Excerpts from the Unpublished Files of Muriel Oxenberg Murphy*:

> He was a fortress, and a fortress of purpose. Like Shaka Zulu, the African chieftain who united the Eastern tribes of Africa, and did so by developing a cleaving, sharper weapon than had been known before, so did Gaddis with his prose. And to do so he sharpened himself daily, quietly, privately, advancing and "getting the work done." He drew the characters of his novels from "back then," choosing from "back then" because in those days for him there was love—the love of oneself, other-enhanced. (*E* 95)

Harsh though this evaluation might sound, and loveless, Muriel's judgment is consistent with Gaddis's own final look back on the final page of his posthumously published work *Agapē Agape*. There we find a final reference not to "my books," but to "the book I wrote then," singular: "my first book, it's become my enemy" (95). *The Recognitions* was the one that absorbed all the love he had to give. *J R*, arguably, is the greater novel, and I will make that argument forthwith. But by the time Gaddis had regrouped for that book he had already been through one marriage; and by the time *J R* was published, and Gaddis was left with both a National Book Award and substantial debt from numerous advances over the years of the book's composition, his second marriage, to Judith Thompson, was nearing its end. The reality of his life with any woman could hardly have matched his imagination of it and Muriel, who can afford such frankness, regards his disposition simply as self-love and world-weariness: "Not an ounce of social conscience in this, nothing more than taking the pen, the pencil, to point out how rotten everything was, and how unfair" (*E* 95).[60] That was certainly part of his authorial makeup, and he may well have hardened with the years, though a desire in him ran deep throughout his life for social cohesion, for the *agapē* of Christian religion that is revealed as a model for humanity, not for lived relations between one man and one woman.

What would go missing after his first novel, even as the postwar expansion of a woman's economic power and political presence would energize some of the most extensive (and personally felt) cultural and material revolutions in world history, was the figure of the Goddess as a counterforce to the culture of progress and rationality. What Gaddis presents in the two fully drawn women in *The Recognitions*, as tentative moves toward an aesthetic alternative to corporate power, would be mostly set aside in the next four decades by the feminization of labor within a rising corporate state. This is not the world Gaddis would have wished to depict when he entered his literary career at Harvard with lighthearted descriptions of social vanities. It is not a world that even the early liberationist movements among women could have clearly envisaged or desired. (An unprecedented expansion of nannies and maids servicing an equally unprecedented concentration of wealth in the United States has been well observed by Barbara Ehrenreich: "And for this," she asked in a late-1980s forum in downtown Manhattan, "we fought to get out of the kitchen?") But it is the world—our current world—whose gradual emergence Gaddis depicts more systematically, with a greater humor and arguably less pathos,[61] than any contemporary author, perhaps precisely *because* of the absence of trust in human intimacy, the unceasing refinement of his own powers of observation and listening, and his familiarity with earthbound, undramatic secrets at the source of power.

Not that Gaddis participated in the paranoia and speculation into assassinations and covert military actions and intelligence operations that preoccupied his more celebrated literary peers, such as Norman Mailer and Thomas Pynchon, Don DeLillo and Joan Didion. The secrets were all there anyway for anyone to see or hear, in the papers (which Gaddis clipped daily), in the prices of things, and in the numbers (the populations, the troops on the ground, the dispositions of peoples in and out of homes and offices). The same secrets are at work today, the same "covert" operations that emerge with the same regularity as sex scandals and governmental agency actions revealed in personal tell-all narratives by former operatives and contractors.[62] None of the secrets, in Gaddis, fit comfortably within the framework of a personal narrative; and none of them have much to do with love.

# Chapter 6

# The Self Who Could Do More

—Criticism is the art we need most today. But not, don't you see? not the "if I'd done it myself . . ." Yes, a, a disciplined nostalgia, disciplined recognitions but not, . . .

Wyatt Gwyon in The Recognitions (335)

Responses from friends to the book's long-anticipated publication arrived throughout the summer and fall of 1955, sometimes along with congratulations on Gaddis's marriage and the birth of his daughter, Sarah. In October 1955 Barney Emmart expressed his pleasure "that all went well" and he supposed "that an heiress is as good as any heir;"[1] Emmart's father sent wishes hoping that by now Gaddis's "search for a satisfactory job has ended with something that pleases you."[2] Gaddis must have expressed his material concerns in a letter to Robert Graves, since the latter's congratulations on the child are followed immediately with an acknowledgment: "yes: isn't it hard to make a living?"[3]

Gaddis heard from strangers as well. One reader in St. Louis wrote to ask how he could "know so *much*? The second time through your novel I began to place a tiny 'tic' or dot beside each line that held something I wanted to look up in the stock rooms, for something I wanted to share with someone—reading it aloud—or something I found unbearably funny or touching. Finally I gave it up because almost every page held a 'tic.'"[4] Another in Radford, Virginia, was impressed by the book "as a possible bringer of good tidings, feet beautiful upon the mountains," though it occurs to the letter-writer that Gaddis "may have neglected the Greeks to the detriment" of the novel's content.[5] He had a letter from the National Jewish Hospital at Denver "written in the interest of the [tubercular] patients whose lives are entrusted to us for medical and surgical care" and who'd circulated a single copy among themselves and asked to receive a signed, autographed copy, "gratis."[6] One Ruth Gaddis Jeffries of Tucson wished to "inquire if by chance your family was from the Eastern branch at Uniontown, Pennsylvania where the 'Gaddis Fort' still stands."[7] A graduate student at the University of Alabama was planning "a comparison of your 'Recognitions' and perhaps some of F. Scott Fitzgerald."[8] An M.A. hopeful at the University of Oklahoma (whom Gaddis answered) mentioned his Jesuit education and time spent "knocking around medieval philosophy and kindred subjects"; he had it in mind to "write criticism that will act as a bridging device between the artist and his potential audience."[9] David Markson, a recent Columbia graduate and a familiar of Malcolm Lowry, would have to wait six years before Gaddis was capable of an answer. Markson had written in an uncanny anticipation of his own eventual, entirely citational antinovels: "What I want to know is, outside of perhaps *The Destruction of the Destruction of the Destruction*, what the hell is left to write? Or read."[10] Another made it known to Gaddis that "Anyone in this day and age who writes a 956 page book and expects anyone to read it has got to be a conceited idiot."[11] There was a letter from the author of a (self-proclaimed) "long novel dealing with a homosexual—I believe it is the greatest book ever written about a 'gay' man." He thought an introduction from Gaddis might help "ward off attacks by the censors." Gaddis would be, "naturally," the "first to peruse the finished product."[12] "With all sincerity," Miss Hilarie Harnell of St. Louis, Missouri, informs him that "I bought your damned book 'The Recognitions' and, having paid $7.50 for it, feel entitled to make the following comment of objection: Why did you 'kill off' Esme! She didn't in reality die—I don't believe it—You just didn't want the possibility of her appearing to disturb the equanimity of the mind. (Whose mind?) Death makes it so safe, so final! . . . and so hopeless!! You're horrid . . . unnecessarily cruel—I won't say selfish—and unromantic. I hate you."[13] Gaddis saved them all, including a chastising letter from his former headmaster, John Kingsbury (who'd only read the review in *Time* and not the book itself).

No better summary of the book's eventual popular reception appeared, in print or in letters, than a whimsical blurb that Barney Emmart sent to Gaddis in a letter of 12 March that year: "Friends, have you read *The Recognitions* by William Gaddis? When this talented young man gave up the pleasures of the Harvard Club, he did it for your sake. He listened for you to endless cocktail party conversations. Ate for you in Tunisia (sheeps' eyes boiled in oil). Suffered hangovers for you in a hipster's hangout located in a moving van. All so that you would not have to budge from your comfortable armchair in Suetville, L.I. Could Thomas Merton say more; could Milton see more; could Beethoven hear more, —for *you*?

Would Uncle Fultie give up celibacy for you, as did Mr. Gaddis? Friends, you owe it to yourselves to read. . . ."

Four decades later, Gaddis recalls how he mentioned to his friend and fellow author Otto Friedrich how he was just then "preening" himself on one of the "infinitely few fan letters that accompanied the publication" of *The Recognitions*. Friedrich observed, "Those are the people who come after you in the middle of the night with an axe,"[14] a line he later incorporated into *Agapē Agape* (55).

It was unlikely that any novelist, this soon after the upheavals of the Second World War, could have achieved the cultural syntheses that elude his characters. Yet the search itself, through fragments that had been articulated by one's modernist predecessors, was being lived through by contemporaries who were able, enough of them, to recognize in Gaddis's writing a way forward, precisely because Gaddis had placed the compositional problems he set himself among so many different characters in the fiction. Few novelists have written so well or so movingly of the imaginative effort that goes into the making of a work of art. However scathing or satirical his presentations can be, Gaddis is entirely democratic when distributing his own creative dimensions among his many characters: Stanley's obsessed revisions of his palimpsest score, Esme's Eliotic "raid on the inarticulate" in her druggy letters and poems (299), the inept strike-overs and desperate plagiarisms that comprise the notebooks of Otto and Ludy, Wyatt's painstaking forgery (adding "layer upon layer" to already established forms [275]), and even Sinisterra's forged currency or Mr. Feddle's wholesale appropriations of completed masterpieces are meant to suggest distinct facets of Gaddis's own narrative performance in *The Recognitions*, his absorption into himself of the perfected expressions and methods of antecedent literature, and his simultaneous reaction against them. Similarly in *J R*, Gibbs's sounding out sentences, the newspapers that accumulate in Eigen's workroom (Gaddis was a lifelong habitual clipper), and the figure of Bast working through the night hunched over a composition "as though listening to bring sounds into being" (286) all hint at the precise balancing of originative effort and passive verbal transcription that sustains the spoken discourse in the even more radical second novel (and what by the mid-1970s is a much more thoroughgoing incorporation of creative practices).

If Gaddis's writing often depicts writers, musicians, and artists struggling with their work, this is largely because such depictions refer us to the creative, as opposed to the popular or convivial, personality behind the novels. Like Melville writing of Pierre at his book, Gaddis defines himself by his project, constructing a coherent personal identity in terms that are quite specific to the aesthetic or technical problems that engage him just then, during the actual writing of the novel. The compositional self, the being that undergoes "the real work . . . the thought and the rewriting and the crossing out and the attempt to get it right," as Gaddis noted in specific reference to *J R*,[15] is the essential personality, the first-order phenomenon, what, in fact, the book is "about."

The process of self-creation eludes biographical definition because Gaddis identifies himself not with the completed work as such but with the possibilities for perfection (and Thomas Wolfe's "billion deaths of possibility") that he may only have glimpsed in the act of writing. This is what Wyatt attempts haltingly to tell his father in explanation for not having finished his boyhood portrait of Camilla: "—There's something about a . . . an unfinished piece of work, a . . . a thing like this where . . . do you see? Where perfection is still possible? Because it's there, it's there all the time, all the time you work trying to uncover it" (57). Wyatt works in the knowledge that every completed line in a drawing, like each typed page in an evolving manuscript, tends inevitably to divert the work from its first conceptualization in the mind of the artist, just as surely as "you can change a line without touching it" by bringing the initial sketch into new and unforeseen contexts (127, 243). But if an idea can be altered by its later embodiment, there is also the chance that further possibilities will have to be sacrificed, even as Melville's Pierre, forced by exigency ("rent and bread") into premature publication, found that "the printed pages now dictated to the following manuscript, and said to all subsequent thoughts and inventions of Pierre—*Thus and thus; so and so; else an ill match.*" The discarded or unrealized possibilities are as much a part of the imaginative life of the artist as those that eventually reach completion— possibly more so. And this is why Melville, in nearing the close of *his* great failed autobiographical novel, could write of Pierre's enterprise that "two books are being writ: of which the world shall only see one and that the bungled one. The larger book, and the infinitely better, is for Pierre's own private shelf."[16]

We might begin to understand, through Melville, why Gaddis—who was otherwise so selective in what he shared with interviewers—took care to preserve and make available to posterity so many of the materials that *went into* the books. The clippings and rejected drafts and even the notes toward anonymous corporate writings are all there in the archive, evidence of all that passed before the self that mattered most to Gaddis at the moment of composition. In this sense, through his own impulse toward preservation, we have a kind of access to the "larger book" that remained on Gaddis's own "private shelf."[17] And there would be, also, the book that inhabited the minds of the readers who identified for reasons of their own with this or that aspect. "Whose mind?"[18] Indeed. One reader might hate him, from the bottom of her heart, for "killing off" a character; another might tick off encyclopedic references; a third would go on to become a major novelist in his own right; and the next might find his own sexual identity confirmed somehow in the imagined life of an author who cannot be known to him, personally. There are as many private shelves as there are readers.

The travel, the reading, the research (in books he found and those he had Edith purchase at Brentano's and Holiday's in New York); the cross-cultural exchanges and missed connections: all that would be formalized and professionalized in later years by graduate programs in a land-grant university system that was beginning a new phase of expansion and would soon explode throughout the United States with the return of GIs after World War II. Writing programs in particular would become hosts to, and arguably put an end to, the unsponsored researches and travels that an individual author could still imagine for him- or herself, in previous decades. The correspondence Gaddis initiated with Katherine Anne Porter; the Majorca pilgrimage he made to meet Robert Graves; a friend, one Miss Parke, who made him known to Evelyn Waugh:[19] these sorts of contacts, entered in the course of things with no urgent thought of professional advancement, are the kind of experience (neither fandom nor formal studentship) that soon enough would be made available (and in Gaddis's eyes most likely, lessened) in writing programs throughout the country.

Younger writers at the time, in turn, could look to Gaddis as a model for a worldly and unsponsored career just as Pynchon may have looked to Nabokov when, as an undergraduate at Cornell, he was able to turn in a short story to a class he had with the legendary author.[20] A decade after Gaddis, Pynchon would interrupt his Ivy League studies for a stint in the navy, which let him see the world without being a mere tourist, and a postgraduate year doing corporate writing at Boeing would have given Pynchon a taste of the life that held Gaddis for more than a decade. Younger writers found in *The Recognitions* a literary life-world unlike any they could find in universities of the time or see recorded in the media: *The Recognitions* was not merely the continuation of the modernist program that was announced so boldly by Joyce scholar Stuart Gilbert on the jacket of the first edition. ("Mr. Eliot's Waste Land was only a small corner of the wilderness so observantly and successfully explored by Mr. Gaddis.") As Ezra Pound had told Sheri Martinelli when she showed him her copy of *The Recognitions*: "You should tell your friend Joyce was an ending, not a beginning."[21] But Gaddis knew this already, and he knew it earlier than the group of young artists and writers who assembled around Pound at Saint Elizabeths Federal Hospital for the Insane.[22] Sheri was foremost among them for six years, until Pound's release in 1958. By the 1960s, not a few accomplished authors would speak of their attendance at the "Ezraversity." In retrospect, Sheri and the other seekers of instruction and access that Pound could still offer definitely have about them the air of an impromptu writing workshop or seminar.

Gaddis certainly shared the modernist impulse to go back in search of alternatives to the present. And the names he resurrected, the Welsh "Gwion," according to Graves, "the equivalent (*gw* for *f*) of Fionn, or Finn, the Irish hero of a similar tale" (*WG* 75); Gaddis had leafed through *Finnegans Wake* and thus knew that Joyce, Eliot, and Graves were each in their separate ways working the same ancient veins for alternatives, for felt differences from the present. And he, Gaddis, surely would have identified, as did Graves, with "someone who styled himself Little Gwion, son of Gwreang of Llanfair in Caereinion, a person of no importance, [who] accidentally lighted on certain ancient mysteries and, becoming an adept, began to despise the professional bards of his time because they did not understand the rudiments of their traditional poetic lore" (*WG* 75).

Gaddis in his early to mid-twenties had been keen himself to become "adept," but over the seven-year-long haul of writing *The Recognitions*, he could not in his own work keep with the continuities and the "mysteries" possessed by poets and painters of an earlier, more spiritual era. "Irony" was the tone he would fall into; and when irony could not do justice to felt inadequacies, nihilism and absurdism and a frantic seeking might take over.

With more justification than the belated "modernist" tag, Gaddis's first novel can be understood as an anticipation of postmodernism in American literature, though even here the similarities have less to do with any self-conscious commitment to experimentation in aesthetics than with a willingness on the author's part to push things to their absurd conclusions and in the process demolish received verities. What Gaddis's early work gave to his and subsequent generations, which they would not yet have found in universities or in bookstores, what could only be seen by someone of Gaddis's background to be degraded by emerging mass media, was something entirely unforeseen and (for several decades) uniquely American. Through his apolitical insistence on craft and care in the face of mass production and private dissembling, and through his powerful influence on the "very small audience" of aspiring writers whom he actually reached (*R* 478), Gaddis may have anticipated something else altogether, without intending it or even appreciating it after the fact. Neither post-modernism nor a regenerated modernism in literature, what Gaddis best realized were all the outlines and many of the practices of the oncoming discipline of creative writing in America.

How else are we to take the extended and detailed and ever so earnest discussions about art among the Village youth and older characters such as the aristocrat-critic Basil Valentine, to whom Wyatt addresses his comments about the "art" of criticism, cited in the epigraph to this chapter? All of the artists, authors, and critics in *The Recognitions* and in Gaddis's New York were finding accommodations within (or variously dropping out of) a vastly expanded commercial culture. Gaddis may have known deep down that his own early excursions far from home were "escapism," as he admitted in a letter to Edith after one of his adventures in the American Southwest; and he was not wholly above superficial needs either: "And speaking of clothes I was looking at an *Esquire* today, and gee—I love the West etc. etc. but do you think there is *any* chance of Harvard in the fall?"[23] The extended working vacations and, later, the years in Europe were unsustainable for someone who insisted on making a living as a writer—unless he wished to renounce totally the world and society that had given him this unique chance at self-development through immersion in past literature, music, and arts.

In his final appearance in *The Recognitions*, Wyatt quotes Henry David Thoreau's injunction to "simplify" and "live deliberately" (900), even if that means deliberately destroying the canvas he's working on, ridding his thought of past works so that he can, at last, do work that is his own. Is it too much to say that in his first novel Gaddis carried his art beyond himself? That he did this precisely by attending to "rudiments of . . . traditional poetic lore" (Graves) while at the same time renewing these traditions in his American circumstance? That his belief in "the self who could do more" was a way of overcoming feelings of inadequacy and the anxiety that comes from being shunted away from the mainstream material paths to success in America? That's one interpretation of the phrase "the self who could do more," but there is another way of reading it: that the work in itself brought out "more" in him than can be accounted for by his own powers, or by the conscious powers of any author whatever his or her social, sexual, or ethnic identity.

"More," then, than a belated modernist or anticipatory postmodernist: the spirit of transcendentalism is a nearer description of the aesthetic Gaddis settled into during the composition of his first fiction, and that his main, male characters at best can approach through fits and fragments. "America is the country of young men": so wrote Ralph Waldo

Emerson of the Transcendentalist Club (circa 1830) in a line that Gaddis used as an epigraph for one of his chapters (169). Emerson went on: our young men are "too full of work hitherto for leisure and tranquility." With no time for solitary reflections and domestic obligations that might concern elder generations, the young Americans of Emerson's time no less than the artists and partygoers in Gaddis's Greenwich Village would live among fragments and channel energies toward more commercial and more creative pursuits. There was one young man in particular, Henry David Thoreau, who would confront his elder with thoughts that may have had an uncomfortable bearing on Emerson's own prosperity and domestic stability: "What you seek in vain for, half your life," Thoreau told Emerson, "one day you come full upon, all the family at dinner. You seek it like a dream, and as soon as you find it you become its prey." This too would be cited by Gaddis in *The Recognitions* (265), and used again four decades later as the epigraph to Gaddis's fourth novel, *A Frolic of His Own*.[24] The circulation and recirculation of literary citations was itself a response of sorts to the fragmentation of American life, and not least the table talk and the everyday speech of ordinary Americans.

But what sort of response was it? Thoreau's elusive remark to Emerson (a man whose hospitality he shared, whose wife he coveted, and on whose land he once resided) was spoken during a walk in the woods, and the topic was (as Emerson wrote) "a night-warbler, a bird he [Thoreau] had never identified, had been in search of twelve years, which always, when he saw it, was in the act of diving down into a tree or bush, and which it was vain to seek; the only bird that sings indifferently by night and by day."[25] Emerson responded jocularly, warning Thoreau that he should "beware of finding and booking" the bird, "lest life should have nothing more to show him." Thoreau's response, that what one searches for will find one out when least expected, differs not so much from his elder's in meaning as in tone and indicates what Emerson, elsewhere in the same essay, calls "the satire" of Thoreau's "presence." Yet it is more than satire, else Emerson would not have recorded the exchange with such care: the tonal difference suggests a difference also in outlook between the two men and a source of tension in the transcendentalist project itself: the one in his domestic comfort, eyeing the cosmos; the other, observing empirical activity in the here and now that goes mostly unobserved yet at any moment can disrupt our everyday domestic arrangements.

J. M. Tyree, who analyses with keen insight the way the Thoreau and Emerson references course through Gaddis's work, points out another tension within the transcendentalist project that also bears on *The Recognitions*. That is the tension within the "Reading" section of *Walden*, where "Thoreau puts forward a capsule theory of the difference between speech and writing. The argument is set within a wider claim that applying oneself to the classics is as rewarding as studying nature itself. Stating that great books must be read 'deliberately'—the word echoes his plan of living deliberately at Walden—Thoreau asserts that there is," as he writes,

> a memorable interval between the spoken and the written language, the language heard and the language read. The one is commonly transitory, a sound, a tongue, a dialect merely, almost brutish, and we learn it unconsciously, like brutes, from our mothers. The other is the maturity and experience of that; if that is our mother tongue, this is our father tongue, a reserved and select expression, too significant to be heard by the ear, which we must be born again in order to speak.

Gaddis's dedication to presenting "the language heard," already apparent in the extended party scenes in *The Recognitions*, would only become more prevalent in his later work, though such attentions would mean little without an equally thoroughgoing commitment to written language, "the language read" (and written by the author) in solitude, away from the talk of the town and away also from the table talk of domestic life.

For many of Gaddis's first readers, and even for later, considered critics, the noise and apparent pointlessness of "the language heard" would indicate little more than an ironic attitude in Gaddis, and his literary citations by comparison only "a means of ridiculing the shallow, materialistic bent of society [. . .] through ironic allusiveness."[26] That may have been his goal in the early stages when he was still thinking of his project under such lighthearted titles as "Blague" or "Vanity" or "Some people who were naked" and his vision of Western society was closer to the art of George Grosz than to the mythography of Graves and Toynbee, the thought streams of Emerson and Thoreau. Doubtless there is no shortage of irony and satire in the novel Gaddis eventually wrote. Yet the transcendentalist background also points to something larger and more consequential: the idea that America itself can be regarded as nothing more, or less, than the speech of Americans. That is how Dos Passos would put it in a preface to his *USA* trilogy of the 1930s, an imagination of the state—or rather the moment-by-moment audible and visible life within the state—that bears comparison with Gaddis's project of disciplined recognition and nearly religious witness in secular times. The dense network of allusions that Gaddis wove into his fictions, both explicitly as epigraphs and indirectly in the body of the text, would be made to circulate, if at all, through the selfsame commercial, convivial, and domestic conversations that constitute our everyday lives. That one should find what one has sought "in vain for, half your life" (in Thoreau); that one might actually complete the work that "[rests] in the hiding places and abysses of perfection" (Nietzsche); or indeed that one should settle for any of "the billions of deaths of possibility, of things done" (Wolfe)—each of these realizations in Gaddis and among authors whose work meant something to him represented a deviation from a transcendental ideal, an accommodation to the real by the self who could do more.

Though of course it is the completed work, the work that reached publication and has since had a life of its own apart from its creator, that validates our interest in the self that could, and did, do more than his many fictive projections.

## Chapter 7

# IBM, Ford, Pfizer, and the Ghost in the Machine

Dear Pat: A very heavy schedule of people, constant talk, talk,
until instructional television seems all that exists and I feel I
cannot stand another word.

William Gaddis in Miami, early 1960s

This letter home[1]—one of fewer than a dozen extant to his first wife—is
written in his formal hand, the same script he'd used when they were
dating and he would write to her at her Barrow Street apartment in Manhattan: "I didn't mean to keep you out listening to that fool piano last
night so late (that's not true of course I did)."[2] An element of Toynbee's
"abandon" can be said to characterize the elopement of Gaddis and Pat
Black, "a pretty woman with a soft-spoken North Carolinian accent" (as
recalled by Harrison Kinney, who knew the couple, helped arrange for
Gaddis's first job as a corporate writer, and eventually talked him into
moving his wife and family out of their lower Manhattan walk-up into
a house in Croton-on-Hudson). After a seven-year assertion of Toynbee's
"self-control" that he needed to complete his novel, Gaddis had married
within months of the book's publication and his first child, Sarah Meares
Gaddis, was born some five months later. A second child, Matthew
Hough Gaddis, followed in 1958. The early years of the marriage were
happy and even boisterous, in summers especially at the family house
on Fire Island, as Sarah recalled in adulthood. Photos show a two-story
windblown structure with what could be a hundred small wood-framed
windows looking over a dune onto the Atlantic. Gaddis himself kept the
windows and the house in repair, though as years went by he would get
his son out there "to help me refurbish for rental again I guess while I try
to sort things out."[3] So long as he was working on salary, or in academia,
he did not hire out contractors for this kind of work. Inside the house
there was never a television; guests were ever present and at cocktail time

there would be, as in Sarah Gaddis's novel, *Swallow Hard*, "so many bottles on the yellow table in the kitchen you couldn't see it" (96).

Less festive, and more annoying to a housewife, might have been the clutter created at a writer's desk, especially early in the marriage when that one piece of furniture had to serve double duty as a dinner table. And the remoteness, nightly when "he goes into that workroom of his . . . and nothing comes out" (*J R* 269), and the feeling (at a time when women were more aggressively finding places of their own in the arts and the business world) that one's own creativity is being stifled: "—And what about me!" Gaddis has Eigen's wife, Marian, complain to their friend Jack Gibbs in *J R*: "—What do you think those nine years have been like for me? You won't give me anything though, will you Jack. That Ninety-sixth Street tenement when you used to come up there for dinner and we had to wait for him to get his typewriter and papers off the card table so we could eat Jack he's still working on that play, he's still rewriting it and changing it and rewriting it he won't let go of it, he won't finish it because he's afraid to compete with himself, it's himself he's . . ." (269).[4]

"The self that could do more" (and did) in *The Recognitions* had turned into a self for the later corporate writer to compete with, a standard set by his youthful self that could not be attained—or would need to be attained in an altogether different way, in a newly corporatizing environment that was itself transforming the country he thought he had known.

The prospect of deliverance through the successful completion of the all-important literary work must have been part of Gaddis family lore. Sarah Gaddis writes in *Swallow Hard*:

> Rollin's [childhood] point of view reasoned that books made money according to pages, and that should mean a lot of money for her father—seven hundred and nineteen pages' worth. But sitting in the blue-green velvet dress that [her godfather] Douglas and Winifred had given her that Christmas and watching the inauguration on television, she took timid sips of New York State champagne and had the odd sensation that Kennedy had won and her father had lost. (96)

Harrison Kinney, who knew the family (their children were friendly with one another, and Kinney joined Gaddis and his son Matthew on a camping outing), recalls the eventual breakup thus: "The requirements of writing Army films led to his frequent absences from home during 1963—usually to Europe. During his absences [Pat] proved vulnerable to the approaches of a married man, to whom my wife and I had introduced the Gaddises. . . . The threat of marital disruption added to William's already harried life. The 'other man' pressed his case and the Gaddises separated. Soon, both the Gaddises and the other couple divorced. During the strained weeks and months that followed, Gaddis, with a glass of Scotch, was a constant fixture in our living room."

Family life and fatherhood for Gaddis, like his early childhood, would be conducted mostly at a distance—during business trips when his children were infants; through letters and phone calls after the divorce, in the weeks and months when they were with their mother. With the arrival of the sixties, technology (and Kennedy) would have been the coming thing—and not technology per se so much as a managerial culture (and mass-mediated politics) that began to permeate the working lives of Americans at every level, including areas that had not been so managed previously (such as small shopkeeping, or grade-school teaching—the latter a particular interest for the new father and a key topic in *J R*). Distasteful as this managerial turn may have been to him,[5] Gaddis was not untouched by the excitement of technological advances. The itinerant dad had an insider's take on these events: "Dear Sarah I am writing you this letter in an aeroplane. . . . Do you think Matthew would like to ride in an aeroplane?"[6] The theme would carry into the 1980s: "I write you (at last) at the end of a long day, during which I earlier spoke with you on the (really miraculous when you think about it) transatlantic telephone."[7]

The only trouble, when he tried to convey a technological enthusiasm for the Ford Foundation project, is that closed-circuit television for classrooms, whatever the inherent merits, was much too familiar for children to get excited about. We all by this time, the early 1960s, had TVs at home, and however much the content and programming might have been geared to educational purposes, children of this era (like those today who have grown up with computers and the Internet) already knew TV as "an accepted routine part of their lives" and didn't "see it as a scientific wonder," as Gaddis wrote in one of his Ford Foundation drafts (WU). To the extent that education relies on universally available technologies, its transformation in the age of new media only supports the unidentified "critic who has said that the child today interrupts his education by going to school."[8] Gaddis (in his drafts, if not often in the finished speeches) saw clearly how television's "novelty and expense have already meant more money and more attention devoted to its technology and those versed in it, than to the teachers and purposes of education for which it is employed" (WU).

The postwar rise and unprecedented expansion of the managerial culture would soon begin the long, slow transformation of educational, small business, and scientific/engineering professions into corporations. The unavoidable material transformation in American culture of this period persisted long after the cultural disturbances of the time could be channeled into largely expressive modes. Those who limit their understanding of American (and an emerging world) culture to forms of personal and "creative" expression in this period are likely to miss the importance of Gaddis's later writing, and the ways that the multiple identities and quests that Gaddis explored in the previous decades, unresolved though they might have been, were transformed universally by a business culture with real traction. The innovations of science and engineering, all of which were essentially in place already by the 1960s, would in effect cease when they were turned toward instrumental ends—televisual and networked communications, touch screens, personal computers, and apps for all appetites. An innovative literary culture, though it would last a bit longer and even flourish during the rise of new forms of conceptual critical writing in the sixties and seventies, would also be channeled, gradually but ineluctably, toward more personalized, minimal forms of expression by practitioners who studiedly avoided the expansive cultural and scientific analyses one finds in major works of this period such as *J R*, *The Public Burning*, *Lookout Cartridge*, and *Gravity's Rainbow*. The growth of the scientific-technological no less than the literary cultures, so distinctive of America during its postwar moment of preeminence, would essentially cease as all growth was given over, on principle, to business and technologies of self-development.

Gaddis however did not just observe and comment on these transformations; he lived them in his own professional dislocation. For a few years, while he was still living with Pat and the children at the uptown apartment (193 East Second Avenue), he looked to foundations as a source of financial support—not least the Fund for the Republic whose representative, Frank Kelley, encouraged him to apply. Along with a somewhat battered copy of *The Recognitions*, the only one he had at hand, Gaddis also enclosed "the brief resume we spoke of, in case something should open up there in your wide part of the world; honestly, when I returned from our fine lunch and 2-hour conversation about ideas, coming back to an office of things was difficult indeed, and even more overwhelming the sense of the stifling limitations of 'business.' Writers will cling to any straw, though mine at the moment word that the Ford Foundation is making a series of grants to novelists. . . ."[9] As with so many aspects of a novelistic "career," we find Gaddis pursuing, on his own through what remained to him of Ivy League, midtown, male networks, a kind of alternative that would not be fully available, or fully incorporated, for another couple of generations (through academic appointments, mainly, that were becoming more and more dependent on the literary or "humanist" candidate's success at getting grants, a success in any case easier to document and measure than "failure that is the precondition for success" in the arts, a recurring phrase in Gaddis's writings).

He needed the twenty years between *The Recognitions* and *J R* "basically . . . to earn a living," as he told a German interviewer near the end of his life.[10] Within months of his first novel's publication, he'd seen the book disappear from the shelves of the bookstores. His prospects suddenly constricted. Like Eigen in *J R*, and like most men in America, he now had to work full-time at jobs he hated, to "pay the bills."[11] He didn't get any help from his publisher; as Eigen's friend Jack Gibbs reminds Eigen's wife (who is planning a breakup): "—Well what the hell Marian, that publisher's a fatuous bastard you know that, he's been sitting on that book for how many years? Blubbering about his loyalty to it pretending it was what did he tell Tom? Very much in print? When the only God damned place you could find it was a rare book dealer's for twenty dollars a copy after they'd remaindered practically the whole first edition? He didn't know anything about this new reprint till he saw one in a window and now it's bringing him some attention he . . ." (269).[12]

Those who knew him well, such as Martin Dworkin (who did a series of wonderful photo-portraits of Gaddis and his family in the late fifties), might have assumed from such oft-repeated denigration of his corporate work that Gaddis cynically took money from the very people he would eventually satirize in the fiction. Dworkin observed, among friends after the publication of *J R*, how "Willie could write the most devastating criticism of the business world in his novels and yet earn money ghost writing for business executives. The President of Eastman Kodak may have reached his position largely due to Willie's speeches."[13]

But what could satire be, in the present circumstances where no position *outside* business any longer was possible? The derogatory observation is recorded in a memoir by Bernard Looks, who does not mention that Dworkin himself had collaborated with Gaddis in at least one corporate project, namely a 1965 "proposal for an instructional TV series that would clarify the real nature of scientific life and work, which [they] felt existing media had failed to convey to a citizenry increasingly reliant on the products of that work."[14] Had it been accepted, the proposal presumably would have been published under Gaddis's and Dworkin's names, which implies a commitment on the part of both to solving "practical problems" of instructional education similar to those Gaddis had researched for the Ford project, like testing "various aesthetic and dynamic techniques of film making in relation to their capabilities to influence individual difference within an audience."[15] Gaddis was to have worked on the script, and Dworkin drafted a letter to confirm the interest of his institution, Teachers College. A third collaborator, Hillel A. Schiller, shopped the proposal around. One of the project's goals was (in Schiller's summary) "to measure the effectiveness of films in motivating interest in and changing behaviour towards science,"[16] an ambition that takes seriously the educational and cultural value of instructional film and that runs against Dworkin's retrospective view of Gaddis's cynicism on such matters.

Gaddis did after all need to know (if not always articulate in ghost-written speeches) the motivating principles behind what he was writing. Surely it is conceivable that, rather than simply depleting his literary energies and more even than providing "fodder" (as he called it), Gaddis's corporate experience provided a technical training of sorts for *J R*. "As for the corporate world," Gaddis remarked during the interview given to the *Paris Review*, "I do read the newspapers, clip things, ideas, articles, and just use them as fodder." A decade earlier in Japan, Gaddis gave this explanation to Yōkichi Miyamoto: "These writings did not show my name. I did not care because all I wanted from these works was the money. In fact, I liked this kind of work better than writing essays or stories for magazines, because they presented a greater challenge."[17] Though perhaps true for the most part, there were projects like the educational film series that, though unpublished, were submitted under Gaddis's name. So, too, were the draft materials he prepared for the Ford Foundation that he eventually would submit (through his agent, Candida Donadio) to the same venue, *Harper's*, he had sought years earlier for his short fiction.

After extensive research, literary scholar Ali Chetwynd concludes that the archive "no longer allows us to accept" Gaddis's retrospective framing of the corporate career "as an entirely separate, merely distracting adjunct to his fiction. It generated writing that he wished to publicly circulate as Novelist William Gaddis'[s], allowed him to develop expertise on select topics, offered opportunities for research-oriented work that he sometimes accepted with only the hope of future pay, and led him to cultivate a reputation-guarding professional pride that both drew on and burnished his other reputation as a novelist." Chetwynd's conclusion is consistent with Gaddis's interest in empirical projects going back to the player piano history (which also was excerpted for magazine publication), and one doubts that Gaddis could have kept going, or even kept his position and livelihood over so many years, without to some degree entering the corporate life-world and internalizing its assumptions.

The archive, more than the interviews, reveals Gaddis even during the corporate years to have been an artist in search of things he could use in his novels—and, more than things, he also grasped (independently of Thomas Pynchon at around the same time, who cut his teeth at a writing job for Boeing) the cybernetic framework for an emergent corporate and managerial culture: as he told two interviewers in 1981, the entropy theme presented a much different image of social, political, and economic change than what were, in some ways, more easy to grasp, dramatize, and narrativize. The theme, Gaddis mentions, "had been on my mind long, long before *J R*—ever since Norbert Wiener's book appeared, *The Human Use of Human Beings,* where he discusses at length entropy in communication. The more complicated the message, the more chance for error, and so on and so forth." His interviewers asked if that made his novels "also apocalyptic"—a fair enough association, given Pynchon's quite different, explicitly nuclear variations on Wiener's great theme (and not for nothing, incidentally, did Wiener advise the U.S. military on rocketry during the Second World War). For Gaddis, although there is certainly something totalizing about the entire entropic tendency of a culture constructed of systems, it's more "about the total fragmentation and chaos, the total chaos which is the last step in entropy, when everything is settled and everything equals everything else. People think of chaos as a battle, you know, but it's not that—it's when energy has finally reached this equilibrium. That's the end of the line, nothing matters anymore, whiskey equals milk, one piece of fiction equals another."[18]

It is fair to say, then, that the corporate years provided Gaddis with more than a set of technological themes or even a powerful sociocultural analysis: the "constant talk, talk" that accompanied the technological and managerial expansions must have influenced the unusual form of *J R* as well, which came to be written, primarily, in dialogue. And where better to feel the expansion of business concern and cybernetic control if not in everyday talk that touches on our every momentary contact with, and mediated separation from, others? The corporate writings themselves had "a foundational influence on the ideas and rhetorical structure" of *J R*, as Chetwynd shows particularly in relation to the opening grade-school scenes that present the musician Edward Bast's hapless attempts to convey, over closed-circuit TV, an understanding of Mozart's creative life. Losing track of the script, Bast cites from memory the letters Mozart wrote to his future wife during their courtship, including the raucous bits about "Burmesquik, where the muck runs to the sea . . ." and other wordplay not usually heard in polite or conventional conversation.

Except in moments when he remembers his scripted instructions, Bast however is not really talking to the children who are purportedly his intended audience on the closed-circuit TV channel, nor to the school principal and teachers and Foundation visitors who happen to tune into the program without his knowledge: he's talking largely *through* the medium, even as many characters in the novel talk through phones and through the noise of crowded offices and fast-food service places that keep people moving and at the same time keep up the novel's action. But at the same time, Bast's inexperience (he is substituting for another teacher), and his own innocence of the ways that power is embedded in the conditions of filmic production, means that he will be speaking largely into a void:

> —um, in the um, his um playful sense of humour yes we, it shows
> us what a really human person this great genius was doesn't it boys
> and um, and girls, and, and you you single child out there his letters
> help you, help make him somebody you can understand too [. . .] to
> humanize him because even if we can't um, we can't rise to his level at
> least we can, we can drag him down to ours . . .

> —See what I mean, there's too much bass in these commercial sets . . .
> and the foot was withdrawn as Hyde tripped over it on his way to the
> set where Mister Pecci stood with a control knob that had just come
> off in his hand.

> —what the um, what democracy in the arts is all about isn't it boys and
> girls and, and you, you . . . (42–43)

Back in the classrooms, the students ask their teachers if they're going to be tested on this.

To realize how successful is the removal of any authorial voice-over in such passages, one need only compare (as Chetwynd does) the above scene from *J R* with an earlier fictionalization that was drafted not for the novel but for the Ford Foundation project that Gaddis never published:

> 'Mozart's middle name was Amadeus which means "loved of God."
> It fitted him,' a classroom teacher in one large-city elementary school
> system reads this morning, preparing to 'shape the imagination and
> appreciation' of her class with the imminent studio lesson on music,
> as suggested here in her Teacher's Manual. 'God blessed him [. . .]
> Mozart's life was like a fairy tale.' And if this teacher knows more of

that fairy tale's particulars, should she share them with her charges? Of Mozart pawning his silver to pay his tour expenses, a career pursued by jealousies, a life haunted by money problems . . . or should she continue to 'foster morality, happiness and useful ability' by perpetuating the fairy-tale of art made as easy and harmless as this education is easy and irrelevant to the life her children will see when they go home from school [. . .]?[19]

A decade after he postulated this fictional teacher for the Ford Foundation project, Gaddis was able directly to communicate what he knows about Mozart through the character Bast—though neither the children nor the school administrators pay much attention. Indeed, Bast himself will learn more from "one single child out there" in particular—namely, his future boss J R—than he's ever picked up from his extracurricular reading in the lives of great artists. Once we have elementary school teachers reading their lessons from manuals and teaching to tests, critical expression ceases to circulate in ways that touch a child's thought or imagination. And this is another reason why Gaddis's formal decision to work wholly *within* the language and life-world of such largely corporate, and corporatizing institutions, goes so far beyond the mere communication of material hardships that creative artists so often experience. The decision to remove his own creative self as a personality within the fiction has cultural implications that even the book's staunchest admirers can fail to notice: What Gaddis was living through was the emergence of a business and political culture that had essentially sidelined critique; it is a culture that not only changed, but which *needed to change*, continually, for its own perpetuation. That distinctive phase in the corporate world system[20] certainly found an analogue in a novel that never for a moment paused, not for chapter or section breaks, and not for the time it might require for one speaker actually to listen to another, or to reflect:

> —No now stop, just for a minute! This, this whole thing has to stop somewhere don't you understand that?
> —No but holy, I mean that's the whole thing Bast otherwise what good is this neat tax loss carryforward and all these here tax credits and all, I mean that's all Eagle is . . . (298)

That is all ownership means for the venture capitalist—in this case, the eleven-year-old J R Vansant, who with Bast's reluctant help has come into control of the Eagle Mills plant in Upstate New York. Control does not mean, for J R, taking responsibility for the plant's production or the welfare of its employees or the town whose economy it anchors or the land and ecosystem it affects: none of that means anything to J R. All he cares about is how Eagle performs as an asset, and that is something that could indeed be grasped by a preadolescent who sometimes puts the decimal point in the wrong place when adding up his millions in costs and expenses, stock holdings and dividend payouts.

The satire was there at the start, and so was Gaddis's conviction that a child could grasp the basic procedures needed (recorded by Gaddis in a 1956 letter posted to himself) "to assemble extensive financial interests, to build a 'big business' in a system of comparative free enterprise employing the numerous (again basically simple) encouragements (as tax benefits &c) which are so prominent in the business world of America today. By taking straightforward advantage of the possibilities which I believe might well be obvious to the eye and judgment of a child this age, brought up on the sets of values and the criteria of success which prevail here in our country today, he becomes a business tycoon." The name "Bast" came to Gaddis in a dream for the character, "innocent in matters of money or business," whom "the boy (named here 'J. R.') employs as a front man." Gaddis was that far along in his thinking as early as 1956, though no mention of the novel's predominant dialogue format was made, in this earliest stage.[21] The idea of a child millionaire, it seems, came to him in a discussion with another friend at the time and throughout his life, the noted filmmaker Donn A. Pennebaker, who recalls starting a film about a young boy who was turning into a mogul by selling comic books and such. Ormonde de Kay and Max Furlaud got involved also, though they never came up with a boy actor. In the end, Pennebaker gave it as a present to Gaddis, who then wrote the letter to himself.[22]

Not all the talk, then, was corporate and inconsequential, however much the heavy schedule of business meetings to no clear purpose must have worn on Gaddis; as we see from his complaints to Pat at the time, he was involved with the Ford Foundation project, sitting listening to talk in meetings "until instructional television seems all that exists and I feel I cannot stand another word." The project would be abandoned in mid-1962 after "time work and travel wasted and a little money changed hands."[23] The Foundation work is called a "fiasco" by Gaddis, yet for all the neutrality and studied impersonality of the bulk of such writing, Gaddis's critical spirit comes through and so does some of his literary range. If he could no longer cite Eliot, Graves, and Toynbee, then Gaddis the corporate writer would still find opportunities to bring in Plato on "the skirmish between education and technology";[24] Thoreau on technology's relation to education ("an improved means to an unimproved end");[25]

Dewey's insistence (against current trends toward testing) that "school must never be isolated from life, the child must always be an active participant"; and Carlyle on an "infinite capacity for taking pains" that can be said to characterize Gaddis's corporate writing as much as his fiction.[26] Gaddis even could get away with a closing reference to Gertrude Stein in his treatment for an IBM "motion picture" on "Software":

> As this voice fades down and under, that of the Narrator locates the essence of software, and the heart of all language and logic systems, in the dying words of Gertrude Stein, when she asked "What is the answer?," and her friend professed ignorance. "In that case," she said, "what is the question?"[27]

Surveying the full archive of corporate writings, one notes how frequently Gaddis lands himself in such conundra: the circling language, the spoonerisms that characterize a corporate system without absolutes, with no grounding in any structure of beliefs or set of values outside itself. (This is consistent with the quality of mind that Katherine Anne Porter had abhorred in Stein and writers of her ilk.) In a position paper for Eastman Kodak, Gaddis cites *Alice's Adventures in Wonderland*, the queen telling Alice "now now faster faster," running to stay still. Instead of using expensive managerial talent "simply to keep the system going," he argues in this draft, human judgment is needed, and a long-term plan that can create some internal friction (WU). But what happens too often is that technicians are chased off the stage by the managers—or those with active expertise are "upgraded," in the words of one document, to management positions and so lose track of how materials are handled in practice. That awareness of the materiality of labor (what Hegel already identified in "The Master and Slave" as the worker's persisting advantage over the owning classes) is the friction needed to keep the system moving, not just running to stay in place or changing for the sake of change. Gaddis in his internal report to Eastman Kodak says as much, even though the language of human judgment that made it into this particular document, Chetwynd notes, is more often revised out from the rest of the corporate work.

We see the managerial logic at work in the school in *J R*, where nobody, not even the teachers, ever mentions "educational content." As Gaddis noted in his *Paris Review* interview: "They talk about nothing but paving the parking lot, about buying new teaching machines and teaching equipment and storing what they already have because no one knows how to use it, and so forth" (67). Gaddis clearly appreciated how education was itself being influenced by the same corporate displacement of practice-based activity with frictionless managerial language. Even the possibility of failure, so necessary to achievement in the arts and in education if one is to overcome the limitations of one's given time and circumstance, was being eliminated by technologies of corporate control. In such conditions a literary sensibility could be at most a haunting presence, a ghost in the machine. Yet the presence is there and it is remarkable that he was able, even in some of the corporate writings, to convey some of the wellsprings of a pragmatic philosophical and literary tradition—the writings of Dewey, Stein, and the rest. That so many literary references were allowed to pass, even in the corporate writings, is a testament both to the respect that must have been accorded Gaddis, Harvard-educated and with a published novel to his credit, by his managerial colleagues, and the esteem held for American and English literature in the culture generally at the time. (The vestigial literary references in the IBM pieces would be unlikely to survive today even in institutional proposals for state sponsored projects in the humanities. As early as 1968, an executive deemed one of Gaddis's industrial film scripts "a little too profound and needed reshaping in a manner that would be informative at a shallower depth" [quoted in *L* 267].)

Although most of the corporate writings were impersonal and technical, Gaddis could not entirely repress a literary impulse. The film sequence for IBM, meant to illustrate a conception from information science—the way an entire city impinges on a man's decision to cross a street—becomes in Gaddis's hands a mini-narrative culminating in the black humor of a crash. Soon thereafter, we're given footage of a collapsing bridge. The environment of noise, accident, uncertainty, and failure so characteristic of Gaddis's fiction may have been more than his sponsors bargained for. This particular script was never produced, though here too the firsthand experience of scripting (like his day-in day-out immersion in corporate "talk") may have influenced the form of *J R*, which in some ways reads like a film—especially in bridge passages that take the reader from one scene to another, as if we are watching the action through a camera.[28]

The Ford experience, of course, was retained for use when Gaddis resumed work on *J R*. (His recollections would be given to the characters aptly named Ford and Gall.) Students in the Long Island grade school are occupied most of the time watching amateur filmed programs far less challenging than Bast's improvisations on Mozart, while administrators count the costs and teachers lose count of the children in attendance on field trips. The children themselves? "—They have a ball," as Miss Flesch, the one "with her topflight track record in curriculum management," puts it (261). The kids are all right—they know well enough how to ignore classroom pablum, how to distill from canned content what they'll need for tests. Something new, though, was emerging in the mid-1970s, even at the preadolescent stage when all that children would be hearing, from more and more ubiquitous and diverse media outlets, had to do with business, and entertainment whose pleasures derived from and fed back into business-friendly lifestyles. The appearance of personal computers, then notebooks, and now handheld and eyepiece devices only completed the universal availability of real business opportunities, requiring no more for their "smart" execution than a sixth-grade education (and briefly focused, multitasking attention spans). That emergent business culture is behind young J R's creation of a million-dollar family of corporations, and Gaddis's decade-long presence in the corporate machine helps to account for his novel's prescience and continuing power.

# Chapter 8

✦

# American Fiction without Recognition: *J R*

—like I mean this here bond and stock stuff you don't see
anybody you don't know nobody only in the mail and the
telephone because that's how they do it nobody has to see
anybody, you can be this here funny lookingest person that
lives in a toilet someplace how do they know, I mean like all
those guys at the Stock Exchange where they're selling all this
stock to each other? They don't give a shit whose it is they're
just selling it back and forth for some voice that told them on
the phone why should they give a shit if you're a hundred and
fifty all they . . .

> J R Vansant, in conversation with his friend, the Hyde boy (172)

One will not find in American fiction a more prescient vision of a collective, corporate life-world than what we have in *J R*, and none of the direct
citations in current fiction of e-mail exchanges, text messages, chat sessions, pings, and tweets have caught so well the spirit of corporatization
that underlies these symptoms. Gaddis was writing about simultaneously
individualized and impersonal deal-making before trading went off the
Stock Exchange floor and migrated online, but the essentials of a virtual economy were already in place, as J R Vansant and the otherwise
unnamed Hyde boy discover when they canvas the ads in the back of a
newspaper. At age eleven, J R has already grasped the essentials of a virtual economy. Even if his own buying and selling was done through the
U.S. post office and the pay phone nearby his Long Island grade school,
he would have no trouble adjusting to the handheld devices used by brokers today, not least by the real-life preteen "self-made millionaires" that
turn up nowadays in the news.

With the Hyde boy, "sending away" and trading is a pastime that
quickly turns into full-time, all-the-time employment performed openly

and with essentially no intervention by any of J R's teachers, coaches, or school administrators. Nobody sees J R. We know little about the boy's mother and nothing at all about his father (who is, like Gaddis's father, entirely absent during the boy's formative years). Neglect, mainly, and nonrecognition are the basis of the free market in an advanced economy. To his class "Six J" teacher Amy Joubert (née Moncrieff), J R himself appears as though he "lives in those clothes of his" and "when you talk to him he doesn't look at you" (246). Amy gets the sense that the boy is not so much hiding something as "trying to fit what you're saying into some utterly different, some world you don't know anything about." Which is to say, the young J R is doing, in business, more or less what Gaddis is doing in fiction, in this very novel where the real action—the rise and fall of personal fortunes and paper empires; the fast, definitive, but half-known transformation of America itself—proceeds steadily within and behind all the recorded talk.

J R "doesn't recognize any other subject, and others can't recognize him. They can't fix him in the space of intersubjectivity, in the gaze of recognition."[1] So writes Michael Clune in a critical evaluation from 2010 that suggests the dramatic move, in Gaddis's own career, away from *The Recognitions* with its lingering faith in the power of epiphanies (even if these only happen, as Wyatt Gwyon suspects, seven times in a lifetime [92]). Within the development of American literature generally, Clune's formulation also separates Gaddis's second book from the "classic post-war figure of the successful market agent," the magnate or entrepreneur on the model of Dreiser's Frank Cowperwood. Unlike Dreiser's titan, who is capable of sizing up every opponent and observing deep trends and likely turns in the economy, Gaddis's youthful entrepreneur derives all his power from observing local, ephemeral opportunities that are "beneath the notice of his elders," Clune writes. "'Buy low sell high,' for J R, simply means noticing that a price for picnic forks is low here, and high over there. The calculations of a Cowperwood are replaced by the careful attention of an eleven year old" (22) As far as the world system of free market economies goes, Clune continues, "this price system is an integral part of his awareness. It is not a system which he might use or not use, as one might use the number system to make a calculation. In this novel, the price system is an interface between an embodied awareness and a global collective. It ensures that J R's choices are coordinated with and shaped by all the choices being made throughout the world" (22).[2]

What we have in *J R* then is not the repression of personal agency and subjectivity that so many critics have seen in this novel, "along with much of the rest of postwar literature," to quote Clune again (22), but something far more significant, namely a *transformation* of subjectivity within the terms of an emergent world system. The intrapersonal communication, which in *J R* is indeed people talking mostly past one another, is by no means the only communication at work in the novel and, indeed, in the present multimediated world in which we actually do live and take cognizance of one another. Going beyond the humanist, humanizing imagination, Gaddis shows what it can be to write realistically in the current world-spanning, media-dominated age. Systems nowadays rarely conform to what we can say about them, whether we are speaking person-to-person or over broadcast and reception media; that is, they rarely conform to our intuitive understanding, shaped as such understanding has been by causal, classical mechanics (of the Newtonian variety, before the interventions of J. Willard Gibbs, Einstein, and quantum theory) and by managed economies and official national languages. Similarly, the modern novel, which emerged out of these same nationalist programs and mechanistic paradigms, has evolved various nonintuitive, antirepresentational stances.

To circumscribe the effects of contemporary systems into what can be known by a single protagonist, a specific community, or an author's own narrative self-projection (however ironical or limited in omniscience) is to drastically reduce the literary work in its critical understanding. When reading Gaddis, we must open ourselves to hybridity, to what he would later term *aporia*, which is to say, the gaps between dispensations—between literature and science, collective experience and corporations, theory and narrative, and "different orders of linguistic imagination."[3] And this implies a significant transformation for the genre of world literature as it engages with issues of power and repression: instead of Big Brother we have little J R (and much, much market-oriented information: what would come to be called Big Data). He's post-ideological—and he does what he does not through any belief system but because he knows "that's what you do!" as he tells his music teacher Edward Bast, who questions the system's morality (and who ends up working for J R, as do many of the adults who once were employed at his school or at the companies he takes over).

For a dollar, his company assumes "this like ninety-nine years lease" of a softball park, "—because I mean who cares what's going to happen in ninety-nine years" (295). Time in J R's world is a medium to be manipulated for present profitability, and his enterprise flourishes—in the logic of abstract economic "growth"—more or less independently of any material base. By the accounting loophole known as accelerated depreciation, for example, a piece of equipment can be said for tax purposes to wear out in less time than it actually takes: "—they call it depreciated acceleration or something only the thing is you can't do it with people see so . . ." (296). J R's vagaries and frequent mistakes in arithmetic and spelling pose no obstacle to his ability to manipulate present "realities" with essentially no outlays of cash, for he has learned (in the formative conversation with industry captains overheard in the executive washroom at Diamond Cable) to "get other people's money" to work for him (109). So long as they are large enough, all "paper losses" can be converted by the J R Corp to tax credits. By means of such "creative accounting" (as Gaddis has one character put it in *A Frolic of His Own*), the virtuality of transactions can be made to fulfill one's personal dream of self-liberation: in an economy that is no longer based on any indexical relation between symbol (money) and referent (wealth, consumable goods), all representation becomes self-referential and seemingly free of material constraints. In a situation where "nobody grew but the business"—Gaddis's title for an excerpt from the novel that appeared in *Harper's*—such unconstrained, nearly alchemical flourishing has produced not individual liberation, but the self-validating collective fascination of a simulation culture.

In Gaddis's later work, a character's subjectivity is trained not so much on other people as on *things*—on what can be bought and sold—and on *communicative networks*, the phone lines, junk mail, office memos, contracts, legal documents, and other media outlets through which talk and text can be exchanged without visual or even voice recognition while collective action is achieved (in Clune's words) "without intersubjective contact" (22). (J R has learned to stuff his handkerchief in the phone mouthpiece so that he sounds "bigger.") This does not mean though that connections, meaningful ones, are not drawn among the characters in the novel: if anything, the verbal and thematic resonances we have observed in Gaddis's first novel are even more richly worked into the fabric of *J R*. Only the connections more often than not are never registered by the consciousness of the characters: these are communicated primarily between the author and the reader, who (as Gaddis remarked in a number of interviews) is brought in as a kind of collaborator in the construction of meaning within and through the novel's systems and networks.

That kind of attentiveness, though an abiding presence in the novel, is no longer even missed by anyone but the artists. The fatherless boy whose mother, a nurse, "works these strange hours," has learned how to benefit from his own neglect. That, and a greed never compromised by sexual desire or adult sociality, is what outfits this preadolescent for a meteoric rise in business. While his elders—the composer Bast, the novelist Eigen, the essayist, physics teacher, and Jack-of-all-trades Gibbs—remain within an earlier economy grounded in recognition, the youthful J R exists wholly in the capitalist present. He doesn't need to look anyone in the eye, he doesn't need to earn or build trust in order to transact, and he won't be detained by anything in the arts. Indeed, his transmutation of the detritus of his culture, as we shall see, is itself a reflection of Gaddis's own accomplishment in the novel (unlike anything that the distracted artists in the book are able to accomplish).

Because nobody recognizes the extent of J R's business activity, they each contribute to it without even realizing it. The grown-ups are in each case available for employment in jobs they hate—an experience Gaddis knew well during his years doing corporate writing though Gaddis, unlike his characters, took the time and effort to inform himself about the conditions in which he was employed and the newly global reach of the limited liability corporation. Like Bast, Gibbs, and Eigen, Gaddis shared a studio with a like-minded friend, Douglas Wood, in uptown Manhattan. (Wood was the Harvard classmate he was out with on the night he was arrested for drunken and disorderly behavior; later an esteemed television writer, he is the model for "Douglas Kipps" in Sarah Gaddis's novel *Swallow Hard*.) It was a place where he could retreat from both business and family obligations, and where he could also store manuscripts and what would become over the years a massive quantity of source materials— much of which, when they found their way to the Queens storage bin for eventual transport to the Special Collections at Washington University in St. Louis, would be in the same recycled food and liquor boxes that he describes in the novel. The growth of the J R Family of Companies, in this sense, is built on the same attention to minutiae within a disordered environment that Gaddis brought from his own Manhattan workplace into the novel itself.

"Curious," Gaddis had written to his British friends John and Pauline Napper, "how some of us who are obsessed with order seem constantly immersed in disorder."[4] Precisely from such disorder, however, he would conjure the meteoric rise of the J R Family of Companies, as reflected by the ever-increasing volumes of mail, office equipment, visitors, telephone calls, and overnight guests received at the apartment. In depicting the chaos, Gaddis comes up with some wonderfully fortuitous effects: at the top of one pile, for example, half covering an electric clock that for some reason runs backward, sits an empty Coca-Cola box labeled NO DEPOSIT, NO RETURN. As the hands sweep a curve from one side of the box to the other, the label is made to comment ironically on the time lost by Bast and Gibbs to the work they do (or fail to complete) inside the apartment. This is only one of the many devices, unnoticed by the characters themselves, that allow Gaddis silently to communicate the book's governing theme of entropy as time's arrow.

There is a further irony in the fact that Bast, who would like nothing more than to be left alone to write music, should be thus implicated in the massive waste and confusion that J R wreaks on the lives of the characters and the nation's economy as a result of the eleven-year-old's voracious gathering-up of "penny stocks and defaulted bond operations."[5] Gaddis even arranged a dinner with a musician in Manhattan just to find out the worst jobs this friend had ever taken to support his music career. So Gaddis could identify with the artists in the book, but even in the worst moments of his own corporate career Gaddis was never so passive as Bast, who (as a favor to J R, "just this once") lets himself be hired out as a front for the nascent business. J R is quick to give out Bast's temporary studio address and number as his (J R's) own Manhattan office, and in this he is only doing better what Gibbs and Eigen had already tried, by receiving mail there from a made-up identity, one Mr. Grynszpan, whose name is on the electric and gas bills. The artists' playful working of the system, however, is nowhere near as effective as J R's. The difference, of course, is that the virtuality of J R's business endeavor is entirely legal, and requires no made-up identities. That and the fact that J R, unlike the artists, plays to win.

Bast is at times wont to think nostalgically of the conditions Richard Wagner, one of his heroes, needed in order to work. He remembers vaguely that Wagner "couldn't concentrate if he looked out and let his eyes follow the garden paths" because, as Gibbs obligingly reminds him, the paths let the outside world in (116). Although Bast himself does not realize it, the artist's romantic desire to stand apart, to cut himself off from "the outside world, the real" (116), may be precisely what contributes to the disorder and disintegration within his own "place of stone" (from Yeats, "To a Friend whose Work has come to Nothing," as quoted all too appropriately by Gibbs on pages 131 and 278). Yet there is something more to this reference (and to similar references early in the novel to Mozart's financial and marital straits), something that goes beyond the material conditions of the artist to the radical, at once verbal, musical, and filmic, form that Gaddis devised for *J R*.

The Wagner reference, occurring early and in the context of a grade school performance of *Das Rheingold* (the prelude to the German composer's lengthy *Ring of the Nibelung*), is yet another way for Gaddis to indicate the world-historical ambitions of the novel we're reading. At the same time he is of course aware of ineluctable differences between a romantic age and temperament and what is allowable in mid-1970s

America for someone like Bast, himself the son of a respected composer and member of a family that (like Gaddis's own) has musical roots extending back to the nineteenth century. We might begin by noting that, like Gaddis's writing, Wagner's music (and the atonal music of followers such as Schoenberg) was regarded as "difficult" in its time—and this has compelled one commentator, Nicholas Spice of the *London Review of Books*, to wonder what in conventional, tonal music listeners have understood. "On the surface, where melody and harmony follow recognizable routines, we feel we know what is being said. But this familiarity is deceptive, if not a barrier to understanding. The compression of information characteristic of much great music, the speed at which it passes, the bewildering density and delicacy of its over-determination, makes it difficult in the way that poetry is difficult."[6] What we find in Wagner is a kind of decompression, an extension of his musical elements over time and through horizontal connections that breaks with familiar musical composition much as Gaddis breaks with conventional narrative. The result, though "difficult" to those familiar only with conventions, can actually bring more attentive readers, and listeners, closer to the composition—the kind of "collaboration" that Gaddis sought in readers, and the (more openly sensual) removal of "the boundary that lies between Wagner's works and his listeners, . . . an experience," in Spice's account, "that may hold a clue to the feeling . . . that Wagner's work is in some sense not altogether good for us" (3).

George Steiner's charge of "unreadability," and the harping on "difficulty" by moralizing reviewers such as John Gardner and Jonathan Franzen, might be understood similarly: as a visceral reaction to a work that so elicits a reader's participation to the point of becoming a collaborator, or a cocreator. As has been demonstrated, there is no serious argumentative support for the "difficulty" claim, yet its persistent influence suggests that Gaddis, like Wagner, is crossing the line of what's allowable—or even *physically* acceptable—in the way that an artist engages not just the mind, but the eyes and ears and sensual capacity of a reader or listener.

In considering "the distinctive character of Wagner's compositional procedures," in which the elements of a composition develop gradually over time and "horizontally" through variations-in-repetition (6), Spice points out that our understanding must develop similarly over time—unlike tighter compositions in classical opera that set out musical themes sometimes within the first few minutes. Gaddis for his part might announce the "money" theme with the first word of the novel, spoken by the attorney Coen "in a voice that rustled," but it is not until the final words, J R's "—Hey, you listening?" that we may fully recognize how many voices and how much rustling of bills and legal documents it takes to form the grand comic opera of an entire economy and communicative system in process. The numerous connections we are able to make from one element to another, over hundreds of pages (as we shall soon see), is entirely consistent with Wagner's technique in the operas, where leitmotifs are not to be gathered informationally, "where we can look up meanings and identifications as we travel through the Wagnerian landscape"; instead, Spice suggests, "we would do better to think of them as staking out a kind of semantic middle ground between music and drama (Wittgenstein called [the leitmotifs] 'musical prose sentences')" (6).

At the start of the novel, as Bast plays the *Rheingold* motif on the school piano, young J R (assigned the role of the dwarf Alberich in Wagner's opera), runs right past the madeup Rhinemaidens of his sixth-grade class, takes the bag of change that their teacher, Miss Joubert, collected from the class, and announces "—Hark floods! Love I renounce forever" (36). The boy runs off with the money, but brings it back eventually so it can be used on his class trip to Wall Street, to buy one share in Diamond Cable (which will be enough to allow J R, as an "owner," to sue the company and start his career in finance). Yet even this development, so easy to recount in retrospect, can be gathered by readers only episodically, never through a narrative voice-over or authorial summary. That slow gathering of connections, as closely paced as possible with the day-to-day development of the novel, creates something very similar to the developing, never fully resolved music of Wagner which (as Spice again notes) famously "enacts the experience of desire, forever on the verge of satisfaction but never satisfied, a state of suspension symbolized by the first three bars [of *Tristan and Isolde*], which 'resolve' the startling discord of bar two—the famous Tristan chord—onto a dominant seventh, itself a discord crying out for resolution" (3).

The sonic discord is consistent with social, cultural, and material dissonance and inequity: "Theft; the breaking of vows, promises and contracts; seduction, adultery, incest, disobedience, defiance of the gods, daring to ask the one forbidden question, the renunciation of love for power, genital self-mutilation as the price of magic . . ." (3). Each of the characteristic Wagnerian themes listed by Nicholas Spice has its counterpart in *J R*.

What Gaddis seems to be getting at in *J R*, particularly with his artists and authors, is the way that the conditions for making art have themselves been transformed along with the economic and material transformations that concern the novel. That is definitely the theme of Jack Gibbs's unfinished, and likely never-to-be-finished work on mechanization and the arts—specifically on "the destructive element" in which the artist finds himself (244). Gibbs is alluding to *Lord Jim*, in which Joseph Conrad has a character (who is a nonnative speaker of English) say: "'The way is to the destructive element submit yourself, and with the exertions of your hands and feet in the water make the deep, deep sea keep you up. So if you ask me—how to be? . . . In the destructive element, immerse!'" (chapter 20).

Where the artists in the novel tend to drown, J R (like Gaddis in his compositional efforts in the novel) is able through immersion and a moment-by-moment integration of voice, vision, and event to make some sense—and surprising sources of both profit and pleasure—out of the detritus and general noise of his culture. Like Gaddis, J R disappears from view, but not in the way that artists, in Gibbs's unfinished magnum opus, are sidelined by mechanization. As Gibbs remarks of Johannes Müller, the German physiologist who fitted a human larynx with strings and weights instead of muscles in the hopes of building an artificial opera singer, the tendency of mechanization was to "get the God damned artist out of the arts all at once, long as he's there destroy everything in their God damned path what the arts are all about" (288). One recording is all it takes, and the artist can be left behind, while his work can then be reproduced, sampled, and remixed without one's ever entering the spirit of its creation. (Yet what are Gaddis's efforts on behalf of Wagner? In the spirit of Conrad? Of Willard Gibbs? These are not mere "allusions" in the self-regarding mode of literary modernism; they are rather ways of inhabiting an earlier aesthetic from within one's own, quite different media environment, closer to the post-digital art of *remixing* that one finds in the work of literary media artists of the 1990s and early twenty-first century such as Mark Amerika, Kate Armstrong, Serge Bouchardon, Mez Breeze, John Cayley, Roderick Coover, Nick Montfort, Jason Nelson, Scott Rettberg, or Steve Tomasula.)

The text Gibbs labors over is drawn from Gaddis's own unfinished treatise on player pianos (from before the time of *The Recognitions*), and while Gaddis may have felt this way at an early stage in his career, his thinking on technology had gone beyond the mechanical, though still human-centered view toward a perspective more consistent with cybernetics and systems thought—the fields he encountered firsthand during his work for IBM, Ford, and other corporations. Gaddis's fabled authorial disappearance, from this perspective, is far from being a capitulation to or even primarily a critique of the mechanistic ideal. Instead, it is an attempt to reconfigure the relation between the author and his audiences in such a way that both are made to inhabit the systems and networks that define our present economy and culture, and that can take us to another place and find other uses for the "frail human element . . . even in the arts" (*J R* 289).

Here, too, Gaddis's aims (if not his sensibilities) are closer to J R than they are to any of the harassed artists in the novel. Apart from Bast (whom J R likes well enough, even as he exploits the musician's innocence of business and finance), the young entrepreneur does not waste energy on knowing, or finding out about, his associates and informants, whether it is a mail-order lawyer or the head of a corporation (Governer Cates) encountered in an executive washroom, who tells him: "—hear more straight talk in the washroom than you will at twenty board meetings . . ." (109). J R's needs of people are informational, not personal. A life lived without recognition: that is what the American system has come to embrace, and the difference between this corporatized world and what Gaddis knew coming of age as a postwar writer accounts for the dramatic aesthetic differences between his first and second novels, *The Recognitions* and its unrecognizable offspring, *J R.*

In replacing a realism based on characters and interiority with a verbal and textual exposition based on systems, Gaddis is not following an impulse toward aesthetic experimentation for its own sake: the transformation in his aesthetic outlook is deeply connected with changes he observed in his native environment. The figure of J R in suburban Long Island is a clear departure from the dysfunctional but still fully invested Greenwich Village sociality of *The Recognitions.* Gaddis, having returned after extensive travel to the Long Island setting he knew as a child, was in a good position to regard the operation of systems on the built environment itself, a landscape and society that would soon enough be unrecognizable to any who had grown up there in the prewar years.

Thanks to the Gaddis Listserv, we are fortunate to have the recollections of a resident of Westrope, near Gaddis's family home in Massapequa, Long Island. An astute reader, Mary Robinson reasonably wonders why none of the many, many critical accounts has ever taken "a woman's-eye view of Gaddis' females." In the absence of any published feminist reading of Gaddis, Robinson intends to "speak up someday about Esme and Esther, Aunt May and Camilla, Agnes Deigh and Big Anna, etc. But today I'm on houses, specifically the Gaddis house on LI, which serves as a model for the Bast house in JR. [. . .] It was a perfectly charming old house, hidden away even then behind privet hedges reaching for the moon, with gnarly old apple trees in the front yard and woodlots behind and on one side of it. In those days there was farmland across the road (Jerusalem Turnpike) and the farmer raised flowers and vegetables. I remember fields of pansies." The land was eventually leased for a shopping center, and this evidently inspired what was (apart from a few letters to politicians) the author's single recorded moment of political activism: Robinson "heard as well that WG himself attended local school board meetings to protest the property tax increases which were, in effect, confiscating his home."[7]

His decision to return, in *J R*, to his boyhood setting points to the personal side of the book, which he was still unable to talk about even when he agreed, finally, to a fairly long interview in a "serious" place (*Paris Review*): "why didn't I say a large part of energy came from revenge on that horrid town that Massapequa became, the vandalism that was really traumatic & c.," he asked his daughter as an afterthought.[8] The incident is reenacted in the novel, when Bast comes home to find "everything smashed broken the whole place torn up" (138). The scene is as personal as the aunts' recollections of their family's musical past yet the whole point of the novel, of course, is how the personal was becoming ever more conjoined with the corporate. During Gaddis's lifetime, America went from a country with vast expanses of rural landscape dotted by funky small towns, to a predominant suburban sprawl. These transformations (and they're not finished yet) have brought numerous cultural and life changes, which go on right before our eyes but somehow go missing in our everyday consciousness and conversation. Norman Mailer, the same age as Gaddis, spent a career denouncing the process as a not entirely metaphorical "cancer" on the American corporate body; Richard Powers, a generation or two younger, humanized this metaphor with his narrative of Laura Bodey in *Gain* (another corporate, corporal novel), and this character's struggle with cancer. But neither Mailer's diatribe nor Powers's appeal to human values, however enraging or comforting each may be, can be said to have made us aware, from the inside, of the patient, spidery operations of suburban development and corporate expansion— less a cancer than a lightly rooted but extensive rhizome.

The ecological and the environmental, Gaddis understood, are also areas of nonrecognition. The land is not suppressed by systems, no more than psyches are suppressed; instead, both the land and human psyches are *transformed by systems.* Lacking Powers's passionate and informed inclusion of ecological themes, Gaddis nonetheless gives an active presence to the suburban environment in the bridge passages of *J R*, such as those in and around the studio behind the Bast house that convey us by roadways, motor vehicles, and occasionally still by foot from the Bast house to the grade school, bank, and train station. In such passages, where the author is anything but absent, Gaddis succeeds where his compeers come up short, rhetorically and stylistically. (No less an accomplishment, he loses the aloof and occasionally aristocratic tone of his narrator in *The Recognitions* and the unlikeable, unlikely mission to "rescue" America and Americans from "vulgarity."[9])

The electric saws outside the Bast house, the laying of pavement over the school grounds, and the ongoing widening of every road traveled in the novel's transitional passages attest to the suburbanizing process that goes on regardless of what people are talking about or what anyone is concerned about at any given moment. Throughout the novel we can hear "the wailing saws of Burgoyne Street" (37), the town's main artery that's renamed Summer Street—presumably because no trees are left to block the sun and no snow or leaves gather beneath the capacity traffic. With "all allusion to permanence" slain (18), the town itself persists in an endless summer. The societal and ecological destruction that accompanies suburbanization is unprecedented: our wars have moved from the sphere of people killing people to the defoliation of landscapes and alteration of entire ecosystems on which human and animal lives depend. Gaddis, who had no experience of fighting in the recent world war, was present for the violence done by systems of administration and control, and this is reflected in settings where the environment he grew up in is made unrecognizable, as if occupied by corporate armies. (Major Hyde, with his fixation on building bomb shelters at the grade school, only makes explicit the corporate occupation that is implicit in the mind of every administrator, politician, and "creative" grant seeker who gathers in the school principal's office throughout the novel.)

Gaddis is systematic, but he's equally (disconcertingly) committed to presenting large systems and broad changes sporadically and in bits and pieces, the way they're actually experienced by most people. Half-attentive adult characters such as the aunts Ann and Julia and the various administrators who know not what they do are prime examples. (Until one day the aunts look out their window to find the hedge missing; or the administrators are notified that the company one of their board commissioned to blacktop the parking lot has covered every acre of land owned by the school.)

Another setting for Gaddis's own extended bouts of writing, the Massapequa studio would itself become in *J R* the backyard studio where Edward Bast seeks to compose his opera, the one place "where nothing happens," you can leave something and know it will be there when you return (69–70). Gaddis felt the same: "How often I think of it, and would love to spend a part of the summer in that large cool room, that seems to me to have so many of my thoughts waiting for me in the high corners and the dark and heavy woodwork."[10]

Of course, this subtly personal sanctuary is *not* left alone. The studio where Bast worked (which is broken into just prior to his meeting Stella there) is based on the farmhouse studio adjacent to Gaddis's family property. The place was well known to the residents of Massapequa, and would have been recognized even during the time when J R walked the side streets in the early 1970s. As he tells Bast:

> —You live in that big old place right after that old empty farmhouse if you turn left, right? This here old house with these little pointy windows and this like big barn in back by the woods? with this big high scraggly hedge out front like? [. . .] That's the only place up there, right? And like right across from it where that guy that raises flowers which used to live in the farmhouse, where he has all those flowers that's where they're having this here new shopping center, you know? (58)

Like Bast in the novel, Gaddis himself had stayed in the studio above the barn for close to a year and in a farmhouse nearby belonging to friends of the family and there managed to push forward on *The Recognitions*, which he'd been working on for much of the previous decade of travel and casual employment in South America, Europe, and North Africa. The more one reads, in letters and notes from this early period, the more autobiographical *J R* seems, even as Gaddis's life, like the life of his characters, becomes overwhelmed by the transformations within his world. It had been suburbanized at first gradually, and then irrevocably during the years when Gaddis was actively writing his first two novels; in *J R* it would be vandalized by teenagers—and entered also in secret by Bast's bewitching cousin (or half sister?), Stella, looking for Bast's birth certificate or some documentation, "just anything," she tells him. Their aunt Julia "thought they must be there in the windowseat." Her husband Norman, the current chief executive and minority shareholder of the Bast family company, General Roll, has been (according to Stella)

> —having some business problems he's rather desperate to get things settled, we . . .
> —Business look everything smashed broken the whole place torn up you're sitting here in the middle of it with a flashlight like a, talking about Norman's business problems all you want is some scrap of paper to prove I, that I'm . . .
> —Oh Edward.
> —What oh Edward what! you, you came out here once to make me look like I, I shouldn't have told you . . . (138)

He shouldn't have told her about seeing her naked at a family outing, in their adolescence. The document she's looking for is meant to
prove that Edward is the legally recognized son of James and Nellie, even
though Nellie, on paper at the time of Edward's birth, may still have been
legally married to James's brother, Thomas, who founded the family business. Early in the century Thomas had produced piano rolls, made mostly
with the help of James's music contacts in Europe such as Paderewski and
Rachmaninoff, the likes of whom Gaddis's great-uncles Jan and Ernest
Williams had known professionally. Those origins appear now as scraps,
"a lampshade crushed, a spoon, a dresser scarf and Piston's Harmony
torn through the spine, sheet music and a player piano roll flung toward
the opened window" (137). We follow Stella's flashlight the way our eyes
might follow a panning camera in a film, as the light "fell on a Bach
Wagner Program of Miss Isadora Duncan and Mister Walter Damrosch
at Carnegie Hall Wednesday Afternoon February 15, 1911, at 3 o'clock—
why anybody would . . . —No I opened that . . . her light swept over
postal views of Cairo, —looking" (137–38).

Cairo, Illinois (pronounced *kay-roh*), was a hometown of Gaddis's
Midwestern relatives on his mother's side. It is one scrap among many,
like the remnants of a golden era in American music before its broadcast
on radio and before its digitization. The scraps do not themselves speak,
although readers might understand, with Gaddis, that the now quaint
piano roll was indeed one beginning of the digital era, with its punched
holes signaling which key should be sounded at what time. As for Walter Damrosch: we have an account of Billy at around age eight, back at
the Merricourt boarding school in rural Connecticut, "standing on an
upturned tin waste-basket, stick in hand" imitating the famed conductor
"before an interested 'orchestra' of children."[11]

The scene with Edward and Stella, filled as it is with Gaddis's own biographical paraphernalia, is connected to a governing theme in the novel:
the dispute over the Bast family's controlling ownership of the General
Roll Company, which once produced player piano rolls that eliminate
entirely the need for a skilled player, while still "insisting the magic touch
of these virtuosos could be preserved on his piano rolls" (63). Norman
Angel has since moved the General Roll business out of rolls for player
pianos; Stella is interested mainly in establishing her share in the business; young Edward wants only to demonstrate by his own work that
he accomplishes in the studio that he has inherited the composer's talent,
not the businessman's acumen. The complexities resolve over the course
of the 700-plus-page novel in Stella's favor (as a result of her husband's
suicide resulting from an inability to cope with his executive position

in the company, and his loveless marriage). Edward mostly neglects his potential business interest, but his boyish and neglectful and passionate nature, which he does share unambiguously with his father, James, comes through in this remarkable scene:

> —I just . . . wanted to look he whispered, his voice like one long out of use gone in abrupt and shapeless fragments that might have framed apology or gratitude, or both, coming down, fighting a foot out of the spread's tear as his shoulders came down to hers and lips delayed at her throat brushed up the scar there, moistened quickly before they sought her own. The opened window beyond was still enough but she turned her face from his so sharply toward it there might have been a light, some sound, some sudden movement from outside to leave his lips lodged at her ear so, filling its convolutions with his gasp of shock at how unseen beneath the spread her hand, unhesitating and without surprise, caress, or brush of exploration found and closed on him swelled to bursting and, silent, motionless, knees fallen wide, led him left thicketed there in dry abrasion as he swarmed over her and clinging headlong wrenched her shoulder in a plunge that left her open eyes fixed on a gap between the rafters where, even in this light, the points of shingle nails showed through in irregular rows, her only sound one that she might have made out of impatience jostled in a crowd, her only movement that sharp turn of her head away from the quaking rise of his, catching the threat of his lips and protest stifled in a bleat against her throat. (139)

The first thing to note about this passage is the myth of authorial absence in criticism of *J R*: on the contrary, a separate, evaluating consciousness comes through with every word choice and every movement depicted. Just as often, without the artifice of either interior monologue or third-person omniscience, Gaddis's voice-over narrator will *inhabit* the consciousness of a character—Stella, in this example, when she senses movement and car headlights outside. (Her husband will enter the barn a few moments later.) Gaddis's outrage especially, which he acknowledged was a source of his literary creativity, is nowhere so powerfully or so beautifully realized than in these bridge passages intermixed within the novel's predominant dialogue. As he lets the business culture speak through the noise and talk of ordinary people, each focused on his or her personal interest, human passions speak mostly through our movements and gestures and hesitancies and the detritus around us from past eras, registered in passages like this one for us to notice, or not. The recognitions are now, definitively, in the mind of the reader in communication with the author; they are no longer for the characters to experience inside the novels and communicate to one another.

In the context of the suburbanized landscape and the more general corporatization of everyday life, personal and biographical elements take on a very specific role. The representations of artists at work and mostly failing at it, have their counterparts in Gaddis's home and work life. One of very few letters depicting his home environment during the years when he was working on *J R* was sent to his second wife, Judith, in 1974. In it, he breaks down his day into hour-by-hour, and sometimes minute-by-minute intervals, to indicate how he's wasting time, and wasting away with her gone (on a business trip, evidently). Here are a couple of excerpts:

| | |
|---|---|
| 08:46 | saw bag with grapefruit, put it by door to remember to give to Jack |
| 08:47 | let cat in |
| 08:48 | poured coffee |
| 08:49 | saw MIL's letter |
| 08:59 | went in to look for stamp for MIL's letter |
| 09:00 | saw work laid out on table, decided to have drink |
| 09:01 | let cat out; decided not to have drink |
| [. . .] | |
| 10:29 | sat down in livingroom chair |
| 10:33 | woke startled by ghastly liquid snoring, decided I had horrible cold and should have drink |
| 10:34 | discovered snoring was being done by dog, very relieved |
| 10:37 | decided not to have drink, went to typewriter in kitchen to work |
| 10:41 | decided I should get some letters out of the way before settling down to work, got paper |
| 10:50 | could think of no one to write to (*L* 287–88) |

We can observe, in *J R*, how long Jack Gibbs holds out before giving in to the impulse to have that drink, although Gibbs, unlike Gaddis, never seems to know the correct time and, each time he has a scheduled appointment, he seems to have mixed up his days. Another difference, as a look at the photo of Gaddis's Piermont writing studio will confirm,[12] is that Gaddis's work is carefully laid out, not sitting on top of a refrigerator under melting ice. Each page is apart and visible, on the desk and taped to the walls of the garage. (Gaddis evidently was more comfortable writing in places suited to manual labor: the studio above the barn in Massapequa where he finished *The Recognitions*, the built-in garage on the ground floor at the house in Piermont.)

The main difference between Gaddis's writing day and Gibbs's, of course, is that Gaddis, unlike Gibbs, *did complete* the work we are reading.[13]

But at what cost? A close friend of the family at the time, fellow corporate writer and James Thurber biographer Harrison Kinney, was there in Croton during the years of *J R*'s composition and knew firsthand the domestic strains that were produced by the book's long gestation and sporadic composition. The final eight years were enough to have their good neighbors wondering, not always to themselves, if the great work would ever be finished; a former supervisor at Eastman Kodak, hoping to lure him back, would send him samples of "work that other freelancers were doing, ending one such letter with a poker-faced 'How is the Great American Novel coming along?' "[14]

During the period when Gaddis and Judith were together, the couple may have been heartened by the series of contract negotiations accomplished by Gaddis's "enterprising" agent at the time, Candida Donadio, "who was able to sell his contract with one house to another, for several thousand more with each transaction."[15] Kinney notes, "Judith put in eight hopeful years with William while *J R* was underway."[16] The couple might have taken encouragement from the example of another Donadio author, Thomas Pynchon, whose considerable sales with *Gravity's Rainbow* in 1973 may have encouraged the Gaddis household about prospects for serious literary fiction on the grand scale. The expectation was voiced, in fact, by Gaddis's editor at Holt, Rinehart & Winston, Aaron Asher, who acknowledges receipt of the latest pages of *J R*, saying, "I'll continue to persist, without making invidious comparisons, in seeing the Pynchon hysteria as a good omen."[17] In the event, however, the publication of *J R* in 1975 left Gaddis with a debilitating debt: $56,500 to his publisher (less future royalties); "to First National City Bank for $2554.89; to Bankers Trust for $2814.24; to Chase for $1450.30; to County Trust for $779.05; and to Chemical Bank with its mortgage on my house for $31,842.73"[18]—nearly $96 grand, equivalent to around $418,000 today. He also had some dental work and tuition payments looming. As he recalled years later, he'd get registered letters saying, "We want our money back."[19]

The familial and personal context for a *succès d'estime* so long in the making, but still so far from economic self-sufficiency, has been captured by his daughter Sarah in a passage from *Swallow Hard*:

Thompkins had won the National Book Award, and a few days later Rollin sat in the darkened auditorium of the Academy of Arts and Letters and watched as he accepted an envelope. There was a moment of levity as Thompkins stepped up to the podium and held the envelope up to the light to make sure the check was in it. The audience laughed, but Rollin's eyes filled with tears. Nineteen years for that laugh and a thousand dollars. He gave a short speech, but she was overcome by how alone he looked up there, as if his suit were too big and he were trying to hold his own. He had worked on the book for two decades. It had sat in closets in cartons under coats, it had been rescued and protected; and yet this audience only saw the glory of the day, the ease and elegance with which Lad Thompkins stepped up to the microphone. (290–91)

Within a year of *J R*'s publication, after a number of tentative separations, Judith had moved out. As Kinney recalls, Judith's "mother took her to Florida for a vacation one winter after her seventh or eighth year with William, and Judith stayed there, getting a job as a waitress." Kinney recalls Gaddis as being "beside himself" after her departure, not least because the "separation" was for so long left indeterminate: "you've cut off any phone possibility," Gaddis wrote to her, after waiting two weeks for a letter and then receiving it Special Delivery. Opening the envelope, he'd half expected to have from her something definitive, for better or worse. As he wrote to her, he expected her to say something like: "—I'm coming back Thursday . . .—I'm coming back in January & get a place in New York . . .—I have some friends here who are going to Mexico tomorrow & have decided . . . then see from your opening line (I feel very badly to have taken so long to answer &c &c) that Special Delivery was only a twinge of conscience."[20]

Gaddis opened his heart at this time (October 1977) to another trusted friend, John Napper:

> In fact Judith's been away for so damned long by this time (since the end of February) that she's rapidly becoming rather an idea than a person. Still a terribly quiet house & somehow a chilly one, wash out one's shirts, cook for 1, nobody to share the small great things of life with like the turning of the leaves, nobody but the fool cat stamping about & shouting for his supper while the porch steps collapse & I add that project to my list of things undone, invitations to stylish openings unattended in favour of sitting here with a glass of whisky & wishing I could write a maudlin popular song (viz. one

current: 'The windows of the world are covered with rain . . .'), you
see what I mean. But frankly there is also a modicum of comfort in
the sense of one less person to disappoint, a personal extension of
the collapse of the Protestant Ethic which I suppose is my eventual
obsession.[21]

Napper was unique among Gaddis's acquaintances in that he and
Pauline had stayed together since they'd married in 1945, and by 1950
(when the Nappers met Gaddis) they'd managed "the marriage and all
that goes with it in London" that Gaddis at the time could only dream
of for himself and Margaret Williams.[22] He'd set aside such notions with
his transnational itinerant lifeways, but both he and Kinney might have
expected, in the 1950s when their children were conceived, that (in Kinney's words) they each "would live a staid Andy Hardy kind of soap
opera domestic life, the children cared for by a doting wife, a world willing to subsidize the talents we both felt we had to offer." Small comfort to
each in their private lives that in their published work they had grasped
(in Gaddis's words) the "major historical readjustment" in the family unit
"for which no single victim or knife-wielder can be blamed, 'blame' itself
having gone out the window with the bath water."[23]

What he was living through, and not just observing in fiction, was
the beginning of the end of patriarchy, and this, too, was part of the
collapsing religious foundations of American society. (The rise of fundamentalist religion, his topic in *Carpernter's Gothic*, would have been
seen by Gaddis as a symptom of collapse.) The "readjustment" might
have been less difficult for him personally if only the pattern were not so
closely connected to what he was beginning to see in social and cultural
pressures exerted on his own children and in an emerging generation of
aspiring writers with no greater cultural remit, or personal commitment,
than their own self-expression. About this connection Gaddis is quite
explicit: he could see for example in Judith's stated desire to be her own
person and learn (in Gaddis's unsympathetic paraphrase) "to take care
of yourself & come and go as you please &c," something very much like
what he was observing in (of all places) the writing workshops at Bard,
which at this moment were barely keeping him afloat financially: "I read
novels (& endless writing workshop stories) about it & look at my own
friends' lives."[24] He could observe similar breakups in the families of men
close to him at the time—Pennebaker and Marc Brandel are mentioned—
who'd married younger women and lost them. In commiseration with
these men, during the months when he was waiting on Judith's decision,
he almost felt as though they had brought their wives up "to prepare

them to go out in the world like we did with our children but here the children come through. . . ."[25]

Even as he conveyed to Judith his own uncertain feelings about their marriage and the hurt caused by her departure, in letters with Napper he attempted to look more generally, and even "sympathetically at these girls' & women's plight." He takes in Napper's evident insight into inequalities that in Judith's case are as much to do with the difference in age as with professional aspiration and he acknowledges "that one 'can't stand still & protected behind someone else', that 'love must be free from dependence' &c &c, & that in essence it's as difficult if not more so for them (Judith) as for us (me) to be participants in this historic watershed between the madness of the Judeo-Christian oppression & what's ever ahead, where surely the Buddhist approach you note must have a place if we are to survive at all."[26]

Far from bringing condolence, the culturally enforced selfishness of it all is what infuriates him finally, "So frankly John I'm a bit sick & tired of people stepping out to 'find themselves' coming up at last with too often, in Cyril Connolly's exquisitely harsh phrase, 'a cheap sentimental humanism at someone else's expense.'"[27]

His later alliance with Muriel, however much it was marked by economic inequalities, would be entered into without illusions and would be largely untouched by sentimentality. Kinney recalls, concerning Muriel: "She liked to give parties and William was the centerpiece, attracting patrons of the arts to her dinner table in NYC and the Hamptons. She was protective of him, often curt with me when I would call as, William said, she was with many of his friends. I would ask him why she always sounded so nasty on the phone; he would simply sigh and say, 'I know, I know.'" When Gaddis was diagnosed with a terminal illness, after sixteen years of cohabitation he and Muriel agreed to part ways. Not a word of explanation (and no sentiment) is to be found in her "unpublished files" (collected posthumously and released in paperback by the vanity press XLibris).

Having in his first two novels presented artists, men and women, in search of authenticity in the arts, Gaddis in his work would now feature (in central characters such as McCandless, Elizabeth Booth, and Oscar Crease) a number of would-be authors in search of their own personal identities but incapable of recognizing (or realizing) the need for involvement with others. Still less would they recognize their involvement with current systems and corporate states that were only reinforcing the separations and nonrecognition that had always been his great theme.

Chapter 9

# The Imagination of the State

—you can't go put a corporation in jail, I mean it would be like
sticking this bunch of papers in jail see so . . .

(*J R* 648)

Lee Konstantinou, one of the organizers of the 2012 Gaddis "Big Read"
at the *Los Angeles Review of Books*, suggested early in the discussions
that J R might have grown up to be Mitt Romney, CEO of Bain Capital,
who in the 1980s and 1990s routinely practiced the kind of leveraged
buyouts, mergers, firings of employees nearing retirement, and sell-offs of
U.S. companies that we've seen J R apply to the fictional Eagle Mills. (The
2012 presidential race, the most costly in history to candidates on both
sides, was in high gear throughout the summer readings.)

J R of course never does "grow up." Although he is a quick study and
there is capital growth galore, he never experiences any *Bildung* in the
manner of realistic novels that trace the education of a character through
adversities and toward an independent adulthood. (That role is taken by
J R's music teacher and corporate front man, Edward Bast.) So J R would
not *grow* to be Romney, whose candidacy will be remembered, if at all, for
the offhand remark to a journalist he didn't know: "corporations are people too, my friend."[1] For Romney, as for J R (who thought there were real
Eskimos stuffed in the Natural History Museum), humans are functional
parts of a corporate system, whose specific embodiment (male or female,
multiracial, able or disabled) are elements that need only to be adapted to
whatever requirements or opportunities happen to arise, or for occasions
of display. Neither Romney nor J R is much prone to a change in personality, or to self-reflection. Both play the system like a game and regard
humans as more or less consequential players. And both are in it to win.

Until they lose—when the only response is then to do whatever it takes
to get back in the game. Romney was a three-time campaigner for the

presidency. J R on the final page of the novel, after the collapse of his empire, has yet another "neat idea" for a start-up. He's undeterred by the fact that, after all his speculative efforts, nobody grew but the business and even this, the J R Family of Companies that the preadolescent "parents," nearly brings down the world economy. As the novel works its way toward the end, none of the artists finish their work, and any hope is glimmering at best. Bast's opera is reduced to a cantata, then to an oratorio, and ultimately to an unaccompanied piece for cello that he writes in silence, from his hospital bed. The fact that over the course of the novel Bast picks up habits of speech from J R ("this here whole," "holy shit," and so forth) indicates another, more mental degeneration— all of which is conveyed without any explicit authorial or readerly access to the character's psychology. As opposed to growth in character, the psychic transformations, very real, are channeled in every case *through* the economic and social systems that each character inhabits, and through the words they use that reveal (to the attentive reader) habits of mind, allowing Gaddis to do away with the whole heavy narrative apparatus of introducing each character every time one enters a scene or dialogue. As Peter Wolfe has pointed out, "Verbal tics and fidgets can do the work of characterization in the novel," a technique arguably that goes deeper than psychological description or stream-of-consciousness narration because the language we use, more than we know, speaks us and not the other way around. "Sometimes," Wolfe notes, "a verbal oddity like [the teenager] Rhoda's saying 'drownd' (376) for 'drown' and 'enchilavies' (599) for 'enchiladas' will identify a character or give insight into his or her social level."[2] Even a character such as Governor Cates, at the other end of the social and economic spectrum, reveals his own roughneck origins with phrases such as "he don't" and a barked "hear me."

This faithfulness on Gaddis's part to the speech habits carried over (in the case of Cates) from a man's formative years to his current position of power can do more than pages of narration to let the readers see past the ninety-year-old mogul to the rough-and-tumble strikebreaker that earned him the moniker Black Jack Cates. And the collocation of "Governor" and "Cates," so close to "Gates," directs attention subtly to the opening and closing of gates by the "sorting demon"—a fiction concocted by British scientist James Clerk Maxwell to convey the microscopic, ever vigilant presence that would be needed for any one consciousness to produce order from the disordered, entropic flow of molecules in a closed system. Yet of course this is precisely the kind of impossibly detailed attention that Governor Cates gives to his business empire, even as his model in life, John D. Rockefeller, was said by Gaddis (in the

1981 essay "The Rush for Second Place") to have been (like Cates in the fiction)

> no idler, no boozer, no skirt-chaser, but a man who saw eye to eye with an ethic that regarded "laziness and idleness as the source of all evil, and the result of a failure to impose discipline," who could feel "the obligation towards property as towards something great, which ought to be maintained and increased for its own sake" and who subscribed to the philosophy articulated in this Sunday school address: "The American Beauty rose can be produced in the splendour and fragrance which brings cheer to its beholder only by sacrificing the early buds which grow up around it. This is not an evil tendency in business. It is merely a working-out of a law of nature and a law of God." (*RSP* 46)

Gaddis thus advances, together with the human dimension of power, themes of entropy, cybernetics, and Social Darwinism that underlie the corporatization of life in America. Discipline at the level of the individual is thus made consistent with a collective unrestrained *growth*: "See it at the corporate level all the time," as the character Hyde likes to say, the same character who's always going on about "what America's all about." And it *is* all about growth, if we grant the largely *uncontrolled* and unregulated tendencies that extend business and its consequences far beyond the scope of any one consciousness. The cybernetic themes also govern the design of the narrative. They are advanced knowledgeably by an author who had worked closely with high government officials, bureaucrats, and generals, but the technological and administrative themes are enacted, not told, and this is all done without ever once relaxing the discipline of remaining true to the way people actually do speak in everyday life.

All this can be conveyed implicitly, from Gaddis to the reader, without our ever having to speculate on a character's motives or to name behaviors with psychological or political abstractions; against the massive, largely unconscious, unrecognizable operations of the corporate system, there is in Gaddis's fiction an achieved intersubjectivity that does away with speculation about questions of character or personal narrative trajectory. Of necessity, any subjective insights happen at a meta level, unknown to the characters themselves who are mostly struggling for a foothold in the corporate system as this comes to dominate not just the offices of Typhon and Diamond Cable, but an American school system that increasingly substitutes closed-circuit television for one-on-one teaching; a musical industry that digitizes sounds that once depended on the touch of a hand or the force of a breath, never exactly the same twice; or an emergent social networking system that creates for an individual (such as the hapless Dan diCephalis) a personal profile: Dan is said to be continually having "trouble with his holes," as his punch-card profile goes missing and eventually he will literally disappear in transit during an experiment in a cross-country teleportation.

This too, the digital profiling of a man's professional aspirations, affirms the overriding insight, unmatched in contemporary fiction, that our contemporary corporate systems are grounded precisely in an emptying out of subjectivity. "—How could I be inside there isn't any inside" (644) is Bast's response when J R informs him that Bast has been sued by stockholders for unknowingly taking out a bad loan against company stock. "—The only inside's the one inside your head" (644).[3] And what is there, inside the heads of the characters, that we are able to access other than language? That is the only access Gaddis allows to a character's psychology, in the diminished world of systems built on zeros and ones. That such a disciplined reduction of narrative is capable of yielding so very much is one of the revelations of this remarkable fiction.[4]

Forty years ago, "Corporations are people too, my friend" was a phrase one would find only in satiric postmodern fiction; now it's our reality. The notion put forward by presidential candidate Romney is not at all metaphoric or cleverly ironic since limited-liability corporations in many instances have the same legal rights as people. Absurd as it sounds to us, and to the adult characters in J R, that is just the state of affairs that has been in place in America since the Fourteenth Amendment to the U.S. Constitution, extending in 1868 the newly universal civil rights beyond black Americans (and all citizens) to incorporated groups. Indeed, an outcry against "the accordance of personhood to Joint Stock Companies that effectively literalized 'corporation' into 'corpus'" was a staple of nineteenth-century realist fiction in England, no less than in America.[5] The world of fictitious capital, as a number of literary scholars of the period such as Anna Kornbluh and David Morier Evans have noted, is a world in which "the speculative mania [is] of such a fantastic kind, that the very names of the 'Bubble companies' . . . look like a sarcasm upon speculation in general." We find this registration, Kornbluh notes, in the "opaque, circumlocutionary, and mumbo-jumbo quality of the actual financial transactions" depicted in satires by Dickens and Trollope. We find it already in *The Way We Live Now* (1875), whose narrative "most dramatically, circulates unattributed speech," and in the oddly named characters that are also found in postmodern fictions in mid-1970s

America. If we listen to Trollope's Melmotte, the speaker of *mal mots*, we may again register an exchange of words that circulate more powerfully than any currency among traders in money markets. Melmotte tells the officers assembled around a boardroom table,

> If I know anything of the world, I know something of commercial affairs. I am able to tell you that we are prospering. I do not know that greater prosperity has ever been achieved in a shorter time by a commercial company. . . . I am able to inform you that in affairs of this nature, great discretion is necessary. On behalf of the shareholders whose large interests are in our hands, I think it expedient that any general statement should be postponed.[6]

Kornbluh notes how "the ambivalent constructions" and carefully conditional locutions of such passages are consistent with the economy of credit, what Trollope in 1875 calls "dealings of unsecured paper" by men who "pay nothing" for everything, write down their debts "on paper," and "even get (their) hair cut on credit." But how many of us today do otherwise?

The discursive supports for such endlessly growing paper empires have not changed all that much since the institution of corporate personhood in the nineteenth century, nor have administrative and political locutions become less craftily ambivalent. What has changed, even as quantity changes quality and credit extends beyond the small world of financial capitalists to we the people, is the capacity of a literary audience to share in an author's outrage at such practices. Once the corporate fiction of personhood became enshrined in law, the mode of satire and an author's undisguised anger could not sustain itself for more than a decade or two. In time, despite regular economic crashes the speculative economy of the late nineteenth century gained not credence, but something much more literary and hence lasting—namely, a *willing suspension of disbelief* by people who understood the fictive terms of their participation in the economy and were nonetheless prepared to enter the fiction: to play the game. And when the state and the corporation take this disposition upon themselves, which had hitherto been the province of printed fictions, "fictitious capital" (Kornbluh) becomes a fact of everyday life and corporate personhood, a part of the realist landscape.

Outrage, Gaddis often remarked,[7] energized him (more as he grew older), and one might think it would motivate anyone who was capable of analyzing an economy so clearly built on legal and linguistic fictions. There are certainly passages where he has characters articulate his own anger, his indignation, but these are mostly presented in blurry-eyed conversations and classroom lectures when nobody's listening to anybody else. If there is something "difficult" about his books, I suspect the source is not to be found in any linguistic or even conceptual challenge posed by the writing so much as readers tiring of precisely these occasionally drawn-out, narcissistic rants by white men of a certain age: by the many youthful selves "who could do more" in *The Recognitions*; by Gibbs, by Eigen in *J R*, usually when alcohol is involved; by McCandless in *Carpenter's Gothic*, as we shall see momentarily; by the ninety-seven-year-old Judge Crease, whose rage is channeled into gemlike written opinions that really do shape our legal fictions. Thankfully, the overall demeanor of Gaddis's work is not denunciatory or even satirical so much as comic. Trollope and Dickens, for their part, might use the circumlocutions of their characters to avoid going very far into the very real economic and legal details that remain operative even in a paper economy. Gaddis, on the other hand, while less concerned with in-depth characterization and narrative voice-overs, accounts for each and every purchase, hire, and trade undertaken by young J R, whether it is the ten dollars he loans Bast (so the boy can later call his music teacher in on the favor), the lawsuit the boy "stockholder" brings to Diamond Cable (that is hidden by the men working under Governor and CEO Cates to protect themselves for having leaked the incriminating information during the sixth-graders' class visit), or each minuscule (but definitive) decision that takes advantage of this or that loophole or tax break or potential Ponzi scheme (built on the serial suspension of disbelief from one investor to the next, until the market reverses and the last generation of investors is left holding the bag).

The unmatched level of engagement with the details of corporate life cannot be contained by satire alone; indeed, as Nicholas Brown has argued, this compulsion in Gaddis recalls another characteristic of earlier, realist fiction—namely, the desire to "delight and teach" readers (*PE* 158). Gaddis educates us not so much in the way we live now, which we can know well enough through cable and network news, reality television, and the many other nonliterary media that have emerged since Trollope's time. No, what Gaddis shows us uniquely, with unsparing analytical fury, are the multiple, half-known ways that legal and financial fictions individually shape our self-imaginings, now and in America.

Gaddis's extensive experience with university writing programs is the topic of the next chapter. But we can note here how the pedagogical was not foreign to his temperament, particularly when he was corresponding with his son and daughter. Not untypical was the way he could spell out, without a touch of condescension, the ways of the newly corporatizing world in a letter for example to Sarah of 5 August 1986. He is relating her brother Matthew's efforts to hold on to a Manhattan rental on 171st Street, and goes on to indicate what is happening to Muriel's building on the Upper East Side: "Pay $2000 a month rent for a ½ way decent NY apartment, or it goes cooperative & you get the chance to buy it for ½ million and then pay $2000 a month 'maintainance', all just nutty."

Young J R of course completely understands the fictiveness of our current economistic culture. He tells Bast not to worry about their company's malfeasance because "you can't go put a corporation in jail" (648). The new reality that corporate personhood is a fiction—and that it *should be so*, is today for many no less plausible than any other fictional construction whereby we much too readily project human qualities onto abstract, corporate (and incorporeal) entities. Gaddis was not alone in this perception; indeed, in January 1986 Donald Barthelme came up with "The Writer's Imagination and the Imagination of the State" for the title of the famed 48th International PEN Congress in New York City, attended by then Secretary of State George Schultz as well as such literary notables as Norman Mailer, Saul Bellow, Nadine Gordimer, Susan Sontag, Mario Vargas Llosa, Claude Simon, and Gaddis himself, who told his compeers,

> We who struggle to create fictions of various sorts, and with varying success, must regard the state with awe, for the state itself may be the grandest fiction to be concocted by man, barring only one.
>
> The collision course on which we as writers frequently find ourselves with this Leviathan lies in the efforts of the state to preserve and protect its own imagined version of itself, confronted by the writer's individual imagined version of what the state—what life in the state, that is to say—could and should, or at least should not be. (*RSP* 123)

The "one," even grander fiction than the state or corporation is of course religion, a central topic of his first novel and again, three decades later (after the postwar rise of fundamentalist religions through a vastly expanded media), of *Carpenter's Gothic*. In that novel, which appeared six months before the PEN conference, the impulse toward collective imaginings, so similar to the church, the state, and the literary novelist, had been much on his mind. Through his character McCandless, Gaddis had already exposed (perhaps too definitively and from too many directions) the wellspring of corporate and religious fundamentalism in "desperate fictions like the immortal soul" (*CG* 157); "any lunatic fiction to get through the night and the more farfetched the better, any evasion of the one thing in life that's absolutely inevitable . . ." (121); and religious "convictions" as just that, residing "in some shabby fiction doing life without parole and they want everybody else in prison with them"(186). He had also already asked whether the idea of the South was not "a paranoid sentimental fiction?" (224), as fictitious as fears of "this great global Marxist conspiracy" (190)—all of this expressed in the carpenter gothic house in which McCandless lives, "a patchwork of conceits, borrowings, deceptions" (227). The latter, at least, while fictitious and derivative, is able to hold together through something like what Gaddis wants to present, in his own fiction, as a *workable* idea of the state:

> Two hundred years building this great bastion of middle class values, fair play, pay your debts, fair pay for honest work, two hundred years that's about all it is, progress, improvement everywhere, what's worth doing is worth doing well and . . . (230)

And that, it seems, is what Gaddis himself (much like McCandless) saw being eroded by the previous long list of not so tangible but patently destructive fictions. So various, scathing, and uncompromising are McCandless's denunciations, of both church and state, that it is possible to miss the one positive, distinctively American value expressed in that last citation. It is the same value, so modest as to easily pass notice, that Gaddis has Thomas Eigen articulate amidst the clutter of the Ninety-Sixth Street apartment on the last page of *J R*: "—Look," Eigen says to an annoying delivery guy, "just do what you're paid for will you? God damn it can't, why can't people just shut up and do what they're paid for!" (726).

McCandless and Eigen (and Gibbs and Bast and every one of Gaddis's partial self-projections) each in his different way ultimately withdraws from any univocal political commitment. Yet they are consistent in a straightforward advocacy respecting "fair pay for honest work" and decent living. That is something tangible, resolutely modest but also a workable foundation for building a society (two hundred years in the making) that is more than the sum of its individuals and that is capable of posing something more than a personal set of values against the vast, impersonal operations that through imitation and mass reproduction render all values arbitrary, and equally inconsequential. One of his closest friends, Martin Dworkin, thought of Gaddis as "aristocratic." He may well have appeared patrician to students and to his literary peers, but both characterizations miss the rough-hewn pragmatism of Gaddis's private outlook. There is certainly something to the aristocratic characterization,

particularly during the years when he was living uptown in the 1980s
and early 1990s, and moving among three or four different properties in
the New York City area that were owned by himself and his then partner,
Muriel Oxenburg Murphy. "There must be a certain irony," he told Sarah
in July 1979, "in my owning a roomy sought-after beach house, & Muriel
owning a large elegant country exclusive stash, & here we are height of
summer heat in a tiny almost airless 1 b.r. (lvg room kitchen bath) borrowed 'apartment' in Sag Harbour . . . (to say nothing of the Piermont
house & her NY layout, we've just figured that in her combined layouts
she commands sleeping for 21, I for 16. . . ."

Along with the irony there could have also been a certain defensiveness
that led him to calculate his own contribution to a lifestyle he never could
have afforded with the middle class income he brought to his cohabitation with Muriel.

The sudden change of fortune must have run against a deeper element
in his character and upbringing, much deeper, for example, than his political convictions, whether they should happen to fall on the conservative,
liberal, or aristocratic side. This is to say, Gaddis's outlook and literary
practice remained all his life deeply consistent with the Quaker religion
he grew up with, and in which he was educated. It's a trait that's easy to
overlook, in that (apart from the elderly Bast sisters) no Quakers appear
in the fiction and his own background is mentioned explicitly only once
in his correspondence, and then in a parenthesis:

> Inhowfar the course of my formal education shaped my later work
> I cannot say; and I believe one must be very much on guard against
> disproportionate inferences and emphases. My own experience was
> rather the reverse of the usual: I went off to boarding school age 5
> or 6, then to public schools from 7th through 12th grade and thence
> to college. The boarding school was a small one, in Connecticut, run
> along lines of what was then described as the 'modified Dalton plan'
> implying a good deal of freedom but very strictly within a New En-
> gland framework of imbuing one with a matter of fact acceptance
> of simply trying to do well what needs to be done; and of taking the
> responsibility for the consequences of one's actions. Its informal af-
> filiation would have been Congregational. (My mother's family till
> her generation were Quaker.) My grades were so far as I recall good;
> but since the climate was a noncompetetive one this was not stressed.
> Similarly, sports were organized little beyond the point of making
> them possible to take part in, and with no more of the competitive
> element than called for by the rules of the game.[8]

He had asked that none of this be used for "biographical" purposes; the questioner, who was researching a book to be titled *Educating Able Learners*, was interested in how his educational background might have influenced his success as marked by the receipt of a MacArthur Fellowship in July of 1982 amounting to $50,000 (roughly $120,000 in 2015) a year for the next five years (*L* 378).[9] The biographical reticence, of course, was itself consistent with Quaker attitudes and offers yet another perspective on his unwavering separation between the social and the corporate, the convivial personality that belongs to this world and the work that celebrates God's creation. Indeed, he was so good for so long at keeping himself out of the public eye that otherwise discerning readers[10] associated his attitude exclusively with the modernist disposition espoused by Eliot in "Tradition and the Individual Talent"—namely that art is not the expression but the "extinguishing" of the author's personality in the work.[11] Eliot was indeed an influence, but we must not forget that for all its definitive modernism, Eliot's position was consistent with a deeply conservative religious temperament. And Gaddis, though he would be a lifelong agnostic, never lost that early sensibility.

Gaddis's Quaker roots, a kind of disciplined self-effacement that he kept close inside him all his life, certainly explain his imperviousness to all manner of modern forgeries and all evasiveness of beliefs in the state, or in religions not grounded in regular, daily, and visible contributions to a common good. How else could he so firmly, and so systematically, reject a culture that increasingly dealt in simulations and false idols? His dissatisfaction with what America had become, through precisely such simulations, could be measured not simply against his own personal imaginings, but against the simplicity of prewar forms and obligations to a community that was real to him, as he notes in the letter to Cox:

> Reviewing the foregoing in the light—or perhaps rather the darkness—of the present day, it's imperative to remain aware how those prewar days, the depression notwithstanding, were simpler times, before so many taken for granted values and obligations were sundered not to be recovered, or reinstituted today in my own strong opinion, in imitation of those earlier forms.

His conservatism, he's careful to say, pulls up short of reactionary as he is well aware of how "Congregational" attitudes from prewar times could degrade into current fundamentalisms, "too often used to justify the perpetuation of entrenched beliefs and material interests in face of the threat of inevitable change." Rather than resist change, the lesson he

carried over from his education led him, as he grew older, to "its pain-
ful embrace in an effort [to] help shape it rather than, all too human,
control it."

> You ask 'did school matter much one way or another?' and of course
> it did: for an instance, the reading I did well out of college was more
> important than what I'd done in college but I should never have done
> it, or be doing it now, without all that had gone before. So it seemed
> to me then and it seems even more to me now that the main purpose
> of education from the start must be to stimulate questions—even
> those to which we've got no answer—rather than answering them;
> and to open every vista even those which are distasteful rather than
> closing them for that reason, only to see them gape open in their most
> destructive features later. (L 389–90)

The final turn of phrase in this key letter for understanding Gaddis
anticipates the title of his last fiction, the posthumously published *Agapē
Agape*. However deeply he inhabited the virtual reality of the corporate
state, the descendant of Quakers and "the boy inside" remained skeptical:
never for a moment, while writing, or while being celebrated by the very
state whose operations he'd imagined (and deconstructed) in such detail,
did Gaddis suspend his disbelief in the state's imagination of itself.

With a MacArthur in 1982 and many other awards and honors coming
his way, along with invitations to prestigious literary conferences and
his partnership with a prominent socialite in Manhattan, Gaddis would
have to come out of his shell somewhat. New York City, the place where
everyone was, or aspired to be, a celebrity of sorts, could in some ways
protect him from more prying, intrusive sorts of public attention. Short
interviews for venues such as *Publishers Weekly* and the *New York Post*
he would do—and he even might be pleased to note how well his words
were represented, "since I can't say I was terribly cooperative."[12] More
to his liking would be an article he welcomed by Louis Auchincloss for
the *New York Times Magazine* in 1987. As he wrote to Sarah with some
defensiveness,

> I know that [his son] MHG will howl & you may too! Everything
> I've always avoided, shied from, a few 'personal details' &c. HOW-
> EVER [. . .] He is a class act, not a celebrity junk journalist a la
> Vanity unFair, real probity, novelist & lawyer, steeped in the world of
> class, money, Edith Warton's [*sic*] world, WASP forthright generous

aristocrat & I say all this *not* for its social cachet but for his crisp approach 'nothing in it for him', not using me to build up his reputation nor his to build mine & not the 'celebrity' trip. It springs from his strong feeling that J R is one of the great novels in its preoccupation with $/USA & his wish (demand!) that it reach a wider audience, rescue it from the academic critics & deliver it to the Middle Class which the NYT Magazine reaches. By the 100 thousands.[13]

Though he would not disdain a wider audience, his approach to the social, whether from an aristocratic, Quaker, or modernist literary outlook, would always be based on communication among like-minded individuals, "a few minds, ever the same" (to cite again the line Gaddis often referenced from Flaubert). In this sense, as far as his own personal life was concerned, he steadfastly refused to generalize his participation in local communities, to anything approaching the idea of a state, be it corporate or political or the remarkable conflation of the two that we in the United States currently have in place. What he sought was more on the order of a literary or cultural *estate*, which he achieved at various times in various ways, from his early participation in the Congregational ethos at Merricourt boarding school in Connecticut to his hard-earned acceptance by upper Manhattan's highest social circles and by literary friends with real influence beyond the appreciation of academics, whose power to keep a book in print and in classrooms and under discussion in journals did not mean that the novels would be widely read in an author's lifetime. The Quaker and the aristocratic, a combination as unlikely as any in his imaginative repertoire, and unlikely ever to attract a large audience, remained central to his imagination of himself and offered a position from which the (increasingly "strong") imitations put forward by states and corporations could be measured in and against his life's work.

A strategy typical of Gaddis, avoiding speaking by making avoidance a theme, marks his entrance into this more public phase. His insistence that writers should be read rather than seen or heard, first voiced in his National Book Award acceptance speech in 1976, made a nice contrast with the speaker who was set to follow him ten years later at the PEN conference—Norman Mailer. With time, however, Gaddis accepted the responsibilities that came with recognition, although he continued to take his creative irresponsibilities just as seriously. William Gass recounted the transformation at the May 1999 memorial service, from the same stage at the New York Academy of Arts and Letters where Gaddis accepted that first National Book Award twenty-three years earlier: "the mysterious Mister Gaddis is actually seen in public, is elected to the Academy, earns a MacArthur, writes a book in less than twenty years. He must be slipping."[14]

In a sense, he may have been. Gaddis must have known that in his sixth and seventh decades he was no longer writing fiction on the order of *The Recognitions* and *J R*. He had scaled back knowingly with *Carpenter's Gothic*, for commercial reasons not for loss of power; and for *Frolic* he would reimagine his carefree youth and transatlantic seeking as a "frolic" among the upper-class, uptown Manhattan society where he suddenly found himself, somewhat as Pynchon has done with his own uptown milieu and Silicon Alley in *Bleeding Edge* (2013). Each author in his eighth decade manages remarkably to enter the brave new world of upscale corporate capital without for a moment compromising their long-term outsider status. Pynchon would appear on an episode of *The Simpsons* (bag over his head, walking past a road sign saying "Thomas Pynchon House Come on In"); Gaddis two decades earlier might have published an interview in the *Paris Review* and had his portrait done by the "$1 million a year" art star Julian Schnabel.[15] Not slipping so much, then, as reassessing and repurposing past accomplishments in circumstances that in Gaddis's case would let an author access resources and connections he'd known of and encountered on occasion but had never inhabited fully, not since his years at Harvard. His sudden elevation to a social milieu whose lifeways he embraced and knew how to enjoy allowed him again to travel and cultivate friendships among accomplished artists, jurists, and business types, with some of the same (though tempered) conviviality he experienced during his youthful travels. (Muriel, characteristically uncharitable, recalled her sixteen years with Gaddis as one long alcoholic haze; Harrison Kinney noted a marked improvement in his dress.[16]) From a professional standpoint, the PEN conference must have made it clear for him, too, the extent to which a newly politicized, more broadly "cultural" approach to novel-writing had entered, as if overnight: "The entire baying and howling of the PEN conference in NY is over," he wrote to Sarah in Los Angeles, "everyone reading papers overshadowed by Mailer's having invited Geo Schultz for the opening, & fighting with the women over their underrepresentation at the close."[17] Always the one for "keeping the peace" at home, he could not have been energized by the political and cultural transformations here openly on display.[18] Certainly panel talks such as Gaddis's were overshadowed by the presence of Secretary of State Schultz, who was accused by Gordimer, Coetzee, and Sipho Sepamla of supporting apartheid. Salman Rushdie, in a memoir written two decades later for the *New York Times Book Review*, recalls how other writers also disapproved of Schultz's presence, protesting that (as E. L. Doctorow put it) writers were being set up "as a forum for the Reagan administration."[19] Schultz had told the assembled authors, in his own presentation, that he and Ronald Reagan were "on your side"—a recognition that the newly corporatizing state was only too willing to embrace (and likely smother) the aesthetic in indiscriminate, nonjudgmental terms. If religion, that other "grand fiction," was separate from the state per the First Ammendment, the separation of literary arts and the state was equally important to Gaddis and the majority of writers in attendance at the PEN conference. Gaddis himself had always held on to the ideal of the artist as the outsider, the one who "comes among us not as the bearer of idées reçues embracing art as decoration or of the comfort of churchly beliefs enshrined in greeting card sentiments but rather in the aesthetic equivalent of one who comes on earth 'not to send peace, but a sword'" (F 39; the passage is from Judge Crease's opinion, *Szyrk v. Village of Tatamount et al.*, citing Matt. 10:34).

But there was more to indicate a sea change in American letters, an embrace of, rather than disarticulation from, statist values: Rushdie recalls many women at the Congress demanding, "with much justification, to know why there were so few women on the panels. Sontag and Gordimer, both panelists, did not join the revolt. It was Susan who came up with the argument that 'literature is not an equal opportunity employer.' This remark did not improve the protesters' mood. Nor, I suspect, did my own intervention—I pointed out that while there were, after all, several women on the various panels, I was the sole representative of South Asia, which was to say, of one sixth of the human race."

Gaddis of course did not join the fray, though he would not fare much better than Sontag and Rushdie, years later in another very public forum when he was asked outright by Mary McCarthy if he could name any important living woman writer in the United States. He thought for a good several seconds, as though he was considering this for the first time, and answered no, he could not.[20]

Sonia Johnson, a literature graduate student in the summer of 2012 at the University of Iowa, notices in a blog how the terms of the conflict between Mailer's celebrity and Gaddis's reticence may have left unspoken a more significant continuity—namely, between what Johnson terms "the oversized dimension and ambition of a novel like *J R* [and] the oversized ego of Mailer's 1970s persona." The PEN conference was not the first professional encounter between these two writers. Gaddis, Johnson noted, apparently didn't know that the ubiquitous Mailer would be the one introducing him at the National Book Award ceremony in 1976. Intending, in his "beautifully written" two-minute presentation, "a self-effacing defense of reading against superficial celebrity, Gaddis awk-wardly apologized to literary celebrity Mailer before plowing on with his prepared speech. He had stumbled," Johnson continues:

> into an old debate in American letters about the role of authorial personality, a conflict more familiarly exemplified by Gaddis's and Mailer's respective heroes, Eliot and Hemingway. Eliot's ideal was the artist's creation as "a continual surrender of himself as he is at the moment to something which is more valuable," while Hemingway raised personality itself to an art form.
>
> Mailer's introductory speech, on the other hand, championed mystic, painful self-examination as the only route to artistic truth, or, to use David Foster Wallace's term, Great Male Narcissism. Mailer was introduced by National Institute for Arts and Letters president Harrison Salisbury as "the most genuine spokesman for his era that we have today," but, if *Publishers Weekly*'s report is accurate, the speech was a flop. Mailer ended with a joke that "various members of the audience characterized later, according to temperament, as racist, sexist, just old-fashioned dirty or all three" (and that was sadly too obscene for the magazine to reproduce).[21]

To Johnson and perhaps several of those participating in the 2012 "Occupy Gaddis" blog, Mailer's public "and pubic" narcissism and Gaddis's privacy and impersonality, "despite their opposition, both seem rather dated. Gaddis's old-fashioned self-denial is certainly less embarrassing than Mailer's old-fashioned chauvinism. But even so, there are some Gaddis advocates who attribute his obscurity to overzealous political correctness in post-sixties literary sensibilities." Steven Moore, for example, had wondered in a review of Wallace's *Infinite Jest* whether Gass's *Tunnel*, published the previous year, was to be among "the last of a dying breed, the encyclopedic American novel that began with Gaddis's *Recognitions* in 1955. . . . Who was left to write such novels, or to read them at a time when some scorn such books as elitist, testosterone-fueled acts of male imperialism?"[22]

Those who regard "such books" in this way are unnamed, and in Gaddis's case it would be hard to name one published critic, since there is as yet no considered feminist, postcolonial, or neoimperialist response to the novels. Current commentators have begun to recognize that the removal of oneself as an explicit voice in the narrative (while disseminating aspects of oneself throughout the narrative, as Gaddis so evidently does) is a subject position unavailable in the Gaddis and Pynchon era to women, or subalterns, who are already lacking in an identity given by a patriarchal or imperial society. The tendency to assert an identity aggressively is the obverse of this condition, one that Gaddis experienced publicly in the protest staged by "under-represented" women at the PEN conference; privately with his second wife Judith's ambition to "find" herself (apart from him); and professionally in "novels (& endless writing workshop stories) about it."[23]

But there have been other explanations for Gaddis's self-immersion in masterworks, less readily reducible to terms of gender—by Tom LeClair, for example, who in 1989 was the first to designate major works by Gaddis (and by Pynchon, DeLillo, McElroy, Barth, Coover, and LeGuin) as *systems novels*, or *novels of excess* whose "mastery" was more about engagement with current systems and structures of communication and control. About *J R* in particular, LeClair stated, "if the economic system of America and life within it are monstrous, the master fiction must correspond to that reality to communicate it."[24] An engagement with systems that exceed the human scale, far from being narcissistic was instead regarded by LeClair as a way of carrying the literary persona beyond the limits of a public, politicized self. Publicity after all, at a time when mass media were watched by everyone, could only bring one deeper into the corporate systems and televisual, radio, filmic, and political forums one wished to contest or, in Mailer's case, occupy and transform through a literary sensibility. This lonesome literary confrontation with broadcast media of the day, however, has also dated, if only because direct participation in the 1970s was far less available to ordinary viewers than are more recent networked, reception media—where one's "public" communications now circulate within a network of many listeners in direct contact with one another, any of whom can respond regardless of one's celebrity status.[25] More than this: any one response in today's social media can potentially turn the discussion in a different direction, or go "viral" in ways that exceed in practice any literary excess or "mastery" that novelists might have once approached in their art.[26]

Another approach to the problem of male literary elusiveness has been offered by DeLillo in his 1991 novel *Mao II*, whose main character Bill Gray, a reclusive novelist living in Upstate New York, resembles Gaddis in some ways. There, as in DeLillo's later novel *Underworld*,[27] the literary imagination is placed in counterpoint not to systems alone but to the crowds that such systems generate, even as the globalizing postwar state has tended to govern not people, but populations: "The Future Belongs to Crowds," DeLillo writes at the start of *Mao II*. In a 1993 essay,

LeClair offered the following list of the different kinds of crowds found there:

> At Yankee Stadium there are thousands on the field looking up to Rev. Moon and thousands in the seats, some looking down, some taking pictures, some at the edge throwing firecrackers. There are the crowds of mourners at Khomeni's funeral that [Bill's housekeeper] Karen sees on TV, and there are the crowds of homeless she walks among in New York. Crowds follow Mao and crowds are killed in Tiananmen Square. Three of the four photos in the novel are of crowds: people crushed against a fence at a soccer game, the spiritual Master Moon and his flock, Khomeni's giant photograph and his followers.[28]

A city, in its network of neighborhoods and buildings, routes of transport and points of interest, can be held in an individual mind. No such mental image forms of a "state." The closest we come to its visual imagination may be in such photos of a crowd during times of unrest. And it may have been precisely the crowding together of shouting, uninvited women at the PEN conference that took Gaddis aback. They had obviously prepared their intervention and knew how to voice their complaint "with much justification," as Rushdie puts it two decades after the event, with the diplomacy of a newly elected PEN president. Does Rushdie avoid the words "righteousness," or "overzealous"? Gaddis in private, as we have seen, speaks of a "baying and howling," making clear his disdain for any open politicizing of social identities and sexual experience—and he must have known that the making public of these human elements would only further endanger the novel in an age of mass media by depersonalizing (and vulgarizing) encounters between the sexes.

What Gaddis encountered at the 1986 PEN conference was in any case a new style of self-assertion coming on the literary scene that had few connections with the outrage that he admitted drove him to write fiction. The voluntary withdrawal of the literary personality was hardly attractive to an emerging generation of women who for the first time had clear routes to inclusion in emerging power structures, and not least the kinds of literary power associated with the New York publishing establishment. At this stage in his career, Gaddis could no longer claim exclusion from that establishment, and hence his elusiveness, as Sonia Johnson notes, makes it harder to read his gender politics than those of a lifelong insider such as Mailer. The outrage, and doubtless a measure of narcissism and testosterone too, must have energized Gaddis's work although he worked just as hard to keep that part private, precisely by redirecting his emotions to his fictions.

His masculinity may have energized his writing, but so did alcohol and tobacco, as he freely admitted to those who knew him well.[29] David Foster Wallace's more expansive selection of mood-altering substances in his own work a generation later may have discouraged the high testosterone displays of his literary fathers, though without the outrage (and the hurt, and the unapologetic masculinity) would we have had the reimagination of the state that Gaddis, Pynchon, DeLillo in *Libra* and *Underworld*, Mailer in his late career CIA novels, Coover in *The Public Burning* accomplished? Would we have had, on the canvas that American writers since Melville have sought to realize, the "writer's individual imagined version of what the state—what life in the state, that is to say—could and should, or at least should not be" (*RSP* 123)? Neither Wallace's, nor his contemporary Franzen's, earlier novels ever seriously engage this larger, long-standing literary mode; instead, their encyclopedism foregrounds exactly what the earlier "systems novel" sidelines—namely, the multiple and unending particularity of hurts and addictions and fragile identities that are the realm, equally, of the corporate state and the bulk of fictions produced in and through academic creative writing programs.[30] It was the program, after all, which produced the generation of writers that followed Gaddis, Pynchon, and DeLillo—who has his character Bill remark, in *Mao II*, on what literature was like "before we were all incorporated."

To directly politicize experiences and subjectivities that have been, one might have thought, a distinctive realm of exploration by the private, literary imagination would have been seen by Gaddis and his (in retrospect, final) generation of powerful New York centered literary cohorts as another win for the corporate and corporatizing state. The state had already appropriated the willing suspension of disbelief, supplanting the literary novel with its own legal fictions of corporate personage and realized capital. Now, in its newly corporate flourishing, the American state was gradually, ineluctably occupying areas of the social itself, through sexual and identity issues that had seemed, to novelists, the proper domain of literary fictions, better negotiated in communications between solitary authors and readers and between men and women privately, not openly politicized or publicized in so-called social networks (not unless one had Mailer's taste for publicized confrontation, or Mao's or Moon's capacity to organize masses). For Gaddis, the reinstitution of creative powers and familiar, familial feelings represented, in his "own strong opinion," a further expansion of the culture of imitations that he had addressed, first in his exploration of forgeries in *The Recognitions* and then, definitively for the corporate era, in his unexampled creation of the "J R Family of Companies." More personalized projections of the fictive, away from the novel and onto the state and its more finely articulated social networks, he would leave to the emerging literary generations.

Chapter 10

# Portrait of the Artist as Writing Professor: *Carpenter's Gothic*

—because what you just said, about being this captive of
somebody else's hopes? and about disappointment? I mean
I think people write because things didn't come out the way
they're supposed to be.
   —Or because we didn't. No . . . his legs fallen wider for
her fingertip twisting a coil of hair —no, they all want to be
writers. They think if something happened to them that it's
interesting because it happened to them, hearing about all
the money that gets made writing anything cheap, anything
sentimental and vulgar whether it's a book or a song and they
can't wait to sell out.

(CG 158–59)

That Gaddis already encountered an emerging generation of literary
aspirants in university classrooms and on national awards committees
has been largely overlooked by scholars. But Gaddis's writing classes at
Bard College, the University of Connecticut, Berkeley, Notre Dame (the
"Sophomore Literary Festival," no less[1]), and Washington University in
St. Louis were the same classrooms that shaped the generation of Wallace
and Franzen and Ben Marcus, whose emergence there may have rendered
them skeptical, and largely uncomprehending, of the previous generation's attempts to resist incorporation. The novelist and creative writing
program director Cris Mazza recalled the way that Gaddis would dismiss
the majority of submissions by younger writers for the 1995 National
Endowment for the Arts competition: "It's not *fiction*," she recalls him
saying time and again. Mazza admits that she, a graduate of the program

in creative writing at San Diego State University, didn't understand at the time what Gaddis meant. She writes,

> Among my few memories of the deliberations that occurred at the large table in the drafty government building on Pennsylvania Avenue, I do clearly recall William Gaddis, seated directly across from me, saying, and not for the first time: "This isn't *fiction*. I know somewhere there's a real guy who stood on this real knoll beneath this real windmill." (Specific details about the story being discussed have been altered in this example.) At the time, I sat nearly aghast. The great William Gaddis was disqualifying a piece because he thought first-person narratives couldn't be *fiction*. He couldn't tell the difference between a persona, a character-narrator, and autobiography![2]

It took Mazza "some years to finally appreciate that Gaddis' comment wasn't a facile assumption that every first person narrative is 'true.' He knew the piece was fiction, was *likely* autobiographic, but it didn't matter. . . . What mattered was that the author purposely wrote as though the piece was memoir, but not for any intrinsic thematic need, but just to make it feel 'real' and therefore gain more audience interest and/or sympathy."

That particular NEA competition brought in 1,100 submissions for a total of 144 grants (as Gaddis noted in his own reflections on the event, which were not published in his lifetime).[3]

Even as the NEA was being defunded by a Congress led by another aspiring novelist of the time, House Speaker Newt Gingrich,[4] the cultivation of sympathy for a protagonist who, more or less, conveys his or her own feelings and experiences without ever for a moment connecting them to social, cultural, or philosophical concerns was becoming the primary means of recognition and self-advancement. That bid for sympathy, a willingness to entertain and be entertained, and placement in the network of writing programs where the authors, most of them, would have studied (a placement often secured through such government and privately endowed awards) had become a condition of writing—protecting writers from precisely the market uncertainties that had torpedoed Gaddis's own debut on the literary scene in 1955, but also creating a field where writers competed directly not for sales but for placement and promotion within a university system.

The shift could be subtle but all the more effective because it altered a writer's sense of his audience, and the expectations that could not help but influence the writing. Speaking to an audience of mostly writing profs and students at the University of Albany in 1990, Gaddis cited Philip Larkin on the danger that awaits a poet on the campus. "If literature is a good thing," as one hopes it will be among academics,

> "then," Larkin continues, "exegesis and analysis can only demon-
> strate its goodness and lead to fresh and deeper ways of enjoying
> it. But if the poet engages in this exegesis and analysis by becoming
> a university teacher"—no offense here—"the danger is that he will
> begin to assume unconsciously that the more a poem can be analyzed,
> and therefore the more it needs to be analyzed, the better a poem it
> is, and he may, in consequence, again unconsciously, start to write the
> kind of poem that is earning him a living."

"And this has all come about," Gaddis remarks, "in my recent lifetime": the chance to make a living "not by poetry" or novel writing but by "being a poet." This in a nutshell is what separates Gaddis and other novelists and poets of the 1970s from the generation of what's been called the Program Era (circa 1984 to our current first-person present). The difference was not only thematic or formalistic; it extended to the protocols for community formation in the literary professions. While many Program Era writers have been generous in their appreciation of colleagues and past authors, those who were recognized and those who were in need of rediscovery,[5] that community-building activity has been made secondary to the need for self-advancement within an institution devoted precisely to cultivating individual talents separate from any collaborative or admitted corporate context. The program also emerged—not always, but often—in opposition to the more conceptual concerns of literary scholarship of the time, even as many luminaries who participated in the scholarly turn to "theory" had lost interest in the discovery and close reading of one's elders and contemporaries, or rediscoveries and recirculation of past authors. Gaddis's own idea of professional engagement was closer to the crisp, no-nonsense generosity that he had noted in Auchincloss, who could afford to keep above the fray through his pedigree and the security of an independent law practice. But of course this species of white male privilege was precisely what the emerging generation of authors, each devoted to the discovery of his or her unique voice and first-person identity, were united against. The new generation recognized themselves, in the final analysis, as competitors.[6]

The ones fortunate enough to make it to the midlists of major publishers were competing, as Jonathan Franzen reminded readers in his *New Yorker* essay on Gaddis, for an ever-dwindling literary audience that

sought primarily to be entertained; but those whose careers were supported by the university and protected from commercial markets were
then placed, primarily, in competition *with one another.*

Gaddis never depicted the writing professor directly. He still held on to
the model he found in Auchincloss and that he held to a degree for himself
insofar as his own work was supported, for several decades, as much by
corporate writing as by teaching stints. That hybrid professionalization
is consistent with the most explicit author figure in his fiction, a geolo-
gist and science writer who has also authored a novel. McCandless, the
know-it-all whose name also conveys an inner darkness, is the one who
expresses the current pedagogy most clearly—though his thoughts on literary art (in the epigraph to this chapter) are not expressed in a classroom
but in bed with his lover, Elizabeth Booth. It's one of many moments
throughout the corpus when Gaddis appears to have a character articulate his own motivations and beliefs: the need to live up to expectations
instilled early in life; a consequent disappointment in the way things have
turned out for his world and for the reception of his work; and, not least,
as Gaddis has McCandless say a moment earlier, a compulsion to write
"[f]rom outrage" (which doesn't seem much diminished even as McCandless, in the same sentence, "eased his leg closer") (158).

The revelations are not new; readers of Gaddis would have heard similar observations from earlier self-projections: from Wyatt, Stanley, Otto,
and Anselm in *The Recognitions,* and from Bast, Eigen, and Gibbs in
*J R.* What distinguishes this account is its context, a sexual and incipient
(though unrealized) romantic encounter that has taken a strange turn
toward what educators today like to call a teachable moment. The care
that McCandless and Liz feel for one another, for the creative potential that they might release in one another as much as for their physical
copresence, extends as well into a concern for what motivates others (and
a condescension toward "these poor people" that perhaps only lovers and
heiresses can express so freely[7]):

> —because I mean I don't think so, I don't think they sell out [Liz]
> said, her voice weighing the idea as though for the first time, —I mean
> these poor people writing all these bad books and these awful songs,
> and singing them? I think they're doing the best they can . . . her hand
> closing there gently. —That's what makes it so sad. (159)

Gaddis's third novel is distinguished by its presentation for the most
part from a woman's perspective. The emergence of the feminine as not
a dominant but a quietly superior force comes through in this novel not

so much from the things Liz says or from any hope she has for worldly achievement. She has none of Stella Bast's calculation (though she tops even Stella when it comes to dissimulation, sequestering cash that she can lend to her brother Billy or use for herself, unbeknownst to her Vietnam veteran husband Paul). She possesses a goodly portion of the sensual nature and brightness of another fictional heiress, Amy Joubert (before the chill comes over Amy after the Diamond Cable corporation falls unexpectedly into her hands and she marries Dick Cutler, which she knew all along was like "marrying your issue of six percent preferred" [214]).

Even as Gaddis had combined his two loves in early manhood, Helen Parker (as Esther) and Sheri Martinelli (as Esme), into embodiments of domesticating and bohemian tendencies in the early postwar period, so would his later depiction of an emerging femininity in corporate America combine aspects of his two wives, Judith and Pat, "one strong and one not so strong" in the words of a friend. Liz's end (tripping against the stair newel while running to pick up a phone and grazing her temple on the sharp edge of one of the antique tables in the Piermont house) brings to the foreground the furnishings that Gaddis's second wife, Judith, had left in their own carpenter gothic house. Before the fatal fall, Liz had been visited by McCandless's first wife Irene and each mistakes the other for the *second* wife. The furnishings of the house in fact belong to the absent older woman—even as those of Gaddis's wife Judith remained in their Piermont home for years after she left him. (She had dealt in antiques during their marriage and would become the director of a small historic house museum when she settled in Key West.) He had written to her, five years after their separation, concerning a problem they'd talked about for a year or so concerning her "things in Piermont":

> . . . the tenant there wants to stay on (despite 2 rousing (& expensive) drain-sewer episodes) but, as she said when she moved in under our temporary agreement, has furniture of her own she wants in & feels like she's been 'camping out' so far: so as I wrote you at the time I've got to clear things up. [. . .] One thing I feel is I just frankly hope that whatever you decide can be managed without your having to come in & do it yourself, for no reason whatever except what just seems to me the needless painful things it would involve."[8]

Gaddis and Judith by the late 1970s had settled into a kind of reserved but attentive communication focused on her reason for leaving—that is, the younger woman's desire to find herself professionally and emotionally. Gaddis's disposition is remarkable in that he adopts a kind of professorial attitude while Judith evidently had done some research in support of her own writing ambitions:

> The material you are digging up sounds marvelous, just made for your purposes & so good it's a wonder nobody has mined it before. What's more important than the material itself though I think is your live enthusiasm for it, of course it's true as you say there's the gap between the best notes & plot in the world & getting them all together in 'readable saleable pages' but unless one's as confidently bad a writer as Jaqueline Suzanne or Sidney Sheldon I think the doubt's got to be there, that in fact it creates the tension necessary to produce anything worth writing & reading.[9]

The realization of her talent would be supported in the same way he might support one of his Bard students (or his own son and daughter, as we shall see momentarily). He goes on in the same letter to write: "I do honestly think from what I ever saw (& have admitted being less generous about than I could have, might have, should have) that you really do have the talent & facility & lyric turn to do it well, & the concentration & pertinacity to do it well if only you can maintain the enthusiasm to do it well with or without encouragement which I hope that eventually you will feel from me."

The displacement of emotional issues, which cannot be controlled, onto problems of literary talent, which can be, is very much a part of the sexual dynamic of *Carpenter's Gothic*. Liz's thought about bad writing, occurring to her "as though for the first time," clearly channels Gaddis's own feelings—as do many characters who don't resemble him at all, whether it's the attorney Madhar Pai in *A Frolic of His Own* discoursing on "critics," "reviewers," and "journalists" (*F* 217),[10] or young J R complaining about "those shits" at the bank who pay interest on the lowest monthly balance, not the average (169–70), or even Liz's husband Paul, who complains about offers by mail for a new loan on furniture that his bank sends him even as the same bank is "threatening to wipe [him] out" for being three payments behind on an existing loan (14). Harvard-educated William Gaddis would not for a moment allow himself, even among friends, to express so bluntly his own thoughts or reveal his own often straitened circumstances that only grew steadily worse over the long years when he "got out of the 9–5 job circuit" and wrote *J R*.[11] So he finds a character who is capable of language adequate to the way he feels, and consistent with all in that character that Gaddis does not and never will share directly. An authorial presence

often can be felt as much in the grumbling of an angered minor character such as Paul, as in more obvious, more articulate personae such as
McCandless or Jack Gibbs. Still more, like a devil in the details, Gaddis can appear in the detritus that accumulates through all the "day
after dayness"[12] that is depicted in *J R*, the robo-bank statements and
junk mailings and conversations overheard in the places where Gaddis
lived and worked during the novel's composition. The detritus in his fiction after *The Recognitions* accumulates like compound interest on a
debt; and his readers do well to look even here, in the mounting trash,
and in his less attractive (but brutally honest) characters, for clues as to
what America is becoming, and what it has been "all about," all along
(in the refrain spoken by the otherwise unsympathetic Major Hyde,
in *J R*).

Gaddis's authorial presence has always been the more effective the
less he intrudes explicitly, as we have seen already in the aloof but never
neutral transitional passages that run all through *J R* and stand outside
its predominant dialogue, places where the book's themes are stated,
repeated, then repeated again much as the leitmotifs in an opera by Wagner. Here is what we find on the very first page of that novel: "Sunlight,
pocketed in a cloud, spilled suddenly broken across the floor through the
leaves of the trees outside" (3). The author is present in these exiguous
passages not as a narrator but as an actively shaping imagination; his
outlook, independent of the recorded talk of his characters, is given not
only in the poetic syntax and the multivalent diction (where sunlight, universal and free of charge, is about to be "pocketed" like money, and like
everything else in this novel about the monetization of everything). About
thirty pages later, a little girl in the schoolyard puts the leaves in her purse
as if they were paper bills (32). We also have the self-conscious equa-
tion of tree leaves and book pages, which are also "outside" the reported
speech and action even as they make such speech and action available to
us in the book we are holding.

The leaves turn up again a decade later at the start of *Carpenter's
Gothic*, whose predominant dialogue is similarly shaped by exiguous
passages of what can only be read, if they're to be understood, as prose
poetry. The novel, after all, was generated from a poem, or rather a line
in Shakespeare's sonnet lamenting "that time of year thou mayst in me
behold,"

> When yellow leaves, or none, or few, do hang
> Upon those boughs which shake against the cold,
> Bare ruin'd choirs, where late the sweet birds sang.

The sunlight, the boughs, even the "sweet birds" were present in the setting that environs the insistent (but comparatively inconsequential) social world of *J R*'s dialogue. The poetry this time, in contrast to *J R*, is clearly focalized around a female observer, namely, Liz:

> The bird, a pigeon was it? or a dove (she'd found there were doves here) flew through the air, its colour lost in what light remained. It might have been the wad of rag she'd taken it for at first glance, flung at the smallest of the boys out there wiping mud from his cheek where it hit him, catching it up by a wing to fling it back where one of them now with a broken branch for a bat hit it high over a bough caught and flung back and hit again into a swirl of leaves, into a puddle from rain the night before, a kind of battered shuttlecock moulting in a flurry at each blow, hit into the yellow dead end sign on the corner opposite the house where they'd end up that time of day. (3)

The shuttlecock, a "birdie" in lawn tennis, is clearly Liz as she shuttles passively among three men (husband Paul, brother Billy, landlord and eventual lover McCandless). She is literally "battered" by Paul, the Vietnam vet who brings the war home by turning it into a kind of command center[13] and by awarding Liz "combat badge[s]" during bouts of domestic violence (22). McCandless for his part, and Billy too, often berate her verbally. As she tells Billy, he and Paul can "—sound exactly the same the only difference is he says your God damn brother and you say fucking Paul but it's the same, if I closed my eyes it could be either one of you . . ." (194). Finally, in this opening scene the "smallest of the boys" is another author figure, a key one: the reticent, sickly boy from Upstate New York appears in the novel repeatedly (even when the boys, or their counterparts, are grown men putting out a fire across the street, a few weeks into the narration). After all these years, this same boy is still presiding over the *Harvard Lampoon*, the smallest among the board of editors pictured in a 1944 yearbook photo, many of them in military or yachting attire. That youthful sensibility, mostly getting in the way but at the same time taking it all in, and learning, is an alternative to the relentless older boys' games, and not least their grown-up language games that can be tough going not just for Liz, but for the reader as well. The repeated appearance by the "smallest of the boys" is also, by virtue of this boy's silence, a figure who holds a potential beyond all the talk and trivia in the book: he is that self who is filled with a youthful joy and frivolity and a *desire to know* how things work in the real world, the "self who could do more" whose lifelong development for Gaddis was the only justification, after he'd mortgaged his own youth on *The Recognitions*, for taking up the task of another book, and then third, a fourth, and a fifth.

By the time he undertook *Carpenter's Gothic*, Gaddis (pushing sixty) had experienced that youthful potential less in himself and, increasingly, in classrooms, where he was brought in as a visiting professor at Bard College and several other institutions in the northeastern and midwestern United States. This turn toward academia in Gaddis's life (consistent with the academicization of literary writing generally during this period) can help explain why so many of McCandless's encounters with so many characters—in the bedroom with Liz, in the smoke-filled workroom with the ex-missionary and current CIA operative Lester, and (offstage) in a New York bar drinking with Billy—have the air of an advisor's meeting, a literary workshop, or a rowdy gathering off campus. Lester makes the connection with his usual bluntness when McCandless points out how his doctrinal book of Genesis is no more or less compelling (as a fiction) than the Chinese creation story of Pangu (the preferred spelling; Gaddis's source apparently spelled it Pan Koo). This is Lester talking (and completing a quotation he already knows by heart, from past encounters):

> —His breath the winds, his voice the thunder, his sweat the rain and dew, one eye the sun and the other the moon and his fleas men and women I've heard it, I've heard it all McCandless I've heard it from you, you think I came up here to listen to it again? You think you're back in one of these broken down schools where you can rave and rant like this? bully and browbeat everybody in sight because that's what you do. Because you're smarter than anybody else aren't you, like this hero you've got in this rotten novel . . . (136)

Gaddis's earlier personae, even such abiding presences as Gwyon and Gibbs, could be located among numerous lesser but also cogent characters who were allowed to move with them in society, among social classes, and across the globe in pursuit of their creator's own worldly and artistic ambitions. Liz and McCandless, by contrast, are seen exclusively in the single suburban New York house based on Gaddis's own residence in Piermont, twenty-five miles north of Manhattan and a bit more than commuting distance from Bard (where he would stay overnight, after his once weekly set of classes). The house's carpenter gothic style (without the apostrophe) was designed, McCandless informs us, "—to be seen from the outside . . . a patchwork of conceits, borrowings, deceptions" (227). The house is a concentration of Gaddis's lifelong themes, but the potential trouble here is that McCandless, the character who mostly conveys the textual logic, himself borders on becoming a patchwork insofar as his identity is itself (in the words of one of the book's more astute critics) "full of mutually contradictory stereotypes: artist, tough guy, scientist, conspiracy freak." Thus observes Nicholas Brown, after having analyzed the incompatibilities of Gaddis's austere aesthetic and sociopolitical ambitions. The latter simply cannot be contained, by either the modernist precept that characters can reveal only themselves or the action that Gaddis restricts to a single setting. Brown nonetheless finds in McCandless's "quasi-monologues" a redemptive quality, one that derives not so much from the modernist tradition of endless innovation, immanence, and aesthetic self-containment but the much longer tradition of the didactic novel: "One is not required to make this observation as a criticism," Brown hastens to add: "in fact, this attempt to revisit the neglected half of the ancient imperative to 'delight and teach' is the novel's great strength" (PE 158).

A certain didacticism during this period was Gaddis's own great strength as a father, as a husband, as a "Visiting Hurst Professor" (Washington University, St. Louis), an "American Specialist" for the State Department and occasional "eminent visitor" to foreign countries, even as a drinking companion among writer colleagues and, occasionally, students. (Are the fictive identities, we might ask, really so stereotypical, unlikely, or contradictory as Brown supposes?) We are fortunate in any event to have one letter from Gaddis to his twelve-year-old son describing (in a way that quietly guides the boy toward his own self-education) a father's first time sitting in front of a conventional undergraduate classroom:

> Well, I got through *my* first day of school! And at last I have done something I never quite had the nerve to do, walked into a classroom with about 15 people simply sitting, waiting; got behind my desk, hung up my umbrella, sat down facing them, and . . . started to talk. I guess they were surprised to hear me start off by telling them I was there to try to teach something that I didn't really believe could be taught, writing fiction. And then go on about some examples of good fiction and bad fiction, and everyone sitting there just looking at me. Silence. Start talking again. Finally I asked a couple of questions and got a couple of them talking, and certainly it will all be easier as I go on, next week and the week after, and when I see some of their work. They are college juniors and seniors, and it is different than teaching at Connecticut was because there I saw each person separately, and didn't sit up in front like The Authority. [. . .] Mainly I hope I can be some help to some of them with their early efforts at trying to write,

though the only point I've pressed on them so far is that the first important and often difficult thing about it is simply sitting down and *doing* it.[14]

With the gender blindness that Gaddis unfailingly practiced in life with prospective writers (if not with his creations in fiction), on this same day he had offered similar guidance to his daughter, who was age fifteen and still in high school:

> Here is a book [Fitzgerald's *Crack-Up*] I've meant to get you a look at since you talked of keeping a sort of notebook journal. Obviously it's not for you to sit down and read straight through but I thought you would be interested in what one writer turned the idea into and continue and expand your own along the lines of catching ideas, impressions, thoughts, images, words and combinations of words and overheard remarks and stories and anecdotes at that instant you encounter them, which is so often one you can never recreate purely from memory and may in fact lose forever. Of course in this case, assuming Fitzgerald never expected these notes to be published, I think you find a lot of material which he would have reconsidered and thrown out and never wanted published; but at least, having written them down, he gave himself that choice, rather than putting himself through those long moments of trying to remember —What *was* it? that remark I heard yesterday, that idea I had last night . . . What is it that makes end of summer at Fire Island unlike anywhere else, and yet like a concentration of the whole idea of summer's end everywhere . . .[15]

With *J R* at that time still in progress, he had certainly not conceived *Carpenter's Gothic*, nor did he even expect to write another book after his second try at a world-fiction. But the much different, more intimate world-spanning sensibility that his Fire Island residence could embody, somehow—a feeling of "summer's end everywhere"—can be taken as an indication of the book's mood even before he had the book itself clearly in mind. By November 1979, however, when he mentions the book for the first time, it appears under the working title "That Time of Year," from the Shakespeare sonnet cited earlier. This time it's the Piermont, not Fire Island, house that holds the emotional charge (and furnishings for a passing life, not least the items left there by Judith). Shakespeare's poem also references a later season but the idea of identifying a place and a "party's over" mood had clearly stayed with him all this time. In this, as in all of Gaddis, we find him following precisely the practice he praised in Fitzgerald, a habit of getting everything down, moods no less than ideas or stories, remarks, and anecdotes. For Gaddis, letters as much as notebooks were vehicles for trying out and recording ideas—maybe more so in letters, since ideas for Gaddis only came alive when they were conveyed to another person, not followed abstractly or tried out on literary peers and potential subjects and focus groups the way a journalist or political theorist or advertising agent might approach an idea. That necessarily interpersonal, basically convivial approach is one more reason why he trusted in the dialogue form to carry most of the conceptual burden of his later work.

In other letters, he'd ask whether Sarah had read either *Candide* or *Ethan Frome*; he wondered what she would think of them ("They are about as different as books can be"), while all the time he would nudge his daughter toward the creator's viewpoint, telling her to be sure "to read E. Wharton's preface to it—which as a coming writer should be of great interest and perhaps some help to you."[16] Writing to David Markson, he recalls "a boy I had at Univ of Connecticut" who was "working on a novel which I greatly encouraged, think publishable & have tried to help him place, he's someone who's never published and I hope to see have a chance."[17] The Connecticut student from 1966 is unknown, but the young men and women who learned from Gaddis directly, whether or not they went on (as did Sarah, and Markson) to publish fiction, found in the figure of the writer a channel for literary understanding that was unavailable elsewhere in the university—unavailable, often, even in literature programs in the United States that increasingly, around this time, moved toward social, cultural, and political themes and away from the close study of individual works of fiction and poetry. Academia itself was undergoing a fundamental transformation at this time based on the same new liberal economic developments that Gaddis was registering in *J R*, and the same introduction if not of televised programs during class time, then of something even worse, namely: programmatic ways of standardizing curricula and measuring performance (of teachers no less than students, diminishing the integrity of that relationship).

That degree of academic freedom, like Gaddis's own "grand dreams of financial liberation in the midst of pounding debt,"[18] proved illusory when students themselves, increasingly, were busy accumulating financial debts during the years when they were meant to accumulate knowledge. Nonetheless, the dream of freedom and movement, that we will do our own work not that of others, persists in the American imaginary, and with models like Gaddis in academia, that dream could live on in the new discipline of creative writing. Still more, the idea that a novelist might come to *know* the culture through his or her work, rather than react to a culture produced in and by other media, helped to set up the field as a bastion, but a bastion precisely against the technologies and media that were in the process of transforming the culture. In other words, what Gaddis did know, directly through his years working in corporations, and what he'd been able to put into *J R* and *Carpenter's Gothic*, was precisely what writing programs encouraged an emerging generation of writers to ignore, or at best know from a distance (by virtue of their location in the academy).

It was not yet the established program that it has since become. It would take decades of sustained professionalization before the *Lampoon*s and *Rammer Jammer*s and (at the tonier end) *Yale Review*s and *Epoch*s were supplanted, or turned serious, by creative writing. By 2012, the number of "campus & hybrid & online accredited graduate degree programs" had reached 270.[19] Prestige, in turn, was replaced by something better described as "cultural capital," since an author's reputation rarely exceeded his peer group in academia and one's books earned tenure for authors, not a direct livelihood or connection to a national or international audience.

If each of those 270 programs were to produce just one published novel or story collection every five or six years, that means forty or fifty books a year just from creative writing, more than any one reader could afford to notice, much less consider reading. Yet the three or four thousand mostly unpublished writing students and instructors, nationwide, renewing themselves over the same five- or six-year period might themselves in time come to replace the general audience that their teachers could have hoped to reach a generation or two before. For such an audience, what "suspension of disbelief" would be possible? What imagination of a world elsewhere? Wouldn't such a reader be mindful, at every page, of the career they'd missed and that another book's author had secured?

In retrospect, it can be argued (and has been argued by the literary scholar Mark McGurl) that creative writing would not have accumulated the credibility (and credentializing power) it has had not so many first-rate writers found refuge, in the sixties and seventies, in academic jobs. For here was the one place where the dream of unsponsored creativity and unhindered intellectual and imaginative exploration, which Gaddis had actualized during his years writing *The Recognitions*, could still be presented as a dedicated function of the university. Here, too, as with his uncanny anticipation in *The Recognitions* of a postwar, postmodernist aesthetic, Gaddis's gradual, unplanned turn toward academia put him around half a decade in advance of the authors whose work he most influenced. John Barth would not arrive at the University of Buffalo until 1966 (he went on to Hopkins in 1973); Creeley, Gaddis's contemporary at Harvard, went to Buffalo that same year.[20] Barthelme returned to his native Houston only in 1980, after more than a decade when an episodic, philosophical imagination fully engaged with the avant-garde in the arts could still be supported largely by a single mainstream magazine, the *New Yorker*. By the time William Gass and Stanley Elkin had set up their program at Washington University in the seventies, they were keen to bring in Gaddis, who was by then the most prestigious writer on the guest lecturing and "visiting" circuit. This was due largely to the continued aura around *The Recognitions* and his National Book Award for *J R*, which, if it did little to increase sales, helped to ensure that Gaddis's second novel would have an afterlife similar to the first, garnering adherents in academia and inspiring yet another generation of writers wishing to engage (and not just cash in on) the transformation of the world on the American capitalist model. Even the relentless exposure of an era's "conceits, borrowings, deceptions," which tried the patience of mainstream readers, likely made him all the more attractive to younger writers who still aspired to do "the real thing," as Gass puts it in his introduction to the 1993 edition of *The Recognitions*. Gass later recalled that when he advocated for Gaddis at a meeting with administrators, Elkin complained with typical brashness that he himself wanted to be "the most wanted writer in America."[21] But that didn't keep him from drafting the letter extending the offer to Gaddis for the Hurst professorship.

Here's how Gaddis himself regarded the situation:

> Speaking of Academia, a really confused land. Bennington you recall months ago sounding quite excited at the possibility of my coming up there; a week, a month, 2, I hear nothing; finally they call, would like me there the bulk of the week (March–June) with a heavier course load than I have now & at substantially less money. Elegant, expensive Bennington & doesn't even get near little Bard's terms. So I said I'd think about it & am going around the house muttering when the mail brings a letter from Washington Univ in St Louis (where Bill Gass is), asking me out for 3 weeks either Feb or April at half the fee Bennington offers for a full term, & with far lighter duties mainly consorting with graduate students as much or little as I like plus a talk or 2, furnished apartment office & (new) typewriter. Plus, the letter itself terribly hoping I'll accept was from a writer named Stanley Elkin who I think is marvelous (novel called *The Dick Gibson Show*) who teaches there.[22]

The life of the eminent visiting professor: Is it not a middle-aged version of his youthful travel? He once styled himself a "tramp, *vagamundo*" in Central America, Western Europe, and North Africa.[23] His dream life of freedom and movement, unlikely even in the 1930s and '40s but for him still realizable, would become (in postwar America) the life of the perpetually visiting artist, living from one grant to the next, and then sitting and waiting, from one semester to the next, to find out if the program and the institute could budget you in. The rise of an itinerant class of untenured writers and literary scholars in the American university system was already under way even this early in the formation of the academic star system, which Gaddis and his compeers in no small way helped to legitimate on the "creative" side. (The largely separate, only occasionally communicating system on the side of criticism and theory, for all its disruption of settled attitudes, did little to delay the fragmentation of commercial, creative, and academic writing in America.) The postwar writers in America, more numerous and arguably better informed than any previous generation in American history, may have been stars among peers and distinguished colleagues; they may have been trophies for the upper administrators who signed the contract; for some students they were surely role models (though many more in Gaddis's case had no idea that the reserved gentleman in the tweed jacket lecturing on "Failure in American Literature" was a National Book Award–winning author). Some writers, such as Robert Coover—who never held a named chair or tenured position at Brown— used the contract system as a way to keep their institutional distance. But all of them, even Pynchon in his well-known switch from engineering to literature at Cornell, can be understood as part of an economic class and emerging cultural phenomenon that helped to inaugurate a system of academic migrant workers. Indeed, Gaddis came to feel that Gass and the others admired him because, apart from the occasional stint (that for two days a week minimally interrupted his private life in Piermont), he'd "been able to stay out (till now)." Gaddis himself admired Gass in turn, in part "because he separates it all clearly & relaxedly in his head ('my public & private selves haven't even shaked hands for many years')."[24] Both authors might have understood their role in academia as maintaining the perception (among students, and also administrators) of a public/private split, the idea that one's self and one's imagination were not wholly shaped by corporate needs, that the inner-driven artist still had a place in society—and if not in society, then in the "small world" of academia that increasingly favored the outward-driven intellectual entrepreneur.[25]

The Washington University offer he "accepted immediately" in part because of his shared views "on what good writing's about plus highly compatible senses of humor" and not least "the prospect of rowdy time with Elkin & Gass."[26] Instead of going from the Village to a job uptown or from a stint in Europe to his mother's studio in the barn on Long Island, for three weeks he would "go from being Distinguished Visiting Prof at Bard to being Hurst Professor at Washington U, then the Lord knows what since being the Hadley Fellow at Bennington sounds less than heaven though if it's a question of the distinction money or none . . . well we'll see. I've also been trying to think seriously about thinking seriously about starting another book & think I may have an approach."[27]

The approach he came up with would produce a third novel as radically different from the previous two as these were from one another: *Carpenter's Gothic* would be conventional in length, constrained in setting, and broken into chapters that are conveyed from a single character's perspective (mostly that of Liz, but once McCandless's and briefly, in the end, Paul's as the outer-directed entrepreneur makes a play for Liz's best friend Edie, using the same line after Liz's funeral that worked with Liz at her father's funeral). There would be no lessening of the book's "difficulty," but Gaddis no longer deluded himself, as he had during all the years of *J R*'s slow gestation and even slower execution, that a wide readership (and ability to support himself and a family through writing) would be possible. As he told William Jovanovich, the publisher of *The Recognitions*, that novel was kept by none other than Jovanovich himself in a cultish limbo by his refusal to relinquish rights. Had Jovanovich done so, Gaddis told him, there might have been "an attractive cheap edition, both at a profit and a decently fair price to the student audience your backlist feeds upon."[28] That secondary, student audience was quickly turning into the only one for serious literature—unless one took the advice that Larry McMurtry offered Gaddis; namely, that an author needed quickly to draft "'a small flat book with a strong narrative line,' as, for example, [McMurtry's own] *The Last Picture Show*, though his luck in the industry since hasn't been all that great either, considering numbers of works optioned, scripts written, films unproduced."[29]

McMurtry's luck was better than Gaddis's had been, despite offers coming over the phone shortly after the publication of *J R* from the likes of David Susskind and one particularly knowledgeable, personable, and persistent producer for the BBC by the name of Jack Gold. The name turns up often in the letters from 1978 to 1981, and Gaddis's hope, and clear economic need, for such an outcome is palpable, particularly as the mass-market paperback rights for *J R* went unsold. To measure the depth of that disappointment, one need only consider how many readers encountered Pynchon's *Gravity's Rainbow* in the Bantam reprint, and then recognize that Gaddis, despite working with Pynchon's agent Candida Donadio, was unable to manage the same for *J R*, published only two years later. In the end, after he had settled for the Knopf backlist, had taken in paltry sales in the United Kingdom, no foreign rights sale, and no film, he could take what must have been a private consolation, on the page, in the irony of Jack Gold's Dickensian name—which seems to have inspired this moment in *Carpenter's Gothic* when Liz encounters McCandless a few days after their night together (and the perspective has shifted from her to McCandless):

> Just this morning, she told him, since early this morning, she'd had a call from a Mister Gold at Saks telling her they'd found her purse and she had to go into town anyway [. . .] and when she went to Saks to claim her purse they'd never heard of Mister Gold, there was no Mister Gold, and —Yes, and while you were there to see Mister Gold they were here to rob the house, they had your keys and your [. . .] (219)

In a slightly more public vein (which would still have been missed by the majority of readers), we can recall Wyatt Gwyon's evident relief in *The Recognitions* that "there was the gold to forge" when he is assured that the painting he had copied at the beginning of his career was really an original Hieronymus Bosch (*R* 689). For all the satire and falling short of a social, aesthetic, and not least religious ideal in Gaddis's first fiction, we find there a capacity still to believe in the necessity of an ideal grounded in recognition among the like-minded (at a given time), and a participation across centuries in an artistic guild (or, with T. S. Eliot, a literary tradition). The inability to hold on to that kind of absolute faith is part of what licenses the universal exchange of values in *J R*'s fictional economy (a fiction that is operative, as we have seen, in the imagination of the state, not just in the work of literary imagination). By the time of *Carpenter's Gothic*, a book written under pressure of making money, the absence of any gold standard of truth is simply taken for granted.

The readership for serious fiction, it was clear, had by this stage of Gaddis's career shifted largely to the university classroom, and this new novel, however it might fare in the diminishing marketplace, would be acceptable for classroom use. By the late seventies, he knew well what students could and could not be expected to read in the course of fourteen weeks and he knew, from stories written by his graduate and undergraduate students, something about the desires of men and women the age of Liz and Billy. He knew for example that nobody needed to "teach the

young outrage," as he would have McCandless say of Billy. At their night
out in New York, he understood that Billy's ire was directed not just at
their father and Paul; "—no," McCandless tells Liz, "he was outraged at
everything, everybody who came before him you think he left me out?"
(229). Gaddis understood also how outrage, in young men especially,
could cause a student to miss the way that energies and rhetorics and pop
psychologies, for all their vulgarity, carried their own insights into the
workings of American society. No other American writer has written so
scathingly about Dale Carnegie as Gaddis did in *The Recognitions*; and
here especially, Gaddis's youthful outrage was energized by his attempt
to work out, for himself, the failure that he perceived in his own father
(whose life spent in offices and high-rise apartments was clearly part of
what Gaddis had worked so hard most of his life to avoid). Yet when he
placed *How to Win Friends and Influence People* on the required reading
list for his long-running Bard course on "Failure in American Literature,"
his intention was decidedly not to go on grinding an axe against Carnegie. Here is how one student, George Hunka, encountered that book
and Gaddis's take on it:

> One of the books I was assigned to write about was Dale Carnegie's
> *How to Win Friends and Influence People*, and at the end of the paper
> I made the mistake (accountable to the arrogance of youth, I sup-
> pose) that the book was "not worth reading" or something like that.
> When I read this in class, it met with a strong negative response from
> Gaddis, who said—and I must paraphrase here, unfortunately—that
> there was something illuminating to be found in every book that had
> as profound an influence on our culture as Carnegie's. I was duly
> chastened and from then on, through my entire reading life, I kept his
> comment in mind. It has saved me from a good deal of churlishness.[30]

Another student, Kevin Begos, recalls Gaddis as being remarkably
"detail-oriented" in his reading, and often more attentive to "structure"
in a student's writing than he was to the student herself or himself. This
structural emphasis (Begos supposes) helped Gaddis in his own writing to get away from plot and conventional characterization—and also
distinguished Gaddis from the Beats and bohemians at Bard as much as differences in temperament. "Burroughs got away from plot," Begos recalled
Gaddis saying, by avoiding fine style and letting his cut-up method take
precedence over the writing. Gaddis (Begos felt) was much more in control of his vision, despite the similar tendency to use idiomatic speech for
pages and pages on end. "He was always attentive to interesting words,"

Begos notes. "Though few of us in the class used them much, one person had a novel in progress titled Falsedge (or False Edge)—can't remember which—which is a technical term for a certain part of some old swords. Gaddis was very interested in the word and praised the student for finding/using it."[31]

Few in his Bard class would have known that Gaddis was acquainted with Burroughs and Kerouac in the fifties, and (some years later) joined Allen Ginsberg on a cultural excursion to Russia. But Begos, at least, recognized in Gaddis a standard of professionalism that distinguished him from the majority of writing professors who often demonstrated no end of self-regard and little of the discipline Gaddis must have brought from his experience in corporations. He wasn't like Ed Sanders, who chose twelve women for his workshop, "all cute co-eds"; or Ginsberg, who chose similarly among boys. As Begos recalls, there were many like that, nice enough guys, some of them famous, who just wanted a sabbatical: "Some stayed and made it a home." Gaddis may have been "among the Beats, he was not *of* them," Hunka said.

Even in those days of smoke-filled classrooms, with ashtrays thoughtfully provided by the Bard College administration, Gaddis took care to sit by a window and asked the smokers (Hunka among them) in the class to collect at his end of the seminar table, "alleviating any irritation our smoke might cause the non-smokers." On occasion "he cadged a cigarette or two (Camel Straights, they were)" from Hunka.

He also served as a one-on-one mentor of students doing senior thesis projects, among them (in fall of 1976 or spring of 1977) Alan Bigelow, who was working on a first novel. Bigelow recalls Gaddis as being "pleasant and patient with me during our weekly meetings, and generous with suggestions for editing and his time conversing about his student's work and direction."[32] Bigelow remembers a story Gaddis told him about what he did whenever he was stuck in the writing process: "I go around the house," Gaddis said, "and find a small chore to do. . . . For example, it might be a broken doorknob. I fix the doorknob and then I get back to work." It was only years later that Bigelow felt he understood what Gaddis meant:

> The metaphor was so embedded, I do not think even he saw it. Just as his subconscious mind had supplied the answer to his writing problem by doing a household chore, his writing mind had supplied the metaphor that I needed as a beginning writer. Fixing a problem in writing is like opening a door. The door handle has to work, though, and sometimes it needs to be fixed.

After he graduated from Bard, Bigelow saw Gaddis one more time, at a reading. "I do not remember where it was, but I am thinking New York City. After the reading, I went over and introduced myself. He immediately remembered me, and without prompting on my part, he mentioned the novel I had been working on as an undergraduate. Now that's dedication."

At a time when, and in a classroom environment where, personal revelation was encouraged, nothing of the sort would go unquestioned in a Gaddis writing seminar. "He never wore stuff on his sleeve," Mary Caponegro recalls. As a senior in 1977, she had switched from poetry to prose in order to take advantage of the program's requirement that each student take on a yearlong project: "The further opportunity to work one-on-one with William Gaddis was awe-inspiring, precisely because he was the antithesis of the showman, and thus the quiet, somewhat awkward, benign exchange of two reserved individuals could evolve gradually into instruction."

He took young women seriously enough that the experience of his class would encourage many to go on to distinguished careers themselves (and for Caponegro, to a position eventually at none other than Bard College). Students might have noticed the particular attention Gaddis paid to one remarkably beautiful woman, the tall dark-haired Liza Wherry (who herself went on to a career in publishing). "Liza, Liza, everyone eyes ya," is how Caponegro memorialized this particular classmate in a story collection.[33] She recalls hearing that in the wake of *J R* he had encouraged Wherry to use more dialogue in the novel she was writing. Gaddis was not blind to a student's attractions, but few supposed this recognition ever compromised his position, or the necessary detachment he brought to the work of each student. Though he may have been at the end of his second marriage, and then newly divorced through several terms at Bard, Gaddis knew to look elsewhere for romantic fulfillment. The role model for another fictional Liz, in *Carpenter's Gothic*, would be (as usual) an amalgam of several women he knew in life, and consistent with what he taught his students: that if one's personal experience could not find a place in the work, it did not bear mention in the workshop.

Chapter 11

# Friendships, and Frolics

I wake at night—that 3 o'clock in the morning business—with
the What do you think you're doing! age 65 starting the whole
mad thing over again? with this trash heap of notes & paper?
Looking at the whole project with 'fear and loathing' . . .
                    William Gaddis to his daughter, 1987

Gaddis's first novel, at its conception, was titled "Blague," "French for
'kidding,'" as he'd told his mother at the time: "but it is really no kidding."[1] His new work would eventually be deemed *A Frolic*, and in many
ways his years living in upper Manhattan were a return, half a century
on, to the select society (and international travel) of his Harvard and Village years. Muriel calls attention specifically to their "serious time" spent
traveling "in Russia and Lithuania, Australia, Bulgaria and, in 1987, in
Berlin. By serious I mean not necessarily long, but eventful" (*E* 61). Never
so carefree as before, the trips were better subsidized through various
institutions not least the "State Department, dragnet for talent, offering
the lure of free trips" that Muriel, at least, felt was a form of payment
"more effective in subduing the strain of the shut-off, shut-in atmosphere
of a writer's indentured household than anything money itself could purchase." In the old days in postwar Europe and at *America Illustrated* in
New York, the United States Information Service had actually given the
prospective novelist freedom to come and go as he pleased so long as
he submitted his assigned articles in good order and reasonable time: "a
piece every 4 or 5 weeks at 200$ a throw," which was enough to live on
in New York in the 1950s.[2] Now, he was kept to a pretty tight schedule,
his trips resembling (to Muriel) "elite intellectual bus tours" more than
the vagabondage that in the past helped to moderate any illusions of
self-control. The present setup did offer him evidence that his work was
becoming more widely recognized, and his "indenture," as Muriel puts

it, was not so one-sided. Even if sometimes his own imagination was in service to that of the state, at least he was not financially dependent on the woman he had partnered with in later life.

The official and international appearances also confirmed that at this high point in his career his work was widely judged as important beyond the elite circle of writers and artists with whom he consorted. Indeed, he may be among the last generation of writers in America capable of reaching a sizable audience in his home country, while also gaining recognition abroad. Except that, as a character in *Frolic* points out, America's "not a country" so much as a collection of professions, each with their own specialized language and functional differentiation. The literary profession, willy-nilly, would consist of writers writing for other writers, and for students and scholars. And the legal profession relies as much as any on obfuscation but also precisions that cannot, and should not, be brought into everyday life.

Here is an exchange in the novel between Christina Lutz and her lawyer husband, Harry:

> —Legal language, I mean who can understand legal language but another lawyer, it's like a, I mean it's all a conspiracy, think about it Harry. It's a conspiracy.
> —Of course it is, I don't have to think about it. Every profession is a conspiracy against the public, every profession protects itself with a language of its own. . . . (284)

There will be no dramatic courtroom scenes in Gaddis's legal fiction of the sort that one finds in work by John Grisham or Scott Turow. The role of the novelist, for Gaddis, is not to displace machinations largely indifferent to humanism with dramas that every reader can grasp; nor is it desirable to clear up too readily or explain linguistic complexities, but rather to inhabit them fully and to bring the human into contact with processes and technical languages that determine our situation, that shape our state, our corporate systems, and our cultures.

The disunity and internal friction among professions within the world's largest power was not then something Gaddis wished to denounce as "specialization" and he would leave denunciations of a work's "difficulty" to journalists whose own specialty too often tends toward talk rather than analysis, the telling of "human interest" stories rather than synthesis, and the canceling out of scientific consensus with a "balanced" presentation of fringe theories. The recognition of functional differentiations within American life is also an opportunity—to craft large swatches of novels for example in the language of theology (*The Recognitions*), or business (*J R*), geological science and public relations (*Carpenter's Gothic*), or law (*Frolic*). It was an opportunity that for around two decades thrived in the work of Gaddis, Pynchon, DeLillo, Didion, Coover, Barth, McElroy, and a very few others, to bring the *didactic* back into the realm of fiction and to represent (with a difference) the cultural and critical discourse of the time.

Gaddis's friendships at this period, more than a clique, represented each of the professions he would reach, and reach successfully on terms they could appreciate without him for a moment abandoning his own authority and autonomy in the profession of literature. This is why being a "writer's writer" is not necessarily the worst fate but rather, today, a necessary starting point for recognizing one's own institutional location so as better to approach others in their distinct locations, culturally and professionally no less than in terms of class, gender, or racial origin—each of which, as we shall see, carries far more consequence when viewed not through the inevitable clash of identities in petty conflicts but through an engagement with professions and languages larger than ourselves.

Of his friends and acquaintances from the forties and fifties, many of them, like him, had gone on to achieve prominence: de Kay, Pennebaker, Gladstone, Socarides, Otto and Priscilla Friedrich, John and Pauline Napper. (As for the women, Martinelli and Parker, their respective accomplishments as an artist and *Liberty* editor were comparatively short-lived, having begun a decade or two too early for these activities to be fully recognized and rewarded.) When Gaddis was young, his evenings with each were given freely and so, occasionally, were ideas for worthy narrative projects—in college rooms, rented houses, and bars. Conversations begun at the San Remo and Cedar Tavern in the Village could be carried over from one night to the next, and across the ocean to their counterpart cafés, pubs, and street scenes in London and Paris. Most of the friends of Gaddis's formative years as a writer went on to positions of acclaim and material security, though not Martin Dworkin, the "self who could do more" whose presence in the fiction (and evidently on Gaddis's conscience) is more pervasive than the rest. Just as Gaddis had expressed concern over his son Matthew's possible reaction to the *New York Times Magazine* feature essay by Auchincloss, he also during this late period continued to worry over what Martin would think—as when, for example, he had a portrait done by Julian Schnabel. As he wrote to Sarah: "The Schnabel business is all pretty wild & wait till you see the thing! I'm already anticipating unkind remarks from colleagues, if it appears somewhere, re someone (me) who has always kept privacy (avoided Elaine's)

suddenly going public —to say nothing of Louis A's piece if they use it . . .
(Again imagine Martin seeing the Schnabel! that I had surely finally sold
out!) But simply enough, with negotiating for another contract on the
next book coming up, why not?"[3]

How many of his nighttime conversations with Dworkin, which Gaddis conveyed to the down-and-out tavern dwellers depicted in lower
Manhattan throughout *The Recognitions*, would have been attempts, sincere ones, to define the role of artists and writers? That is where Gaddis's
and Dworkin's worldly aspirations took shape, in conversation and a
sustained, mutual challenge, in the glory days of Greenwich Village circa
1952. The conversations continued even into the corporate years: "I've
come through a few of those late-night world-settling sessions with Martin Dworkin," Gaddis had written in a letter late in the 1950s, when he'd
hoped, with Dworkin's help, to continue his pre-*Recognitions* assignments at places like *America Illustrated* magazine.[4] But neither Gaddis
nor Dworkin would have recognized the terms for artistic success that
emerged suddenly in New York in the 1980s when all was clarified: anyone, or anything, could be an artist if the emerging art market deemed it
so. The transformations in New York at the time have been captured by
the British historian Tony Judt, who arrived in Manhattan "just in time
to experience the bittersweet taste of loss":

> In the arts the city led the world from 1945 through the 1970s. If you
> wanted to experience modern painting, music or dance, you came to
> the New York of Clement Greenberg, Leonard Bernstein and George
> Balanchine. Culture was more than an object of consumption: people
> thronged to New York to produce it too. Manhattan in those days
> was the crossroads where original minds lingered—drawing others in
> their wake. Nothing else came close.[5]

"We are experiencing the decline of the American age," Judt recognizes—
and his analysis, as a definitive historian of postwar Europe, is among the
very few of the era that, with Gaddis's, carries a wide-ranging, documentary authority. The difference between them is mostly temperamental, as
Gaddis (a New York native) observes decline not so much with Judt's
"bittersweet" mood but with a combination of energizing anger and cor-
rosive humor.

Those late-night alcoholic conversations among producers of art and
culture in the late forties and fifties were taken to heart by Gaddis, and
must have helped shape his lifelong distrust of "abstraction" in the arts
that could so readily move a mediocre or untrained or plagiarizing artist

into notoriety. He already had one of the young pretenders in *The Recognitions*, Max, hold a private opening at his apartment for *The Workman's Soul*, which was nothing but a laborer's shirt (the actual shirt, not a rendition) placed on a canvas. Gaddis himself four decades later would place, on the cover of *Frolic*, a reproduction of a painting by Sarah, not mentioning that it was done when his daughter was a child of five; and no one at Scribner noticed the error on the spine for the paperback edition of the National Book Award–winning "A Frolic of His of His Own."

That kind of inattention was anathema to Dworkin, and became all the more so to his protégé. Dworkin may have been only a year or two older than Gaddis—but what a difference in one's twenties in New York, when each year counted so much toward, or away from, professional recognition and potential worldwide acclaim. And besides, Dworkin with his completed Harvard degree and established position in a downtown office of the United States Information Service had already "done more," though by the time Gaddis did come through with a work of his own, both men would each be faced with the melancholy of not yet having fulfilled their potential: Gaddis, confined for the next two decades to corporate writing and itinerant teaching, and Dworkin, settling in at Columbia's Teachers College, his poetry developing in private while he published mostly criticism in middlebrow journals. By the late 1970s, when Gaddis was back in the high life and doors were again opening, those same doors seemed to have shut for good on Dworkin—a fate that Jack Gibbs in the fiction anticipates with his reflections on that favorite word of Gaddis's, *Torschlusspanik*, the fear of doors closing, of being left on the shelf, one's books unread and oneself alone and unmarried, eating a chop in Queens as happened to Gaddis's father.

Dworkin all his life was generous with ideas to his own detriment. He would go so far as to itemize "38 conversations" between himself and Gaddis that appeared in *The Recognitions*, but who else was keeping accounts, in those days? Certainly not Pennebaker, whose original idea for a film about a boy millionaire, "J. R." (with periods, no less), was only several years later noted down by Gaddis for legal purposes, to protect himself in case word got out and somebody tried to scoop him. The idea was gifted to Willie by Penny. No wider public acknowledgment of his source was ever given, but Pennebaker, unlike the unsuccessful Dworkin, was never heard to complain. Mike Gladstone for his part was only amused when his own self-inflicted accident was given to the character in *A Frolic of His Own* who ends up suing himself as the owner of the car that ran him over when he was attempting a jump start. This character, hapless Oscar Crease, became a vehicle also for Gaddis's novel-length reflections on the problem of intellectual property when the aging community college teacher goes on to sue a Hollywood filmmaker for the unattributed, uncompensated use of his unpublished Civil War play in a schlock film titled *The Blood in the Red White and Blue*. The postwar, posthaste, gift economy that enabled the free circulation of such generative ideas, and the truly village-like streets and shared lofts and affordable night scene that brought prospective writers, artists, filmmakers, and actors into regular casual contact—all that, the context for an entire literary generation, was precisely what the new cultural economy of the 1980s was eliminating now that millions of dollars were at stake in any passing thought or modestly remarkable experience or widely sympathetic self-presentation that could be turned into an "original" media production.

Gaddis, who had gone off on quests of his own (and doubtless some frolics) for long stretches after his dismissal from Harvard, could nonetheless hold his own by virtue of his literary achievements even if he found himself for most of his adult life (and also, as we shall see, at the end of his life) in much more precarious circumstances than his cohorts, materially and socially. The long years in relative obscurity with at best modest means that even the National Book Award in 1976 did not much improve suddenly ended when he took up with wealthy Muriel Murphy, a "high class rediscovery from those days before my first marriage, whose encouragement of my callow infatuation then would have deprived the world of Sarah & Matthew, so perhaps Mother was Right, perhaps everything does happen 'for the best,'" as he informed William Gass, adding moments later, after stepping away from the typewriter, that "the 'phone rings with Muriel from NY saying a cousin may be leaving a home (staffed) in London for a few weeks so should we consider London rather than Haiti. I tell you."[6]

Back then in the mid-fifties ad hoc Village scene, Muriel was (again, by her own estimation) "a self-fancying expert working at the Metropolitan Museum who recommended who would or would not be taken into the collection" (*E* 45). In those days, "in the red-hot center of creativity and the avant-garde," she would not have made too much time for a locally respected but widely unrecognized minor novelist. He may have been, in Ormonde de Kay's recollection, "aggers-baggers about Muriel. But at that time, so was half the male population of New York of that age group."[7] Back then, just as Gaddis never quite made it into any Harvard clubs, he would not have been invited to join the Eighth Street Club, for example, whose young artists courted Muriel. For her part, she felt honored by the invitation to join the "Eighth Street toughs" and she coveted "the Seal of

Approval" even if she must have suspected, even then, that the downtown artists were only "seeking advantage or currying favor from an official at the Metropolitan Museum." By the time she united with Gaddis thirty-five years later, now with an NBA to his credit, she was in a position to advance careers less directly, if no less definitively in her uptown salon, which gained her the reputation of "promising young hostess" (Muriel's quotations):

> [The salon] came about through Hans—not Hans Hokensen, Buddhist sculptor, not Hans Hoffman, Abstraction's leading exponent, but Hans Namuth, the photographer—through greeting him on the street, saying "come play chess tonight. Duchamp and Tini are coming," through his response "Can't," and, finally, through my reply, "We'll do it again next Thursday. Come at 7." And so the so-called "Salon" began, with open-house chess being played every Thursday night. (*E* 77)

Thus was Gaddis suddenly placed in the center of Upper Manhattan high society, whose members had fulfilled their potential and were all receiving their due. His acquaintances, and occasional friendships, as he approached his seventh decade would be with the likes of the aristocrat-lawyer and novelist Louis Auchincloss; the "$1 million a year"[8] art star Julian Schnabel ("a large forthright generous fellow I got quite fond of"[9]); Nobel laureate Saul Bellow, whose novel *More Die of Heartbreak* Gaddis would review in the *New York Times Book Review*; Carol Phillips, an old friend from the sixties who had become editor of *Vogue* and founder of the Clinique line of fashion products; and later Salman Rushdie, whose beach party may have had some of the fifty-plus invited guests and the many servants wondering, with Muriel, just how secret Rushdie needed to be just two years after the Ayatollah's 1989 fatwa. First among Gaddis's new friends was the visual artist and famed *New Yorker* illustrator Saul Steinberg, who appears to have been largely responsible for Gaddis's membership in the American Academy of Arts and Letters. Steinberg was also "one of the background figures who recommended candidates for the MacArthur Foundation's 'genius' grants, and he worked tirelessly to ensure that Gaddis got one," according to Steinberg's biographer, Deirdre Bair.[10]

At a period of semi-depression in Steinberg's life, friendship with Gaddis came as a source of comfort, from "another man who did not speak until or unless he had something intelligent and interesting to say." Steinberg "was, however, wary of what he assumed was Gaddis's ferocious intelligence, because he had a great deal of difficulty whenever he tried to

read one of the novels, none of which he had yet succeeded in finishing"
at the time he met Gaddis. Like Gaddis, Steinberg was impatient with
avant-garde posturing, even as he established himself and his own career
as a reference point for the avant-garde in the arts. "'To draw without
seeking truth,'" Muriel recalls him saying, is "'to practice at drawing,
something like idling or mindlessly running scales at the piano without
playing music.' . . . The artist developed his craft, but the viewer is mis-
used" (E 114).

That was Muriel's view, informed by a wide acquaintance with artists
who doubtless were looking out for themselves if they were speaking
with a staffer at the Metropolitan or an uptown hostess unafraid to pull
strings, or pass along judgments, in private—a practice that continued
posthumously, in that her *Memoir* is said to be taken from her personal,
"unpublished files." Gaddis's own view of the avant-garde in writing, or
what it had become since the informal adventures that he knew firsthand
in his Village years, can be gleaned from a description of one night out in
Manhattan when an old friend, Mathilda Campbell, Duchess of Argyll,

> arrived in town so for reasons of old time friendship not Art I went
> with her down to some confused & I thought all quite unnecessary
> number at the old Phoenix Theatre, some sort of tribute to William
> Burroughs with readings some nonsense music & Allen Ginsberg all
> of it the avant-garde which is suddenly just old hat. That was Fri-
> day night, they had a big number last night scheduled to end up at
> Studio 54 the big disco everybody wants to go to because you can't
> get in, but I thought I'd had enough so skipped that, probably it
> all ended up with lots of artistics & Ginsberg taking off his clothes
> which may have been a romp 20 years ago but would hardly be an
> edifying sight now.[11]

The evening was redeemed for him, however, by the chance location of
the theater across from his old apartment building on Second Avenue
and Twelfth Street, "& looking up at the windows [. . .] & remembering, Christmases & that cage elevator & old Henry in his cap. This of
course is the season for such things & for so many people a hard one to
get through, rather than being able simply to look back & realize how
marvelous it all was & how lucky to have it, something to do with that
'living every every minute.'"

It was a line Gaddis would often cite in letters (without a trace of
irony) from the distinctly *non*-avant-garde American dramatist Thornton
Wilder in *Our Town* (1938).

In the extended Christmas scenes in *The Recognitions*, moving between uptown Manhattan and the downtown art world, Gaddis let his narrator interrupt the festivities (and much in the novel that was forlorn) with the observation that "we are drawing away from one another, that we share only one thing, share the fear of belonging to one another, or to others, or to God" (105). Gaddis is feeling the same way in this epistolary reference to Wilder in the winter of 1978 as he approached his fifty-sixth birthday (which fell each year in the midst of holiday celebrations, making neither the celebrations, nor the birthday, wholly his own). The Wilder allusion is indeed a refrain in letters sent to his closest family members—as he urged himself, and them, not to be like the people in *Our Town* who find it "difficult sometimes simply to stop and live 'every every minute.' "[12] Thornton Wilder, and Gaddis's own disposition toward a Quaker ethic: together these constitute the homely essence of Gaddis's avant-garde aesthetic. Implicitly, he appeals to his readers, as he does to his family members, to recognize that every minute is one that "we do all have together in this life."[13] It is the heart of his message in *The Recognitions*, it is behind the broken families in his second novel and their reconstitution as the "J R Family of Companies," and it would again be the theme of his final reflection on *agapē*, the Christian ideal of brotherly love.

If Wilder's American small town dwellers are too caught up in the business of life (and the business life) to attend to every passing minute, it is unlikely that many among the American reading public could attend to the every, every detail in Gaddis's work, each of which nearly always connects to other details in a carefully layered structure. Simple as Wilder's homespun advice might seem, it is the essence of the defamiliarizing principle of art—one that does not, like that of Ginsberg and Burroughs, take us away from the everyday through ecstatic performance, but rather brings us in.

Burroughs and Ginsberg, whatever one thought of the culture that grew around their work, their personalities, and (indeed) their persons, were clearly *placed* in the public imagination, in a way that neither Gaddis nor Steinberg ever were, and this too accounts for the deeper friendship between the two men. If they were "avant-garde," it was in each case a distinctively *middlebrow* avant-garde that, like midlist fiction by the late 1980s, was no longer of interest commercially to publishers or gallerists. Art of the order of Steinberg's, conceived in the spirit of Picasso and Klee, Beckett and Joyce but still capable of reaching a large audience through the *New Yorker*, would be increasingly bound for museums; serious fiction, possessing a similar range of "disciplined recognitions" (in Gaddis's case) was bound for academic writing programs. Steinberg's fame—he

was "the man who did that poster," *View of the World from 9th Avenue*—
kept most people from seeing his art *as* art, in an institutional context.
And Gaddis was no easier to locate: his anticipation of postmodernism
in literature and ruthless description of the corporatization of American
life in its every aspect, from business to school to family and friendships,
could hardly be absorbed by institutions (journalism, a corporatizing academia) that were operating largely *within* those powerful cultural modes.
"Difficult," in such a culture, was the only term by which he could be
widely known, and thus his work (and its challenges) could be routinely
and repeatedly ignored.

Steinberg did eventually, on a second try, finish reading *J R*, and he
communicated to Gaddis an interest he discovered in the Austrian novelist
Thomas Bernhard—whose relentless negativity suited Steinberg's mood
following the death of his long-standing part-time lover, Sigrid Spaeth.
Steinberg's dejection was not helped either by the transformations under
way in America, which affected him personally, for example, in the corporate buyout and editorial downgrading of the *New Yorker*, his home
base for half a century.[14] He was also affected by the commercialization
in the 1980s of the Manhattan art world, from which he certainly ben-
efitted financially, though his position and his powerful representation by
the Andrew Wylie agency allowed him to keep a certain distance. Steinberg would recommend "Wily Wylie" to Gaddis, and the agency would
continue to work closely with the Gaddis Estate in the preparation of his
posthumous publications and the disposition of his archive at Washington University in St. Louis.

On the publication of *Frolic* in 1994, Gaddis inscribed a copy "to
Saul": "With gratitude and affection." "Gratitude is a serious word,"
Steinberg observed. "It's meant," Gaddis responded (*E* 116). In another
letter sent a year earlier, Gaddis crossed out the word "generosity," and
replaced it with "friendship" in reference to "this burden on your friendship which you have shown to both of us," Gaddis and Muriel, "in so
many ways over so many years." Part of that burden is Gaddis's having
asked Steinberg to read, and presumably respond to, the manuscript of
the deposition section of *Frolic*. The letter itself is typed on the reverse of
a discarded draft page, in which Gaddis had woven passages of Longfellow's *Hiawatha* into the narrative; references to Updike and Eliot appear
in two postscripts, the latter indicating a return to "where I came from."[15]

There could well have been a measure of resentment on Gaddis's part
in any hint that he owed the recognition he so richly deserved, on his own
merits, to his friend's position in New York circles of power—the very
institutions, and not least the *New Yorker*, which had for so long excluded

Gaddis himself (even as his own eye for verifying every, every detail was trained during his year working there as a lowly fact-checker for the magazine). How much of a toll these exclusions (from the inner circles at Harvard, from the *New Yorker*) must have seemed when he observed others, such as Steinberg and Gaddis's fellow *Harvard Lampoon* alum John Updike, who managed to work within the system and gain its recognitions. How ambivalent, the gratitude to such friends? We have seen Gaddis express similar, though modulated, uneasiness about the portrait done by Schnabel and the *New York Times Magazine* feature done by Auchincloss. The conviction that such active support came from each man's heartfelt respect for, and grasp of, his unique accomplishment nonetheless enabled Gaddis graciously to accept his preferment, so long in arriving.

That did not mean that Gaddis, from his newfound position among the empowered and the influential, was inclined in the least to let up on his critique of what his own country had become. Certainly we note a shift where his central characters now tend to come from the upper classes. Even if these characters are, like Liz Booth in *Carpenter's Gothic* and Oscar Crease in *Frolic*, denied full access to their inheritance and their presumed heritage by negligent fathers, they move within spheres of empowerment more easily than any of Gaddis's previous characters. They are placed, in their dwellings, mostly away from the center of things—Liz in the carpenter gothic house where Gaddis himself lived with Judith and then alone, in Piermont; Oscar in Muriel Murphy's Wainscott home in the East Hamptons. But the personal dramas of the characters unfold, through PR and legal maneuverings, in the sphere of power and influence that Gaddis himself now could know from the inside, in the Upper East Side apartment Gaddis also shared with Muriel (where he places the attorney Harry Lutz and his wife Christina, Oscar's stepsister in the novel). Many of the legal situations were derived through personal acquaintance. Steinberg would remark, for example, how he could have lived off the proceeds of each knockoff of that one poster had he received commissions that were owed him by U.S. copyright law. And this is only one example of intellectual copyright, so consistent with Gaddis's long-standing interest in forgeries and the decline of American values through imitation, that he could have derived from everyday conversation with the likes of Steinberg, the lawyer-novelist Auchincloss, and definitively the millionaire "attorney, art collector, and bibliophile" (*L* 422) Donald Oresman, who sent Gaddis as a gift the entire 81-volume *American Jurisprudence*, "every sort of case & human foible & precedent one might imagine so there may be a spark [for a new novel] somewhere there & enough reading to see me well through the Twilight Years."[16]

Out of this reading would come not only the inspiration for but also much of the language that went into the several depositions, briefs, procedures, complaints, and judicial opinions created for *Frolic* with the same exacting verisimilitude Gaddis used when working out the public relations gambits for *Carpenter's Gothic* and the economic transactions in *J R*. During the writing of *Frolic*, Gaddis regularly showed work in progress to Oresman and a number of other literary-minded legal professionals of his acquaintance. He much appreciated their "repeated assurance" that the lawyers' commentaries on the drafts were meant "only to clarify 'real world' law not direct my course," as he wrote to law clerk James Cappio, "but that I might wish to know the former & where I'd strayed intentionally or otherwise (artistic license? sheer sloppiness? plain ignorance?) . . ." He goes on to quote Oresman, who had counseled him at the start not to get overly attached to legalistic details: "Did getting *Arrowsmith* medically correct make it a better novel?" Gaddis appreciated the well-meant words of caution, but knew at the same time that a detail or distinction, in the real language of an operative discourse—be it law, economics, technological systems, or even aesthetic theory—was precisely what stimulated his unique imagination. He also knew that in any case he would never be rid of "this damned affliction as witness *J R* (what Bill Gass despises as) 'verisimilitude' or its semblance wherein events in the 'real' world of business (read, the law) while not plausible are essentially possible, ie an 11yr. old 'could' buy up by mail the controlling majority of a defaulted bond issue at 7¢ on the dollar, &c."[17]

The collision between real-world, professional language and his own novelistic language protected him, in his self-estimation, from the excesses of postmodern playfulness that he has Judge Crease describe in one of his opinions. The formidable ninety-seven-year-old, father of Oscar by his first marriage and stepfather of Christina by his second, has been appointed to rule on the suit brought by the Village of Tatamount, Virginia, against Szyrk, "a sculptor of some wide reputation in artistic circles" (30), for having placed in their domain the seventh in a series of steel structures, *Cyclone 7*, which entraps a neighborhood dog, Spot. Where classic sculpture might have expressed a "beauty synonymous with truth in expressing harmony as visibly incarnate in the lineaments of Donatello's David, or as the very essence of the sublime manifest in the Milos Aphrodite," Szyrk's structure requires something more of viewers, even educated ones who might be "unprepared to discriminate between sharp steel teeth as sharp steel teeth, and sharp steel teeth as artistic expressions of sharp steel teeth" (34). As Gaddis's attorney friend Oresman was capable of apt references to Sinclair Lewis's *Arrowsmith*, in his written opinion Judge Crease can move with assurance from citations of Ruskin to Stravinsky to Euripides to Keats, Tolstoy, and Melville. He will have no truck however with current "theory that in having become self referential art is in itself theory without which it has no more substance than Sir Arthur Eddington's famous step 'on a swarm of flies,' here present in further exhibits by plaintiff drawn from prestigious art publications and highly esteemed critics in the lay press, where they make their livings, recommending his [Szyrk's] sculptural creation in terms of slope, tangent, acceleration, force, energy and similar abstract extravagancies serving only a corresponding self referential confrontation of language with language and thereby, in reducing language itself to theory, rendering it a mere plaything, which exhibits the court finds frivolous" (34–35).

Frivolous such language games may be, but they are nonetheless consequential in that any modern profession is "self regulating," as the sympathetic character Harry Lutz says of his own legal profession (310). A self-creating, self-referential language is in fact what enables a profession to function autonomously or, as Harry puts it less generously, as essentially "a conspiracy against the public, every profession protects itself with a language of its own, look at that psychiatrist they're sending me to, ever try to read a balance sheet? Those plumes of the giant bird like the dog cornering his prey till it all evaporates into language confronted by language turning language itself into theory till it's not about what it's about it's only about itself turned into a mere plaything the Judge says it right there in this new opinion . . ." (284–85).

The cagey Justice is no less hesitant than Gaddis himself when it comes to recycling a good phrase, or savoring the twisty little passages of his own written documents that he knows will remain, many of them, operative as law and as precedent for future practice, even if only a few devoted legal scholars will ever read them closely past the date of their submission to the court. Crease is the absent hero of *Frolic*, or rather the one whose presence in language carries more weight than all the talk and deliberations staged in the novel. The opinions, drafted painstakingly by Gaddis, are meant to place Crease in the league not of "white-shoe" attorneys working in "blue chip" firms like Harry's Swine & Dour but of eminent judges in the tradition of Learned Hand, Benjamin Cardozo, and Oliver Wendell Holmes. Judge Crease especially admires Holmes, extolling his "dedication to the reason and practicality of the common law in its lack of sentimentality" (460).

The separation of law from theatrics, however difficult to conceive in the present era of legal soap opera and reality television, is no less fundamental than that of church and state. Such functional differentiations among professions and spheres arguably are the foundations of a modernity that is particularly American. Holmes is noted for his insistence on this very separation in a popular anecdote about "—Justice Learned Hand exhorting Holmes 'Do justice, sir, do justice!' and Holmes stops their carriage. 'That is not my job,' he says. 'It is my job to apply the law' " (285). The distinction is registered in the novel's first line in another "old saw" about getting justice in the next world, "in this world you have the law" (11). And that's not such a bad thing since, as Harry recognizes, calls for justice inevitably descend from idealism to stridency and, ultimately, to "opera." As he tells Christina, "—The ones showing up in court demanding justice, all they've got their eye on's that million dollar price tag. [. . .] it's always the money. The rest is nothing but opera . . ." (11).

Although money is "just a yardstick," it is also social and subjective because, as Christina suggests, "—It's the only common reference people have for making other people take them as seriously as they take themselves . . ." (11). But money for all its moment-by-moment measures cannot be in the final instance a way of determining or describing communication among persons, and between persons and the state and professions the state recognizes and supports. That power belongs, in the law, exclusively to a textual domain that consists of written opinions whose preservation in living archives enables practitioners to apply received judgments over time, and to alter past judgments in light of changing circumstances. The changes moreover can be monitored by the profession and judged by historians more objectively than can other verbal communications—with the exception of literary works, which also, in a different register, record human speech acts and recirculate past writings. The power of imaginative writing, while never so rigidly systematized as in law, is nonetheless available (as legal writing for the most part is not) for a continuous comparing of our own present subjectivities with those of humans who came of age, spoke, wrote, and lived in earlier generations. And this is possible because both we and they experience the world through the medium of language, a language whose changes in style and content over time are themselves indications of how subjectivities have changed. That is to say, how we have changed.

Those changes over time are the cognitive content exclusively of novels, poems, and dramatic scripts. The imaginative writer who captures those changes in the language of business and media is capable in this sense of observing and communicating the rise and fall of state power and subjective states of individuals during a given historical present—not least the period of "American decline" discerned by Tony Judt and delineated by Gaddis. So long as the culture is able to archive written texts that can then be referenced, read, and taught, that capacity for tracking changes in the language of one's own time is a reason for a work of fiction to claim for itself validity through the ages.

Nowhere in *Frolic* is this power so evident as in the scenes from nature, in the pond outside Oscar's house, that occur with increasing frequency late in the novel:

> Neither the red scream of sunset blazing on the icebound pond nor the thunderous purple of its risings on a landscape blown immense through leafless trees off toward the ocean where in flocks the wild goose Wawa, where Kahgahgee king of ravens with his band of black marauders, or where the Kayoshk, the seagulls, rose with clamour from their nests among the marshes and the Mama, the woodpecker seated high among the branches of the melancholy pine tree past the margins of the pond neither rose Ugudwash, the sunfish, nor the yellow perch the Sahwa like a sunbeam in the water banished here, with wind and wave, day and night and time itself . . .[18]

While all this is happening outside, a natural ecology mostly unobserved by humans, another medial ecology plays out in much the same way during late-night scenes when the television runs for hours unwatched, or half watched as a character emerges from sleep:

> the black body necklaced with a blazing tire turned out to be at a crossroad in Soweto and now, poised at a casement window, a lady in impeccable negligee stirred by a gentle breeze over phantom breasts smiled serenely on the unruffled landscape of a country morning after a satisfactory bout with an overnight laxative in the day's early light, mist rising on the pond out there and the smell of —some more coffee? Ilse? (270)

Typical of Gaddis's later style is the absence of transitions between a televisual reality and a textual reality; nor is there a need, even, for the presence of a human consciousness to register what's going on in home or natural environments: we move from a news report on distant, war-ravaged South Africa to the cloying intimacy of a laxative commercial, whose early morning light *becomes* the light "out there," beyond the television frame. The actual, real "environment" in the land around the Wainscott home is experienced as an overlay of various times and multiple media, even as the movement of perch in the pond becomes another form of light passing through a medium, a "sunbeam in the water." The language of such passages inhabits, at the same time, in the present light of day, the epochal time of wildlife (much of which nonetheless will cease in a not too distant future), and the cultural past of Longfellow, whose words from *Hiawatha* course continually through many natural descriptions. It was a poem Gaddis read for the first time at age eight or nine; half a century later, the same words were still present in his mind and would become a presence for readers, through his writing and institutions of literary art that persist even in periods of cultural decline and ecological decimation.

Another way that Gaddis would overlay past and present subjectivities is through the repurposing and presentation in *Frolic* of a play he'd drafted over thirty years earlier—all but the last act—under the title *Once at Antietam*. In it "the central figure hires substitutes on both [sides] . . . one from the south and one in the north, and they're both killed in the same battle . . ." (as he remarked to the "New York State Writers Institute Seminar," April 14, 1990). Regardless of its inherent literary interest (the play was termed "rather stiff" by Gaddis himself[19]), *Antietam* becomes yet another referential document for the courts and lawyers to pick apart while Oscar's copyright infringement suit is under litigation. Gaddis simply could not let unfinished work—the Civil War drama, the player piano history—remain on his shelves. These works were composed in the continuing rush of creativity and concentration after his completion of *The Recognitions*, before he quite recognized that the commercial failure of that novel would make it hard to find a publisher, and an advance, for such demanding and uncategorizable works. The recycling of unpublished writing into his own later work (right up to the reworking of the player piano history in the posthumously published *Agapē Agape*) participates no less actively in the self-regulating, self-defining, and self-reproducing circuits of expression that Gaddis, and his characters, perceive in the world of mutually distinct professions and largely confrontational personal relationships.

Such circularities exist everywhere in modern society and in Gaddis's novels, which, as we saw in Tom LeClair's earlier remarks, "correspond to that reality to communicate it."[20] In doing so, Gaddis asserts over the wastes of the world, and among minds that are mostly inattentive to language and to one another, a kind of literary mastery appropriate to the era. Oscar sues himself after he is run over by the car he owns. He also brings a products liability action against the car maker, Sosumi ("So Sue

Me"); another character refers to an Isuyu (28). He had once mailed a copy of his play to himself in a sealed envelope, recalling Gaddis's self-mailing of the précis for *J R* two decades before its completion. In Oscar's play, the characters battle one another in the Civil War: both are stand-ins for the man who hired them to fight in his place, one for the North and one for the South. When one kills the other, he goes on record as having killed himself. (Scholar Peter Wolfe notes that "The play's two leading figures, William and Thomas, have Gaddis's first and middle names"—an instance of postmodern self-consciousness if there ever was one, and there are many such in Gaddis, as we have seen.[21])

One of Gaddis's most perceptive readers, Wolfe also points out how "the separateness that menaced the people of *The Recognitions* has returned with a rush in *Frolic*." Wolfe rightly references the four deaths in the novel, and the absence of births. Each death takes place away from the novel's action, and each is experienced without the slightest significant pause for mourning by the characters. Christina, devastated by the sudden loss of her husband Harry, begs Oscar please to let go of his own legal preoccupations for just a moment while she tries to take in Harry's death by heart attack from overwork. And Oscar himself, who had been estranged for decades from his own father, hears about Judge Crease's demise through a television news report. "Oscar," Wolfe notes, "is so full of his own rectitude that he complains endlessly"[22]—but this is precisely the kind of endless self-assertion that is encouraged in people in the world of confrontation and litigation that takes people away from the lived moment—Wilder's "every, every minute" whose fulfillment is all that can give a person equanimity to face the moment of death, in oneself and in others in whose perceptions and consciousness we also exist.

How then does Gaddis as an author avoid the self-protective self-absorption that can push so many of his characters into conditions of separateness? Does he not, as Wolfe supposes, enforce the "loveless ontology" experienced by his characters "by withholding help from the reader"?[23] Of course there are moments of sanity in the novel, when Christina (mostly) brings the men around her down to earth and away from their legal preoccupations. And not only the men: she keeps Oscar's younger girlfriend Lily in check even as Lily quietly discourages the older woman's increasingly heavy drinking; Christina also moderates somewhat the excesses and intergenerational marriages of her millionaire childhood friend, Trish Hemsley, who brushes her off with quips: "—Teen, at our age marriage is half the fun at twice the price" (16). These moments too, of course, require no small attentiveness on the reader's part. Do we notice when Lily (without a word spoken, or a narrator to tell us) ignores

Christina's request to bring her a drink and makes her tea instead? How often do we notice these things in our experience among the people we know and converse with in life?

With such small, accumulative details distinct to novel-reading and the coordination of everyday acts of attention, Gaddis rejects traditional representation, and rejects perhaps narrative itself if by this we mean a way of connecting our own and others' past experience to our present condition, a way of living that is supposed to be superior to the episodic, moment-by-moment life that we are given. Instead of a life narrative with ourselves in the role of protagonist, or the communication of some authoritative vision or life philosophy, we have in Gaddis (and in an entire tradition of nonnarrative fictions by Proust, for example, by Joyce or Musil[24] or Cervantes for that matter) a unique opportunity to coordinate our perceptions with those of another mind. In this sense, crucially I think for any appreciation of Gaddis's accomplishment, while reading we continue (while never completing) the process that went into the composition of the novels. That is especially true when Gaddis willingly (and with such evident enjoyment, in this late work) brings his own interests in language into contact with the language of law, as understood by men and women he trusted who (like him) worked primarily with language on a day in, day out basis.

Around the time he was nearing completion of *Frolic*, Gaddis set down, for himself apparently, a somewhat similar life outlook. His thoughts are imparted on half a page of the 8½ × 13" paper he typically used for manuscripts. The text is single spaced:

> Perhaps in my 70th year the time has come to set forth some attempt
> at a cohesive 'philosophy' that this accumulation has tried to express:
> > in the essentially comic attempt to impose our vanity on a world
> > of chance
> > and take refuge in the notion of the unswerving punctuality of
> > and the clumsy attempt to impose absolutes
> > and fight cause and effect
> > and the desperate notion that we are put here for some purpose
> > in order to find answers to questions which not only have none
> > but no reason to have any and in fact have not been asked
> > its meaning only in its very lack of meaning
> > and the unbearable prospect of a disorderly universe
> > tag ends of the thoughts of others
> > which cannot compete with the serenity of dawn
> > conceived only in fear of the end

The years, as though they've accumulated apart from him somehow, are what come to expression through him but nowhere near so powerfully as when the organizing, arranging author seems absent, imposing nothing of his own (no beliefs, no "absolutes"). Mostly our communications and the thoughts in our heads, like the voices on late-night television, go unheard even as the teeming life in a pond either goes unattended or (too often) is actively thwarted by our own ecological interventions, our institutionalized competition with a natural serenity. Most of what we assume is our own thought, Gaddis understood, will be "tag ends of the thoughts of others." But not the literary work: that is the site where one's own thought and the thought of others can be carried forward, in textual form, to other minds at other moments in time.

The interaction among "a few minds, ever the same" (Flaubert) extends beyond the confines of literary practice and engages with the practice of one's contemporaries in fields that have consequences in the construction and continual reconstitution of social, legal, and conceptual norms. No less necessary to his own self-worth and peace of mind was the chance to bring his novelistic practice into direct contact with the practice of lawyers whose work he respected and whose good report he coveted—more than that of reviewers, critics, or the steadily increasing cohort of graduate students writing dissertations on his work. On reading the letters that were placed in the archive at Washington University in St. Louis, it came as a surprise to his immediate family that Gaddis gave to scholars so much of his letter-writing time, and so much reflection on the wellsprings of his own work. Sarah, for example, "found his letters to scholars interesting, considering he was known for being unwilling to discuss his work" ("Afterword," *L* 531). Around the same number of letters to established and (more often) aspiring scholars appear in the later sections of the collected *Letters* as there are letters to lawyers. The former, however, are clearly efforts to correct past misunderstandings (among reviewers, "calumnists,"[25] and opinion setters); always respectful, these letters to scholars do not however have the spirit of camaraderie that shows forth, during this period, with lawyers whose personal quest to get things right, to restore order (even where social justice was unlikely) echoes his own literary project and reveals the one side to Gaddis's personality that consistently links the man and the literary artist. The contact between the legal and the novelistic also ensured that neither profession would devolve entirely into "self-regulating conspiracy": for it is the unique potential of language that it is able to cross over among professions, and among minds.

Fittingly, the most authoritative and apt critique of *Frolic* at the time of this writing was done not by a journalist, a critic, nor a literary scholar, but by the law professor and practitioner Larry M. Wertheim. "*Frolic*," Wertheim notes, "contains much substantive law. But for the fact that they are purely a creation of the mind of William Gaddis, *Szyrk* and *Crease* would be the sort of judicial opinions which might be discussed as serious propositions of the law in a law review such as this"—namely, the *William Mitchell Law Review*.[26] The literary canon of English language novels is not often favorable to lawyers, and in Gaddis's own personal canon, which is bereft of admirable people, *Frolic* is notable, "if for nothing else . . . for its favorable portrayal of at least one member of the legal profession"—Harry Lutz, whose interest in the law, we learn from his obituary late in the novel, was "inspired by a growing sense of injustice which he later ascribed to his reading of Dickens" (527). In the midst of spoken communication that is "often interrupted by other unattributed dialogue, the author's narration, a telephone conversation, or the omnipresent television programs and commercials," and in the absence of a settled home life or collaborative work environment to create faith in the reality of other subjectivities, Wertheim supposes "The only way the characters can really ever communicate with the outside world is by litigation." In conclusion, Wertheim finds *Frolic* to be "unique in the works that are studied in the fields of law and literature. With its numerous invented judicial opinions, pleadings, and fictional deposition transcripts, *Frolic* creates an entire imagined world of law and lawsuits unlike anything found in any other novel."[27]

Much the same can be said of each novel by Gaddis. The fact that it is said about this one, by someone outside the self-congratulatory circle of literary authors and well-placed friends, bodes well for Gaddis's continuing relevance to readers in general.

# Chapter 12

# His Master's Voice: *Agapē Agape*

> . . . have been concentrating on the studio, getting painted &
> bookshelves up and pretty much taking my time getting all
> my books over there which is proving a very good & calming
> experience, so many of them I've had for 50+ years & each one
> of them recalls something, some time, some idea or aspiration
> or aborted project & I somehow feel very content & whole
> sitting there and looking at them in their shelves probably for
> the last time & the feeling that lurking somewhere here is this
> another book still waiting to be written.
>
> William Gaddis in East Hampton, 1995

Gaddis's letter to Sarah appears with five photos he had taken of the
Admiral's House on Boatyard Row in East Hampton, "boatyard across
the way reminiscent of Piermont."[1] Anticipating visits from his immediate
family, Gaddis wrote, "Can live all on 1 level but upstairs studio-bedroom
always there": as the studio above the barn by his boyhood home, he
knew, was always there while he found his way around the western United
States, Cambridge, Central America, France, Spain, and Greenwich Village, and just as the Alan Ansen house was there for him in Hewlett
when he needed a quiet season to revise the first novel and the Piermont
garage was there for him during the writing of *Carpenter's Gothic*. The
properties inherited and purchased by Edith, and then given to him, reinforced his self-confidence and helped ease over financial hard times, so
his thoughts would turn to his son and daughter as he settled, with no
woman in his life, into the small house in his native Long Island.

In fiction the ironical "place of stone" (Yeats) was there for Gibbs
in the Ninety-Sixth Street apartment in Manhattan, and the studio in
Massapequa was there for Gaddis in life as for Bast in fiction, where an
idea could be left indefinitely, and still be found there after years away.

"[L]urking somewhere," in the places where he'd begun earlier work, were generative ideas for the next one, "this another book" whose attempt after the unlikely achievement of *The Recognitions* never quite seemed plausible to him (though he knew its pursuit was inevitable as death).

*Agapē Agape* is Gaddis's swan song, his most concentrated fiction and the one work where he risks a direct address to the reader. The distillation of a project that occupied him throughout his professional life, this final fiction began as an exhaustive social history of the player piano in America, whose lineaments can be read in the thousands of notes, clippings, working papers, drafts, and snippets that Gaddis left at his death. Organized roughly, like all of his manuscripts and background materials, into numbered cardboard boxes, the remains of his research match the narrative description: among the working papers, one finds a chronology from the player's invention in 1876 to 1929, "when the player piano world and everything else collapsed." Handwritten reminders, in a hand whose changes can be discerned over half a century, appear in the margins, or on whatever scraps of paper he had around. "Chaos theory as a means toward order," reads one note among the strips and folders that Gaddis would refer to when composing his last work. After a career spent imagining in detail the vast systems and multiple voices of an emerging global culture, Gaddis at the end would reflect primarily on his own private system of assembling materials and putting words down on paper.

As with all of his books, for *Agapē Agape* much of the working material was cut out from popular magazines and newspapers. (Even the high literature, art, music, and technology references that made him seem forbiddingly "erudite" to some readers often came out of daily papers, or were sent to him by acquaintances; possibly more came to him this way than from books.) Often Gaddis would combine strips on a single topic or under a single date and tape them all the way along one side, on a single long page. When correcting galleys and typescripts, he would insert words and small phrases by hand, but he preferred to lay in new material in typed strips cut with scissors. Composition, for Gaddis, was a distinctly material practice, involving a literal organization and arrangement of found materials, even as his narrator struggles literally to hold himself together. In a sense, the writer becomes the page on which he's writing: the wreck of an old man in *Agapē* has rusting staples in his legs, and his skin is like tissue paper from the drugs he's been taking. He worries that his books will be left on the shelf, unread, while his unpublished research molders in the boxes stacked around him. But as long as he goes on reading, revising, adding to the manuscript, he will stave off death and madness and keep the work from becoming "what it's about": entropy, chaos, loss, and a mechanized culture good at discerning, disseminating, and commercializing identities, but indifferent to the cultivation of particular, individual talents in communication with one another.

When he was ill and powerless he would practice calligraphy—from the time in his teens when he was sent home expecting to die to his final drive home from the hospital when he told his son and daughter, truly: "I'm not going to be here tomorrow." The writing that took him outside of himself, to the extent that he would cease to think about his own mortality, is the theme he would come back to, obsessively, in the very last working papers and at the last page of *Agapē*: "Discover yr hidden talent," "yr unsuspected talent," "disc secret talent" all appear on one page of notes, along with "the self who could do more" (three times, with variations). The note-taking evidently continued weeks and months past the time when he'd declared the manuscript finished[2]—confirming a lifelong habit he had of writing past a book's end. That's how it went with *The Recognitions*, which Gaddis completed half a century before, when he still had on his desk pages of "outlined notes . . . for spinning out the novel's conclusion."[3] And the succeeding books each took off, in their turn, from the leftover drafts of work that preceded it until, at the end of his life, Gaddis determined to transform his accumulated research into one gemlike meditation without false illusions or consolations.

The player piano history, had it been completed, would have been an impressive coda to the fiction. As scholarship, it would have put Gaddis belatedly in the tradition of those North American writers on media and technology—Lewis Mumford, Elizabeth Eisenstein, Marshall McLuhan, Neil Postman—who could perceive technology's aesthetic consequences and wellsprings. Much of what Gaddis intended, as scholarship, had already been accomplished by Hugh Kenner in *The Counterfeiters* (1968). As a conceptual work, the history could scarcely have rivaled Walter Benjamin's "Work of Art in the Age of Mechanical Reproduction" or Friedrich Kittler's *Discourse Networks*. Gaddis knew this, as his letters attest; he also knew that his contribution to the study of mechanization and the arts had already been accomplished, indirectly, with his novels. But the accumulated research of half a century weighed on him during these final years, demanding an outlet. He worked hard on the history through 1996 and early 1997, when he discovered that he would not have long to live. By that time, however, he had already decided to reformat the work as a fiction, having finally realized that his own raillery on the subject was more interesting to him than "a dim pursuit of scholarship headed for the same trash heap I'm upset about in the first place," as he told his son Matthew.

Once he had finally set aside the history, Gaddis used his boxes of snippets to create a character who had obsessions identical with his own, whose lived experience and efforts at composition could dramatize both the possibilities and "the destructive element" within an emerging technological order. Later, in 1998, when he was commissioned by Deutschlandradio to write a play suitable for broadcasting, he responded with a fragment unlike anything he had ever written: a one-act monologue entitled *Torschlusspanik* (which, as noted earlier, means the fear of doors closing, of opportunities lost, of staying single, and—not least—of going unread). The work was translated and broadcast on 3 March 1999, three and a half months after Gaddis died. At his death, a somewhat longer typescript of eighty-four pages, intended by Gaddis for posthumous publication, was sent to his agent under the same title he had used for the history: *Agapē Agape*. His last words sound and read less like a deathbed utterance than one from beyond the grave—less a lament, finally, for his own passing than an honest expression of fear at where technology is taking the world.

The voice Gaddis found for his last fiction is unique but not without literary precedent. In the early nineties, on the recommendation of Saul Steinberg Gaddis began reading the novels of Thomas Bernhard and sensed in this near contemporary from Austria not only personal affinities but a model for his reconceived project, a minimalism that allowed him to transform (rather than abandon) his accumulated research. The shift from scholarship to fiction would be accomplished by giving musical form to the work itself. Rather than reiterate music history, Gaddis would invite the reader to experience the work's musicality; his lifework would be understood not by following his labor and his logic, but through listening to his voice and its several modulations. Bernhard's musicologist in his novel *Concrete*, writing a biography of Mendelssohn-Bartholdy, aims at a "major work of impeccable scholarship" that would leave "far behind it and far beneath it everything else, both published and unpublished," that he had ever written.[4] Gaddis at a high moment may have felt the same about his player piano history; most of the time he more likely suspected that his research would ultimately be left to "some beleaguered doctoral candidate"—as he said to me in a letter of 1989 when my own doctoral studies were getting under way at the University of Toronto (*L* 454).

Bernhard's *Concrete* and *The Loser* are not only cited by Gaddis; they provide narrative models, or, as Gaddis's narrator would say, plagiarisms in advance, "like my own ideas being stolen before I even had them."

Bernhard's subjects were Gaddis's subjects also—musicology, home-state excoriation, and Glenn Gould as the hidden talent who could do more than his fellow students, Wertheimer and Bernard's narrator in *The Loser*, causing both of them to give up piano playing. Also, the brevity of Bernhard's work was made to order for Gaddis's reformatted fiction—this and the single narrative voice capacious enough to express subtle shifts in mood and occasional surges. More specifically still, this stripped-down style was consistent with the effects of prednisone, the drug that both Gaddis and Bernhard had taken for relief from emphysema. To his son Matthew, Gaddis would recall waking up singing after his first use of the drug, and its jag is consistent with the peculiar pacing of the narrative he left us, the meandering, hallucinatory quality that suddenly comes to a focus on one particular object, one item within the field of vision capable of absorbing attention and momentarily freeing the body from pain and breathlessness.

Bernhard is certainly a far cry from the meganovelists—Pynchon, Joyce, Melville—whom readers usually associate with Gaddis. But the fiction Gaddis cites with affection and admiration—George du Maurier's *Trilby*, Tolstoy's *Kreutzer Sonata*, John Kennedy Toole's *Confederacy of Dunces*—and his public expressions of admiration for the talkative novels of Saul Bellow, Norman Douglas, and Ronald Firbank should widen the literary context within which his own body of work might now be read and appreciated. What he particularly admired in Bernhard—and in writers as diverse as Joan Didion and Evelyn Waugh—was the economy of style, the ability to write expansively without wasting words. That stripped-down quality was just as important to Gaddis's own aesthetic as the highbrow satire (in Douglas and Waugh), the predominant dialogue (in Firbank's anticipatory "camp" novels[5]), the entropic vision (in Didion's *Slouching toward Bethlehem*), or the apocalyptic destruction in Yeats's "Second Coming" (a favorite poem of Gaddis's, whose high-toned mysticism he had once dismissed but then came to appreciate after reading Didion[6]). Unique as *Agapē* may be, it can attune readers to qualities of voice and economies of style that have largely gone unnoticed in Gaddis's earlier work.

Where the continuities between the earlier and later fiction stand out most clearly is in Gaddis's previous depictions of artists and writers—characters who, through their appetite for destruction and self-destruction, fail on their own terms. "Overwhelmed by the material demands" their art imposes, these characters—as Gaddis said in the *Paris Review* interview—generally fail "to pursue the difficult task for which their talents have equipped them" (71). Most often they cannot focus

their energies and—like Gaddis at work on the player piano project—
they have trouble finishing things. In *J R*, as we have seen, Gaddis would
show Jack Gibbs working fruitlessly on sections from Gaddis's own early
drafts for the project. Gibbs's friend Thomas Eigen, like Gaddis, has written an unpublished play on the Civil War, the same play that would be
recast and worked into the structure of *A Frolic of His Own*. Recycling
his own work, and the work of others, was consistent with Gaddis's overall aesthetic; he was, in many senses, an ecological novelist who at the end
cringes to think of "what we destroyed" and who could not bear to see
things wasted—not money, not talent, and certainly not the unpublished
products of his own creative energies.

At the end of his life, by concentrating his epic research into a novella,
Gaddis was following a pattern he had already worked out for his other
persona in *J R*, the young composer Edward Bast. Unable to ward off the
demands and distractions of life in corporate America—the materialistic
world of "brokers, bankers, salesmen, factory workers, most politicians,
the lot"—Bast undergoes a gradual reduction of his musical ambitions.
As Gaddis said in the 1987 interview:

> Bast starts with great confidence . . . that confidence of youth. He's
> going to write grand opera. And gradually, if you noticed [. . .], his
> ambitions shrink. The grand opera becomes a cantata where he has
> the orchestra and the voices. Then it becomes a piece for orchestra,
> then a piece for small orchestra, and finally at the end he's writing a
> piece for unaccompanied cello, his own that is to say, one small voice
> trying to rescue it all and say, "Yes, there *is* hope." (PR 71–72)

In Bast too Gaddis concentrated "the grand intoxication of youth" (*PR*
58) at once ridiculous and wonderful that had seen him through the
composition of *The Recognitions*, a book whose successful completion
(and initial commercial failure) haunts the historical project that Gaddis
returned to, fifty years later, in *Agapē Agape*.

Instead of a self-generated cosmos to place over against the material
universe, Gaddis imagines this "one small voice"—although it is easily
lost in so vast and noisy a novel as *J R*. Now that the voice has been
isolated and made to speak out in *Agapē Agape*, readers might arrive at
a fuller appreciation of what Gaddis was trying to do in his lifelong literary engagement with the materials, systems, and specialized languages of
corporate America. The single voice that emerges out of competing voices
and constraining media is not simply the voice of "artistic individualism"
struggling vainly against commodification by the capitalist machine.[7]

Gaddis does not fool himself into imagining that he can oppose his art's power to the power of the material world. What he can do, however, is to coordinate his art with the vast systems and structures that now shape our world. And we, in turn, can fashion new images of ourselves within that world by reading, by listening, and by attending to how these multiple voices and worldly materials have been heard and organized by the author.

Rather than opposing an artistic individualism against an impersonal, collectivist technology, Gaddis investigates their common historical roots as creative collaborations. From Vaucanson's mechanical loom for figured silk to Jacquard to the drum roll on the player piano to the punched data card on the first computers: in part, the digital age owes its existence to the arts. Yet Gaddis, who continued to tear out and save anything he came across on the subject after he had abandoned the original project, found scant acknowledgment of technology's debt. The "frenzy of invention" that culminated in the player piano in 1876 seemed intent rather on removing the artist from the arts altogether, just as the century ahead sought to eliminate the very possibility of human failure as a condition for success in the arts. "Analysis, measurement, prediction and control, the elimination of failure through programmed organization"— Gaddis had set the terms and cultural context for a "secret history of the player piano" as early as the 1960s, when the double-take-inducing title *Agapē Agape* first appears in his papers. The title turns up again in *J R* as the unfinished "social history of mechanization and the arts" that overwhelms Jack Gibbs by becoming what it's about: "the destructive element." *Agapē*—the community of brotherly love celebrated by early Christian writers—has come apart (agape) through mechanization and a technological democracy that reduces art to the level of light entertainment, a spectacle for the gaze of the masses. Ultimately, the "vast hallucination that's everything out there, and that you're all part of" (85)—Gaddis addresses his readers here directly—derives from nothing but little gaps. Sprockets in a film strip, patterns of holes in punched paper, microscopic etchings on silicon.

As noted earlier, Johannes Müller's experiments exemplify the economic rationale for technologizing the arts; as Gibbs points out, the German anatomist "—Thought opera companies could buy dead singers' larynxes fix them up to sing arias save fees that way get the God damned artist out of the arts all at once, long as he's there destroy everything in their God damned path what the arts are all about . . ." (*J R* 288; Müller is mentioned again in *AA* 16). A variation on Plato's banishment of artists from the Republic, the imposed condition of the outsider became a central theme in Gaddis through the early years of commercial failure and, with renewed irony, at the end of his life. In early 1998, a year after resuming his work on the player piano history, Gaddis discovered that he was very ill. His son Matthew, who did some minor office work for him during this period, recalls the context in which Gaddis set to work on his final fiction:

> While discussing his options with an estate planning lawyer, he real-
> ized that if he should require extended care he would lose his house
> and savings within two years. In order to receive money from Medic-
> aid he would have to become a financial non-entity. His reaction was:
> "Talk about the elimination of the artist. I have to be turned into a
> non-person in order to exist."[8]

Within weeks of the estate-planning conference, Gaddis returned to his original idea of "the raving ranting concerns of a single character" who became known as "the man on the bed." Gaddis briefly considered making this character a modern-day King Lear, the father of three daughters who apportions his estate and tries to secure his rights to a digital technology patented in the 1920s by a small company manufacturing cash registers and player pianos. Matthew recalls the evolutions of this character:

> The father of the man in the bed was a holder of the original patent.
> The two daughters charged with filing the suit know that it is frivo-
> lous and will be dismissed by the courts, but pretend to go along with
> it in order to get their father's money. The third daughter of course
> objects, and offers to care for her father ostensibly so that his wealth
> can be saved—so that it won't be taken by lawyers, doctors, taxes,
> and nursing homes. Her real purpose is simply to be with him while
> he completes his last treatise. Her father suspects this Cordelian fig-
> ure of objecting to the lawsuit because it will sap her inheritance, and
> promptly turns her out.

In the end, Gaddis discarded most of the Lear structure as too literal: "What happens to Cordelia? She gets killed in traffic? No. No." Losing interest in broad social satire and the sustained allusiveness of a modernist novel, Gaddis instead became possessed by something more in a gothic vein: the thought of creating a dying man who in turn creates doublings of himself—all for the purpose of explaining his obsession to his "detachable selves" and to the world before he dies or goes mad. Through all his research on the player piano, Gaddis relentlessly documents an

American culture of simulation in which technology has become the only imaginable solution to problems it created in the first place. The same demonic circulation that can sometimes put computer operators "at the mercy of the systems they've designed" would inform his narrative of a mind devouring itself in endless self-reflection. But something happens near the end of *Agapē* that enables Gaddis to imagine an escape from the technological hall of mirrors. Hurried by the sense of his impending death and finally unable to avoid identification with the biological, abject, material "Other" of his imagination, Gaddis for the first time in his career risks a direct personal address—to the reader, and to the ghosts, demons, philosophers, and fictional characters he holds in conversation. This identification with his "detachable selves" makes possible the astonishing final pages, when the man in bed speaks, evidently without irony or satirical intent, of what he has been able to hold in belief: "Finally I really don't believe any of it" (90) except for the evidence of the senses and memory and now, when they are to be lost, in the reality of the youthful "self who could do more," and its work.

"The self who could do more": this phrase from a verse by Michelangelo appears in Gaddis's first and last books: "*O Dio, o Dio, / Chi m'a tolto a ma stresso / Ch'a me fusse piu presso / O piu di me potessi, che poss' io?*"[9] Rejecting the standard translation as pedestrian—and just as Stanley in *The Recognitions* attempts his own translation (322)—Gaddis near the end of *Agapē* offers a version of his own: "it's fifteenth, sixteenth century Italian nearer poetry, Who nearer to me Or more mighty yes, more mighty than I Tore me away from myself. Tore me away!" (94). Everything depends on the language, on the living author's struggle with a past artist's words and on the future reader's ability to hold in mind two opposed meanings—*O Dio* and odium, heaven and repugnance. A capacity for imaginative projection into the life-world, thought, and language of another person, whether living or dead, through music, literature, the visual arts, or conversation—this is the ethical burden of *agapē* in the arts.

The theme of a nearer, "more mighty" self had a grip on Gaddis, obviously. And although he cites many models in history and in literature—Socrates, Michelangelo, Glenn Gould,[10] Tolstoy, Wyatt Gwyon in his first novel—at the end of his life he was preoccupied with one "exalted friend" and mentor, who had been crucial to his work on *The Recognitions*. Next to a passage in the notes citing "Bitter age (me)," "my youth," and "the self who would do more," Gaddis has an arrow pointing down to the letters MSD. Martin S. Dworkin, as we have seen, was in the fifties a widely published critic, photographer, and editor who pushed Gaddis, himself unpublished, to a standard he would not have achieved on his own. Later in life, when their fortunes were reversed, Gaddis was able to look back and see that Dworkin all along was using his own incipient failure as evidence of integrity while Gaddis's eventual (though long-delayed) worldly success was constructed as a sellout or, worse, intellectual theft. The accusation is again noted by Gaddis in a frail hand: "You have let me down"; and two years after Dworkin's death in 1996, Gaddis continued to feel a "need to speak with those no longer here." The accuser never stopped haunting Gaddis's conscience.

The theme of intellectual property is made explicit in the final and perhaps happily discarded attempt at giving context for the "insane project" that Gaddis, in the end, let stand alone. Within months of Dworkin's death, Gaddis composed a conversation in a hospital corridor between a man and a woman, friends of the "man on the bed" who can be identified not as Lear, and not as Gaddis, but as Dworkin.

Here is the alternative opening Gaddis drafted:

—Nobody here.

—Must have taken him down for one of their procedures. They'll probably bring him back stupefied, like the kangaroo.

—The what?

—You'll see. Beautiful out there isn't it, those great trees and the sun in the leaves, almost makes you want to believe in God.

—It's the, what?

—Makes you wish you believed in God I said, those great trees and the leaves. Try to talk some sense to him he'll just lie here looking out, all those leaves he'll say, how can there be so many leaves, look at them. How can there be so many! Will you look at this mess? Papers, books, scraps of notes piled up everyplace, the night table, the windowsill, the only chair it's like the apartment he used to have, every chair and table piled with books, newspapers, no place to sit down when he'd ask me up to visit in the middle of the night. Day started late afternoon and stayed with it till dawn when he was still teaching, marking papers, writing out comments on some muddled student's essay twice as long as the essay itself, he'd get in a frenzy because he cared, because he cared so deeply not for the student no, for the ideas. The word got around and finally only three signed on for his fall course so they dropped it, dropped him, sheer matter of cash flow. He wanted to be a great teacher, was a great teacher but needed great students. Same thing here isn't it? Same thing gone over the edge in this insane project of his, here it is, right on top, listen. Opens right up with "No but you see I've got to explain all this because I don't,

we don't know how much time there is left, have to finish this work
of mine when I get this property divided up," you see?

The "leaves of the trees outside"—all that is "outside" the voices and
systems at the start of his greatest novel, *J R*—are all there is, this time
around. They are the same leaves, whose turning he regrets having to experience alone, during the autumn after he'd been left by his second wife:
"nobody to share the small great things of life with like the turning of the
leaves," as he told his lifelong friend John Napper.[11] The desire to believe
in a god who can produce "so many leaves" in excess of any one person's
need, not least the need to assert one's personal identity within a God-
given plenitude, quickly turns to a reflection on the leaves of pages that are
equally beyond our ability to grasp or organize. The kangaroo in the discarded opening is later identified, in the published version, as "Huizinga's
kangaroo" in *Homo Ludens*, and this too bears on the religious concerns
of a man on his deathbed. But he's hardly prepared to embrace belief; the
kangaroo is meant to suggest more of a collapse of all distinction "when
one doesn't know belief from make-believe," as Gaddis's narrator says (*AA*
19). Belief for Gaddis was always in danger of tilting more toward a religious rapture that is unreasonable and asocial, something more pagan than
Christian and grounded in the element of play as (in Huizinga's words) a
"kind of frenzy or delirium which is neither conceived nor born in a man's
soul except by the inspiration of heaven. It is alien to us, its spell is wrought
from without; it is a transport, an infinite rapture away from reason and
natural sense." When one "accepts a sacred identity between two things
of a different order, say a human being and an animal. . . . [T]he identity,
the essential oneness of the two goes far deeper than the correspondence
between a substance and a symbolic image. It is a mystical unity. The one
has become the other. In his magic dance the savage is a kangaroo."

At the time of their early conversations, it seemed to Gaddis as if there
was nothing Dworkin "didn't know, nothing you hadn't read," but Gaddis, the onetime "wide eyed youth," is now capable in his final days of
questioning the shade of the perpetually older man: "Did you really know
the things that I thought you knew?" And does it matter, finally, where
an idea originated in the uncopyrightable act of creative transformation?
Possibly Gaddis did take another man's ideas and perhaps, in a sense, he
wrote another man's book; but that "other" self was as far distant from
Dworkin as from Gaddis himself. Through the compositional process
threatened on all sides by the chance of error Gaddis became something more than what either he or Dworkin had been. With Dworkin he
was always the lesser talent but the initial distance between himself and

Dworkin proved no greater, at the end of Gaddis's life, than that between the dying man and his own "youthful self who could do anything." It was partly Dworkin's example that had seen Gaddis through the thousand-page *Recognitions* "without fear." And Dworkin, who had preceded him to the grave by two years, was again on his mind as *Agapē Agape* finally came together, a living shadow to go with the proliferating fictive doubles. The intensity between the two men had never gone beyond the intellectual—"No the passion was. . . . No no no nothing like that no, first thing people think now don't even think, just take it for granted, the intensity of it the excitement the intoxication."

In notes Gaddis made while concluding his final fiction, Dworkin appears as both an "enabler" and an "accuser," an intense teacher whose intellectual generosity exacted a psychic toll: "that was always his thing, the accuser, you've let me down, you've betrayed me; my 'dialogues' with him (he talked) were so important to me to feeling able to do what I did (REC) unafraid." Dworkin was always older—only by a year or so but "an overwhelming difference" in the prime of creative development: "those years were packed with his mind, his lust for knowing everything." This one-sided dialogue finds its answering voice in the fiction. The intensity of a lifelong conversation gets carried forward into old age, and the shared thoughts promise to survive death, because these men really believed— they were creatively driven by the faith—that literature and the arts were the place where a few unique minds could meet in a kind of fellowship.

Although the material on Dworkin never found its way into the final draft of *Agapē Agape*, Gaddis preserved in the published version a conversational impulse similar to what had seen him through the composition of *The Recognitions*. Feeling a "need to speak with those no longer here," Gaddis this time channeled his thoughts into a series of imaginary conversations—Walter Benjamin in dialogue with Johan Huizinga, Nietzsche communing with himself in his final mad days spent mostly improvising on the piano, and the man on the bed in direct conversation with various characters from fiction: Svengali (from *Trilby*), Hoffmann (from Offenbach's posthumously published opera), Pozdnyshev (from *The Kreutzer Sonata*). In each case music, the art most conducive to unspoken fellowship, is the medium and occasion for the conversation. Its appreciation is best expressed by two people together, listening and keeping quiet for as long as the music lasts. But the agitations that such listening might cause were understood by Tolstoy, an author whose role as a secular prophet dismayed Gaddis but whose work he never ceased quoting. Music in *The Kreutzer Sonata* is a source of dangerous emotionality and physical connection. Tolstoy's narrator, Pozdnyshev, complains that piano recitals initiated "the greater part of the adulteries in our society."[12] But music is also recognized as creating a separate place where one experiences emotions and sensations that are less easily defined:

> "How can I put it? Music makes me forget myself, my real position; it transports me to some other position not my own. Under the influence of music it seems to me that I feel what I do not really feel, that I understand what I do not understand, that I can do what I cannot do. . . . Music carries me immediately and directly into the mental condition of the man who composed it. My soul merges with his and together with him I pass from one condition into another, but why this happens I don't know."[13]

The experience Pozdnyshev struggles to define is neither exaltation nor entertainment. It is something akin rather to the mental communion enacted by Gaddis in *Agapē Agape*. Against all forgeries, simulations, and wastes of the world, this was the one consolation that Gaddis held on to during the last stages of composition: that the life of the mind in collaboration with other minds, the fraternal love that he felt in his recollection of a friend no longer here, and the disciplined recognition of the achievements of past writers would give to his work a staying power beyond his own, finally human, powers of caring and invention.

The day before Gaddis died, Matthew called John Sherry, a friend and coeval living close by in Sag Harbor, to say they were going to bring him home from the hospital that afternoon. Sherry recalls that Gaddis's condition had deteriorated markedly from a previous visit a couple of days earlier. His hand was pitiably frail and his voice was so enfeebled that Sherry had to lean close to make out his words: "Matthew's getting the ambulance and we're going directly to the crematorium." Sherry was unsure whether these startling words indicated confusion or gallows humor. "But," he adds, "Willie was not much given to confusion where words were concerned."

That day, William Gass received a message that Gaddis wanted to talk to him, but the hospital operator gave him the wrong number in Long Island. The tragedy of lost messages pursued Gaddis to the end. And his own refusal to give up self-control: on the ride home from the hospital, he again insisted on being driven to the crematorium. At home, after all the attentions of a hospice worker and his immediate family's discretions, he asked his daughter Sarah if anybody understood what was happening, and he was visibly relieved to have his knowledge confirmed. When the hospice worker assumed a best case scenario and told Gaddis he could take care of this and that tomorrow, he put a stop to the charade: "I'm not going to be here tomorrow. I'm finished here. I'm going *tonight*." Later that night, as his son Matthew recalls, he said that the woman's upbeat attitude reminded him of the time early in his first marriage when a vacuum salesman had visited him and his wife Pat, insisting that they consider leasing the machine when they barely had rent money that month. Nothing they could do or say would get the man to leave. And here was Gaddis now, with a heart collapsed by emphysema and a body poisoned by chemotherapy—with no currency of life left—and he was again being sold something he could not afford.

Gaddis's life ended, like his last fiction, not in a melodrama but in a direct confrontation of the moment, an acceptance—or rather, an active embrace—of death in its materiality. That night, he took two glasses of vodka and some cigarettes—his first in years, which he inhaled as if they were giving him breath, not taking it away.[14] Later in the night, after taking a light sedative and sleeping briefly, Gaddis sat up in bed, raised his arms above his head, and started making small waving motions. Through most of the previous day, his voice had been too weak to hear on the phone, but he had enough strength to go on conducting into the early morning hours. As a boy, when he didn't know his schoolmasters were watching, he'd taken the role of Walter Damrosch, conducting an "interested orchestra" of playmates at the Merricourt boarding school. He died on the morning of 16 December 1998, two weeks before his seventy-sixth birthday.

At his death, he left four novels, the final novella in manuscript, and enough essays and occasional pieces to be published as a book. His archives were stored at first in a warehouse in Long Island City. (His one fear as we have seen, as he grew older, was that he would end his days, like his father, "eating a single chop in a room in Queens.") In good order, the papers were sold to Washington University, St. Louis, and at Gass's suggestion placed in the Special Collections there. Within a year, his closest longtime friends at his home in Sag Harbor, John Sherry and Saul Steinberg, had died, and so had his first wife, Pat. Gaddis himself had always sympathized with William Faulkner's "ambition to be, as a private individual, abolished and voided from history, leaving it markless, no refuse save for the printed books." Yet the letters, collected for publication in 2013, and the archive itself are now part of that history. And just as any literary work is fulfilled only in the absence of the author, this posthumous reflection on *agapē* and the art of fiction is all one could have asked of Gaddis. Its continuation, and the ages-long literary conversation he engaged and extended, now depend on us.

NOTES

## Introduction

1. "Postmodernism" may have been the name that for a decade or two was applied to these diverse writers. Regardless of its usefulness as a term of periodization (and we have yet to come up with a better one for our present cultural state), postmodernism, once named, is then easy for media to dismiss in their (distinctively postmodern) search for the next big thing. I heard Coover make these remarks in March 2007 at a Paris conference put together for the retirement of Marc Chénetier, who helped bring American fiction into the French curriculum.

2. Smith introduced Gaddis to the New York State Writers Institute at the University of Albany, 4 April 1990; a few years later, when *Frolic* was about to be published, Gaddis had a half-hour conversation on National Public Radio with Smith.

3. Walker, 18.

4. See his response to the editors of the *Iowa Review* in *L* 495–96.

5. In the fullest, definitive response to Franzen, Michael Ravitch notes how much of literature this quite conventional social realist author is ready to dismiss, including Virginia Woolf and Samuel Beckett along with those I've mentioned. Clearly Franzen is attacking not merely Gaddis nor difficulty in fiction writing but the retention of *any* literary standard against which present practice might be judged.

6. Green, 1. We can sympathize with Green's critical engagement with all those who incompetently reviewed Gaddis's first novel, and (to varying degrees) every succeeding book each with its complex network of mostly unacknowledged enfolding of other literary texts. Yet, in the average reviewer's misrecognitions and predictable complaints about "erudition," "elitism," "difficulty," and "inaccessibility," can we not also hear the half-articulated voice of all those readers who, recognizing only that some kind of allusion is being made, sense all too well that they are being left out? There can be no power in quoting a literary source out of context for readers who never granted authority to that source in the first place. It was Pierre Bourdieu who argued, after literary modernism had become an established part of the university curriculum, that its aesthetics of quotation protected the legitimacy of an elitist culture by discomforting, even excluding, readers who are not able by education or social position to place a quotation with ease.

7. Gaddis cited by Helgesen, pagination unknown.

8. To Edith Gaddis, 9 August 1950 (*L* 155–56; hereafter letters not cited as *L* can be assumed to be at WU).

9. To Warren Kiefer, 28 July 1974 (*L* 292).

10. Dr. Bernard Looks describes how Gaddis's close friend from the 1950s, Martin Dworkin, after contributing early to Gaddis's knowledge became a lifelong weight on the more successful author's conscience; see "The Novelist and His Mentor."

11. Gaddis described himself similarly in a letter to William Gass dated 25 June 1993: "And so I will hope to appear at your doorstep much like Prince K. in D[ostoevsky]'s *Uncle's Dream* arriving at Mordasov 'so decrepit, so worn out, that as one looked at him the thought instinctively occurred to one that in another minute he might drop to pieces' having, last week, a 10year lithium battery pacemaker installed beneath the clavicle as a cautionary step before next week's shaving of the prostate with other repairs to follow ('the Prince had made a brilliant debut, he had led a gay life, flirted, had made several tours abroad, sang songs, made puns, and had at no period been distinguished by the brilliance of his intellectual gifts. Of course he had squandered all his fortune, and found himself in his old age without a farthing')" (*L* 489).

12. Kerouac, 534, 536.

13. Coe, 8.

14. Ben Marcus is here summarizing Franzen in *P* 380.

15. As he wrote to his mother at the age of twenty from the U.S. quarter boat in St. Louis where he'd found work, "The boys here are a ripping bunch, and the food good and plenty (4 meals a day). And they all think I'm an Arizona cowboy! We do have fun!" (to Edith Gaddis, 21 April 1942) (*L* 32).

16. Conversation with Mike Gladstone over the course of the year 2011.

17. The excerpt appeared in *Harper's* June 1975 issue (47–54, 59–66). On page 719 of the novel, the phrase NONE OF US GREW BUT THE BUSINESS appears on a passing truck that also pictures five dwarfs who are house painters.

18. Konstantinou points out how almost nobody, from the time in the early sixties when *The Recognitions* was first reprinted, approaches Gaddis without first having been a fan of Pynchon. That is true for me, who attended university in the 1980s, as it is for undergraduates who find their way into my courses in contemporary fiction. It was no less true for Richard Powers, who told critic Stephen Burn he "read *The Recognitions* in 1980, having recently dropped out of graduate school and got [a] job working as a second-shift computer operator in an isolated facility on a renovated, nineteenth-century wharf in Boston. I had recently read *V.*, and I could feel the direct genealogy. The book just amazed me, and I am still living with it and working my way through all the material he opened up for me" (*LS* 164).

19. Remarks to the New York State Writers Institute at the University of Albany, 4 April 1990. When he was invited by an editor at Scribner's to blurb John Aldridge's *Talents and Technicians: Literary Chic and the New Assembly-Line Fiction* (1992), Gaddis has something to say about "the material under fire here." Like Aldridge, Gaddis had his patience tried by "Raymond Carver's 'story' ["A Small, Good Thing"] about the birthday cake, manipulated sentimentality &c & I looked in vain in these pages' exploration of the self fulfilling/defeating plague of Teaching Creative Writing—my own brief & depressing foray among undergraduates to witness—for the debt Carver apparently felt to a major minimalist in terms of talent John Gardner whose numbing influence seems to persist beyond the grave" (to Erika Goldman, 7 November 1991) (*L* 475).

20. In "The First Belgian Radio Television Interview" with Johan Thielemans, taped August 1984 in New York City, Gaddis discussed the way word processing might be consistent with his own compositional techniques: He points out that his work "involves immense piles of notes and trying to organize notes, really." He

recognizes that word processors might eventually "simplify what I do, which is to try to get a theme which I am going to develop fifty pages later and then reappear forty pages later and finally come to a head in another hundred pages. So I generally do make very elaborate outlines and then do what a word-processor does in the most crude fashion, which is to take a pair of scissors, have pretty much of the material that is going to be involved in the next scene in the book, and write it down in little snippets and then cut them up and then lay them on a table, and move them around like a puzzle until there seems to be a flow in the dialogue or in the events, and then write that in a rough draft and then rewrite it and then rewrite it and then possibly throw it out—I mean this too can happen." Thielmans thought of it as "a collage-kind of exercise" but Gaddis rejected the arbitrariness of most visual collages; as we'll see in the chapters on *The Recognitions*, the "palimpsest" is a better figure for the process, since the elements are more layered than spread out, with varying nuances of meaning and also narrative flows emerging from the conjoined materials. I discuss print anticipations of new media writing in "The Processual Page: Materiality and Consciousness in Print and Hypertext."

21. Lisa Siraganian discusses the shift of the art world from its center in Paris to New York, as this is portrayed in Gaddis's version of the Greenwich Village scene (*LS* 101–14).

22. Dick Dowling, who Denham also dated a few years later, went on to write a novel titled *All the Beautiful People*.

## Chapter 1

1. Coen tells the aunts that his name is spelled without the *h* but the sisters pronounce it "Cohen"; evidently they did not catch the correction. Are we, the readers, any more attentive?

2. Hazel Bond to Ida Williams, 5 May 1937.

3. A. L. Meredith to Ida Williams, May 1937.

4. Kabel, pagination unknown.

5. A. L. Williams to Ida Williams, 18 February 1935.

6. *Union City Times Gazette* (Indiana), 10 February 1947—an obituary of Ernest Williams by an unknown author.

7. Puffenbarger. Online at http://wvmea.tripod.com/jp99-5.htm.

8. Handy, D4.

9. Ibid.

10. *Union City Times Gazette* (see note 6).

11. As recalled by WG's Harvard acquaintance and later Village companion Ormonde de Kay in an interview with Charles Monaghan.

12. Park, online at http://theunarchivable.blogspot.com/2007/09/piece-on-sebald-gaddis-and-bernhard.html.

## Chapter 2

1. Conversation with Sarah Gaddis, June 2010.

2. Smith, 38–39.

3. Ibid., 36.

4. Excerpts of the letterhead and sidebar for stationery used by Ruth Beardslee Kingsbury, B.A., and John Howard Kingsbury, M.A., who went by "Uncle John" and "Aunt Ruthie" at Merricourt. Arguably, the school could represent an

early example of the corporatization of family life, which would become Gaddis's signature theme in *J R*. But the attentiveness and the pace of communication (by letters, in visits) allowed for a mutual recognition among parent, child, and surrogate aunt and uncle.

5. To Edith Gaddis, 21 March 1931.

6. To Edith Gaddis, 12 May 1931 and 28 March 1931; to Dr. Wilson (first name unknown), 10 March 1931.

7. To Edith Gaddis, 3 April 1934.

8. To Edith Gaddis, undated.

9. To Samuel E. Williams, 13 February 1933.

10. To Edith Gaddis, undated 1935.

11. To Edith Gaddis, 1 February 1931.

12. To Edith Gaddis, 23 February 1932.

13. Ibid.

14. To Edith Gaddis, 15 January 1930 or 1931.

15. To "Granga" (Ida Williams), 31 December 1934.

16. To Edith Gaddis, 24 October 1933.

17. To "Granga," 19 September 1934.

18. To S. E. Williams, 9 December 1930 (*L* 15) and 3 January 1931.

19. To S. E. Williams, 2 December 1930; cf. letter to "Granga," Easter 1933, when the pen evidently broke "and Mom's getting it fixed." A picture of the pen, and cap, is included. A fascination with the materiality of writing runs all the way through his Harvard years when they released "the new Parker '51' pen . . . gee they're *something*" (undated, from Cambridge). In later years he would complain in letters about mechanical problems with certain typewriters.

20. To Edith Gaddis, 25 May 1930 or 1931.

21. To Edith Gaddis, 31 December 1934.

22. To Edith Gaddis, undated 1934 or 1935.

23. To Edith Gaddis, 28 April 1932.

24. To S. E. Williams, 7 October 1932.

25. To Edith Gaddis, 10 October 1932.

26. To Edith Gaddis, 16 November 1931.

27. To Dr. Wilson, from Cape Cod (on stationery from Gifford House, Provincetown), 1930 or 1931.

28. To Edith Gaddis, 26 September 1932.

29. To June R. Cox, 24 January 1983 (*L* 389).

30. Undated letter to Edith Gaddis at the start of a school term, likely the autumn of 1933.

31. Ruth B. Kingsbury to Edith Gaddis, 4 April 1932.

32. William Gass recalled McCarthy's decision in his memorial speech, "Memories of Master Gaddis," 152.

33. To Edith Gaddis, 26 January 1942 (*L* 25).

34. Gaddis's settler origins are clear on the mother's side, as described in chapter 1. My own researches have not uncovered any links between Gaddis's father William Thomas or his grandfather William and a still earlier Thomas Gaddis (1742–1834), an officer in the American Revolutionary War known for a fort he built as a refuge from the Indians in Uniontown, Pennsylvania.

35. Gaddis, drafts of "Ernest and the Zeitgeist," WU box 127, folder 450.

36. Looks.

37. Ibid., and conversation with Mike Gladstone, 2011.

38. In his expanded *William Gaddis*, Moore regards the whiskey-drinking, cigarette-smoking, and determinedly absent Judge Crease as "a portrait of the artist as an old man" (176).

39. The conceit derives from Flaubert and is cited in Gaddis's final fiction, *Agapē Agape* (50).

### Chapter 3

1. Gaddis's daughter Sarah based the character Lad Thompkins on Gaddis in her novel *Swallow Hard* (1990). There, the adult Thompkins appears as similarly spare and uncommunicating. Sarah imagines an early meeting with Sally Anne, based on Gaddis's first wife, Pat Black: "she watched Lad Thompkins, watched the cigarette travel its measured distance. Apart from that movement there was nothing extra about him, no flesh or gestures, he was so contained that his reserve fell short of grace" (26).

2. To Edith Gaddis, 29 March 1949 (*L* 129–30).

3. The rapidity of his heartbeat was noted during one of his periods of hospitalization at Harvard when he was age eighteen, but (as he told Edith) "I've had that for a couple of years" (3 November 1941).

4. Kinney, online at http://www.williamgaddis.org/reminisce/remhkinney.shtml/.

5. Arvid Friberg, e-mail to Steven Moore, 27 December 2007; the father and personal friend of Gaddis was also named Arvid.

6. Friberg, e-mail to the author, 31 March 2014.

7. Friberg, e-mail to Moore.

8. Conversation by phone with Friberg, November 2012.

9. To Edith Gaddis, 2 January 1942 (*L* 21).

10. To Judith R. Cox, 24 January 1983 (*L* 389).

11. To Edith Gaddis, 17 January 1942 (*L* 24).

12. To Edith Gaddis, April 1942 (*L* 29).

13. To Edith Gaddis, 6 April 1942 (*L* 30).

14. Pennebaker, 158. That Gaddis was as careless about driving in his youth as he was about fighting is indicated with good-natured humor in his high school yearbook next to his senior picture: "You can't tell what his car'll do next, / Or what Bill's going to say, / His manner always carefree, / And his motto 'toujours gai.'"

15. To Edith Gaddis, 21 April 1942 (*L* 32).

16. To Edith Gaddis, 25 July 1942 (*L* 35).

17. To Edith Gaddis, 7 June 1942 (*L* 34).

18. To Edith Gaddis, 17 January 1942 (*L* 24).

19. To Edith Gaddis, 21 December 1948 (*L* 113).

20. To Edith Gaddis, 29 January 1948 (*L* 87). Accurate though his judgment might be, the desire to set himself and his work in opposition to American society in order to "rescue" it from "vulgarity" (to Edith, 4 May 1948 [*L* 103]) is one of the least promising stances he adopted during his early formation as a writer, and his ability to drop this particular stance is crucial to the success of his second novel, *J R*.

21. In a letter to Moore, Gaddis doubted his old Village friend Vincent Livelli's recollection that he returned from Central America wearing "my 'unimpaired

right arm in a sling', but Vincent's image is lively enough that I won't argue" (3 January 1983 [*L* 368]).

22. To Michael (last name unknown), 13 December 1986 (*L* 427).

23. To Edith Gaddis, 15 January 1948 (*L* 82). Bernard Winebaum and Jake Bean were Harvard/Greenwich Village friends.

24. To Edith Gaddis, April 1942 (*L* 30).

25. To Edith Gaddis, 16 January 1943 (*L* 43). The albumin in his urine indicated a kidney condition, the edema was in the legs. The doctors' inability to treat or explain either occurrence, like their predecessors' mystification during his youthful illness, makes for a refrain in letters home from Harvard: "they wouldn't let me out til this morning because of it (has been 3+) albumin tests. However had to practically fight my way out this am and am going to see Dr. Contralto in the morning. Am going to tell him that if he wants to incarcerate me up here I'd just as soon leave . . ." (9 November 1941). His time away, in Texas and Arizona and Colorado, gave him at least the feeling of overcoming his powerlessness: "I think it's foolish to try an urinalysis—besides have no place to so just tell Williams and all his buddies to find some other where to peddle their bottles and pills—I'm all thru with them" (15 August 1942) (*L* 37).

26. To Edith Gaddis, 19 October 1941 (*L* 19).

27. To Edith Gaddis, 21 April 1942 (*L* 32).

28. From Ida Way to Edith, 9 June 1942.

29. 21 November 1941, sent from "Broadway, Bethpage," a town not far from Farmingdale, Long Island.

30. To Edith Gaddis, 10 December 1943 (*L* 50).

31. Ibid.

32. To Edith Gaddis, 17 February 1944.

33. To Edith Gaddis, 11 February 1943 (*L* 44).

34. To Crystal Alberts, cited in *PE* 237.

35. To Edith Gaddis, 11 February 1943 (*L* 43).

36. To Edith Gaddis, 19 February 1943 (*L* 44).

37. To Edith Gaddis, 12 February 1944 (*L* 51).

38. To Edith Gaddis, undated (March 1944).

39. To Edith Gaddis, 27 February 1944 (*L* 53).

40. Broyard, "Remembering William Gaddis in the Nineteen-Fifties," 13. Jean Campbell is not mentioned by name or described by Broyard, possibly because the "Radcliffe girl" he himself went on to date was still alive in 1995. It was in any case Broyard's practice in his many memoirs to leave unnamed, or alter names of those he knew who were still alive, notably "Sheri Donatti" for "Martinelli" in his posthumous publication *Kafka Was the Rage*.

41. To Edith Gaddis, 10 March 1948.

42. To Edith Gaddis, 12 November 1942 (*L* 40).

43. To Edith Gaddis, 4 October 1942 (*L* 38).

44. To Katherine Anne Porter, 7 April 1948 (*L* 96).

45. To Edith Gaddis, undated (early 1942).

46. To John and Pauline Napper, 12 December 1951 (*L* 199).

## Chapter 4

The chapter epigraph is from a letter to Edith Gaddis, 12 January 1948 (*L* 81).

1. To Edith Gaddis, 28 November 1944 (*L* 55).

2. To Edith Gaddis, 1 August 1945 (*L* 57).
3. To Edith Gaddis, 4 August 1945 (*L* 57).
4. To Edith Gaddis, 13 March 1948 (*L* 92).
5. Ormonde de Kay interview.
6. Ibid.
7. Letter to Edith Gaddis, December 1947 (*L* 77).
8. Kinney, "Reminiscences."
9. To Edith Gaddis, 6 March 1947 (*L* 59).
10. To Edith Gaddis, 8 April 1948 (*L* 99).
11. "The Novelist and His Mentor." Kinney for his part recalls walking with Gaddis in New York and running into Baumgarten, "a young-appearing, thin, intellectual woman who had been the spark behind *The Recognitions* at Harcourt, he told me. She was then with another house. She shared his disenchantment with Harcourt."
12. To Edith Gaddis, 11 May 1948 (*L* 105).
13. To John Napper, 15 December 1954 (*L* 217).
14. To John and Pauline Napper, 10 August 1953 (*L* 209).
15. Letter to James Cappio, 21 May 1993 (*L* 488). Peter Wolfe notes how this trait of negligence is assigned each of the artists in *J R*, whose exaggerated self-regard is accompanied, tellingly, by a nihilism that is wholly within the system of waste and neglect that their art supposedly offsets: "Eigen is as careless with his unfinished book as Bast is with his musical score and Gibbs is with his racetrack winnings [not to mention his sole copy of "Agapē Agape" that he leaves on a refrigerator in the Ninety-Sixth Street apartment where he works over the manuscript haphazardly]. Self-blamers all, they fight success" (181).
16. "The Novelist and His Mentor."
17. Sonia Johnson, in her dissertation chapter on Gaddis, squares these moments of self-consciousness in the novel with his "apparent surprise about the actual reception." She finds in Gaddis something Mark McGurl (in *The Program Era*) notices in Flannery O'Connor's fiction, that is, a representation of failure designed, whether consciously or not, and whether successful or not, to stave off actual failure.
18. Even here, in the economics of the thing, Gaddis was fully aware of the real possibility of failure. As he wrote to John Napper in England (30 March 1954), when the "10-pound manuscript" was submitted at last to Harcourt, Brace, "It comes we find to some half-million words, some thousand printed pages, some 7$–10$— (the £3 novel) per copy I'm afraid, which assures it against anything so vulgar as a popular success." In the event, the book "was priced at $7.50 at a time when most hardback novels cost between $3.00 and $5.00" (*L* 214, 215).
19. Letter to Edith Gaddis from Mexico City, 3–4 May 1947 (*L* 74).
20. Ibid., *L* 75.
21. Berkley interview, 57.
22. Kerouac, 534, 536.
23. Headnote in *L* 211. For more on him, see Steven Moore's introduction to Ansen's *Contact Highs: Selected Poems 1957–1987* (Elmwood Park, Ill.: Dalkey Archive Press, 1989).
24. To John Napper, 4 January 1954 (*L* 212).
25. To Edith Gaddis, 16 November 1950 (*L* 168).
26. To Edith Gaddis, 19 January 1948 (*L* 83).
27. To Edith Gaddis, 16 November 1950 (*L* 168).

28. Denham, quoted in Darius James, "Sleeping with the Bad Boys," *Books and Publishing* (supplement to *NYPress*), 30 April 1997, 13.

29. Letter from Alan Ansen, 25 January 1955.

30. Ibid.

31. Letter from Ansen, 30 January 1955.

32. Letter from Ansen, 18 February 1953. Gaddis and Ansen befriended Burroughs around the same time in the early fifties.

33. Letter from Ansen, 27 February 1954.

34. Letter from Ansen, 8 February 1954.

35. Letter from Ansen, 30 January 1954.

36. Letter from Ansen, 1 January 1954.

37. Letter from Emmart, written on "Duke University" letterhead, subheaded "The Parapsychology Laboratory," 26 June 1954. Since Emmart's father in another letter to Gaddis mentions this department without a hint of irony, we can assume it existed.

38. Letter from Emmart, undated.

39. Letter from Ansen, 7 December 1953.

40. Ibid.

41. Ibid.

42. From Grant Dougdale (of Harcourt, Brace & Company), 13 September 1956. Other letters throughout the year are signed by the secretary Rita Gorse (later, Rita G. Moran) and Denver Lindley, who in December sends "the final check from the mysterious lady. I have, by the way, finally met her and found her very charming. She intimated that perhaps in the fullness of time it would be nice if she met you. Will you let me know how you feel about this?" In the archive, I found no record of Gaddis's response, and the only words from the "mysterious" donor are those cited in a letter from Lindley on 6 July 1956: "I am happy that this small assistance has had a positive effect, and you may tell him, if you wish, that the manner in which he has accepted this relationship and its meaning has had the same heartwarming result with me."

43. Taylor, 38.

44. Many episodes in *The Recognitions* are set on Christmas Eve, a time that, as Wolfe observes, "emphasizes the isolation, coercion, and panic fostered by today's America. . . . Individualism breeds aggressiveness in Gaddis. Because each person stands alone in a competitive society, he or she lacks the fellowship that quiets fear" (292).

45. The "church gimmick" that Ellery concocts is a show like *Lives of the Saints* or *Let's Get Married*. Taylor observes how Ellery's "formula" of "staging events as if they were real" anticipates by several decades the rise of reality television (44). The anticipation of televisual "reality" is done with a full awareness of its absurdity and basic lack of interest in the well-being of participants—when, for example, in *J R* a politician's staged rescue of Rhoda out on a skyscraper's ledge ends in his mistakenly pushing the teenager off, to her death.

46. To John Napper, 4 May 1951 (*L* 195).

47. To Edith Gaddis, 27 December 1948 (*L* 117).

48. Franzen, 267. As noted in the previous chapter, there is plenty of evidence that ordinary, educated readers less influential and less well placed than Franzen have had far less trouble seeing the synthetic, organizational work that is there,

such as those early readers who followed Jack Green's early 1960s *newspaper* articles in defense of Gaddis, or readers who more recently posted their commentaries, page by page and scene by scene, during the summer 2012 collective reading of *J R* hosted by the *Los Angeles Review of Books* at http://tumblr.lareview ofbooks.org/post/25730564051/occupygaddis-began-as-a-hashtag.

49. Stanley quotes from section 277 of *Beyond Good and Evil*: "It is too bad! Always the old story! When a man has finished building his house, he finds that he has learnt unawares something which he *ought* absolutely to have known before he began to build. The eternal, fatal 'Too late!' The melancholia of everything *completed*!" Accessed from http://www.williamgaddis.org/recognitions/27anno1 .shtml.

## Chapter 5

The chapter epigraph is from a letter to Edith Gaddis, 11 April 1949 (*L* 132–33).

1. To Charles Socarides, February or March 1948; Moore identifies this letter as the earliest "to explain the essential idea and plot of *R*" (*L* 88).

2. Letter to Napper, 27 September 1950 (*L* 162).

3. "The Second Belgian Radio Television Interview" with Freddy de Vree, taped May 1988; Johan Thielemans conducted the first interview in 1984.

4. The "Naked" title mentioned to Porter in a letter from Panama, 7 April 1948 (*L* 94).

5. To Edith Gaddis, 29 January 1948 (*L* 95).

6. To Katherine Anne Porter, 7 April 1948 (*L* 95).

7. De Rougemont's summary of Platonic love is quoted in Moore's online annotations to *R*.

8. What Wyatt doesn't tell his youthful competitor and doting admirer is that the novel concerns (as Moore writes in his annotations) "the relationship between Adolphe, a young man, and Ellénore, a count's mistress (which has its parallel in the relationship between Otto and Esther)." Gaddis confirms the context and stressed the key point "that Otto has not read it & is vainly & sublimely unaware of the parallel" (letter to Moore, 12 June 1983). Would the vast majority of potential readers be any more aware? Gaddis must have known, the deeper he got into the project, how exclusive his practice was becoming. But like another author cited in the novel, the like-minded American satirist Charles Fort, he may not have given a damn (literally, if "by the damned I mean the excluded" [Fort is mentioned on 81]).

9. Recounted in an unsent letter to Steven Moore, 18 July 1998 (*L* 527).

10. Broyard, "Remembering William Gaddis in the Nineteen-Fifties," 13. Broyard knew what it was, in this era, to live in a condition of self-imposed secrecy. He never, during the Village years (when he knew Gaddis) or in later life, told any of his acquaintances that he was black; and even later he would tell his fiancée, Sandy Nelson, only after he was outed by two close friends. His immediate family, all but one of whom (the older sister, Shirley) was light skinned, had moved from New Orleans to a black neighborhood in Brooklyn. But no one, except for Sheri Martinelli on a surprise visit, ever looked into this background and not even Broyard's posthumous account of the visit (in *Kafka Was the Rage*) mentions the likelihood that she, Sheri, or others in the Village might have known about his origins, or suspected. Besides, as Henry Louis Gates Jr. mentions in a

largely sympathetic account: "wasn't that why everybody came to New York—to run away from the confines of family, from places where people thought they knew who and what you were? Whose family wasn't in some way unsuitable?" ("The Passing of Anatole Broyard," 194). Even if Broyard could sense Gaddis's reticence, so would Gaddis in *The Recognitions* note his own suspicion, likely shared by many others, that Broyard himself was hiding something. What Gaddis writes about the character Max (one of Otto's competitors for the affections of Esme) could apply equally to Broyard (who preceded Gaddis in the pursuit of Sheri): "He always looked the same, always the same age, his hair always the same short length," seemingly "a parody on the moment, as his clothes caricatured a past at eastern colleges where he had never been" (*R* 525). Worse is his "unconscionable smile," which intimates "that the wearer knew all of the dismal secrets of some evil jungle whence he had just come." Gaddis, with an abbreviated but actual past at an eastern college, was able in time to turn his own personal reticence to account in a major (though at first commercially unsuccessful) novel. Broyard, for his part, was expected by many in and out of the publishing world to produce a very important autobiographical novel, though he never managed to publish in his life any but book-length collections of essays from his long tenure as a reviewer and essayist for the *New York Times* and the *Times Book Review*.

11. To Katherine Anne Porter, 7 April 1948 (*L* 93).

12. Ibid.

13. See Denham, *SBB* 253.

14. Letter to Katherine Anne Porter, 21 January 1948 (*L* 84–85).

15. Letter to Katherine Anne Porter, 7 April 1948 (*L* 94). Porter's letter to Gaddis doesn't survive.

16. Letter to Katherine Anne Porter, 21 January 1948 (*L* 84).

17. *New York Times Book Review*, 14 July 1974, 27–28. Tanner's critical judgment was seconded in 1977 by George Stade in the *Partisan Review*: he was reviewing Norman Mailer's biographical essay on Henry Miller, *Genius and Lust*, and there he noted how Mailer, whom many recognized at the time as "our main man of letters," was nonetheless "not the first novelist of his generation. That title belongs to William Gaddis; Joseph Heller is a contender, and Ralph Ellison has been a promising challenger for twenty years. These men do not write novels in a couple of months, or even a couple of years" (623). As early as January 1955 in a letter to Gaddis, before the novel was published, Robert Graves was already calling *The Recognitions* "the great American novel of the 50s."

18. Graves writes: "According to the Clementines, whose religious theory is popularized in a novel called *The Recognitions*, the identity of true religion in all ages depends on a series of incarnations of the Wisdom of God, of which Adam was the first and Jesus the last" (160).

19. Gaddis in a letter to his mother from Costa Rica contrasts the modern tendency toward personal development and self-expression with the alternatives found in Toynbee's *Study of History*: "Because that brilliant man has somehow the meaning of meaning, and never in a smart way, you know, like so many of the books now: how to be free from nervous strain, how to write, how to read, how to be a Chinaman like Lin Yutang, &c &c" (4 May 1948 [*L* 101]).

20. Bildow toward the end of the book is shown departing for Europe, "to get laid," although his wife, ashore, discovers he's left behind his medication for

erectile dysfunction. Viagra would not be widely available until the nineties but there is very little that Gaddis's novels do not anticipate, so systematic was his observation and his clipping of obscure developments in the daily news, and so thoroughgoing was his ambition to tell everything because that was, for Gaddis, "the frantic point. That it all *happened*" (letter to Socarides cited above, n1).

21. *Swallow Hard*, 37–38.

22. To Edith Gaddis, 17 December 1950 (*L* 178). It was a familiar jibe, about "the small-town boy" from Massapequa. More convincing at this time, and what proved consequential, was his sincere desire to return to the refurbished studio there, which he was put in mind of after a visit to the Sussex home of John and Pauline Napper: there, he thought of his mother often, as he told her: "how much you would like this house—an old mill house, parts of it 700 years old! and fireplaces in almost every room, much of it though enough like the studio, and a similar way of life. It is proving to be one of the most pleasant Christmas holidays I've ever spent" (27 December 1950 [*L* 178]).

23. To Edith Gaddis, 20 April 1942 (*L* 30–31).

24. In this respect, the embrace of *The White Goddess*, while signaling a rejection of Gaddis's own modernity, was in no way a rejection of literary *modernism*. Eliot himself published Graves's book in 1948 and the "mythic method" that Eliot described in Joyce and his own poetics—a continual juxtaposition of past and present literary formulations—was a way for these writers to question implicitly, and at times challenge, the rationalization and industrialization of modern life. Not infrequently mythic figures might be projected as a feminine counterforce to rational modernity. That rationalism would come to be embraced *by* women, as Esther embraces commerce and professionalism a full generation before the emergence of second-wave feminism, would come as something of a surprise to Gaddis (as we'll see in his reactions to protests by the underrepresented women authors at the January 1986 meeting of the International PEN Congress, the global writers' association).

25. I owe this observation to Stuart Moulthrop (e-mail of 29 April 2011).

26. Letters to John Napper, 27 September 1950, and David Ulansay, 30 July 1993 (*L* 162, 491).

27. In this respect too the Reverend Gwyon resembles Graves as the latter was depicted in *Tuning Up at Dawn*, a memoir by Robert's son, Tomás, as summarized and cited by Sue Stuart in the 9 January 2005 London *Telegraph*: "Robert worked upstairs in a book-lined room, off-limits to the children, but his son remembers the sounds he made: 'The clink of his pen as he dipped it in the ink well, the scratch of his writing, and the creaky chair scraping the floor when he got up. There was always the feeling that something was going on in there.'"

28. http://readingwilliamgaddis.wordpress.com/ (see post dated 7 June 2013).

29. To Edith Gaddis, 4 May 1948 (*L* 103).

30. Based on his own experiences, Gaddis rejects the sentimentality of another interwar novelist of travel, spirituality, and sexual exploration: Somerset Maugham. In his May 1948 letter to Porter, whom after a single exchange of letters he could trust in all respects, the literary as well as the worldly, Gaddis notes how the "good American" in *The Razor's Edge* may have been "a rootless American, a life I know well enough. But good? Because he was disinterested; that is fine, but I don't remember his doing any acts of disinterested goodness; he wanted to marry

the girl who had turned up a whore—that saintly complex, but it has been done so many times and better explained as such than simply shown as a picture of goodness. And what girl who has gone that far wants to be 'saved' by being married, none that I have known, they usually have their futility pretty well in hand" (*L* 106). In another letter, of 4 January 1954, to his longtime British friend John Napper, Gaddis mentions "some broken glass and a nameless blue-eyed girl on Thursday night" in the town of Hewlett where he was revising *The Recognitions,* but otherwise "sticking pretty close to this infernal machine" (*L* 211).

31. To Edith Gaddis, 4 May 1948 (*L* 103).

32. Ibid.

33. To Edith Gaddis, from Puerto Limón, May 1948 (*L* 105).

34. De Kay's recollections are quoted in *L* 122 from his online interview.

35. To Edith Gaddis, from Paris, 9 July 1949 (*L* 144).

36. Ibid.

37. Ibid.

38. To Katherine Anne Porter, May 1948 (*L* 107).

39. To Edith Gaddis, December 1948 (*L* 120).

40. To Edith Gaddis, 29 July 1950 (*L* 153).

41. To Edith Gaddis, 15 August 1950 (*L* 156).

42. To Edith Gaddis, 6 July 1950 (*L* 153).

43. One wonders if Sheri, then thirty-five, would have appreciated hearing that she was "still beautiful" in her friend's eyes: "yes: even then [when they were both spending time in the Village] I could not understand other people taking your presence for granted and still I cannot, nor understand, no one weeps looking at you, I will." Letter to Sheri Martinelli (in draft, unclear whether sent or not), from Massapequa, summer 1953? (*L* 206).

44. Letter to Edith Gaddis, 13 March 1948.

45. Letter to Edith Gaddis, 9 July 1949 (*L* 145).

46. Letter to Edith Gaddis, undated 1948.

47. Letter to Edith Gaddis, 20 August 1950.

48. Moore, "Sheri Martinelli: A Modernist Muse," 36.

49. To Steven Moore, 18 July 1998 (*L* 527), in response to "Sheri Martinelli: A Remembrance," *Anais* 16 (1998). The letter was unsent, and later found in Gaddis's copy of the journal that published the expanded version of the essay (cited above).

50. Broyard, *Kafka Was the Rage,* 133, 137.

51. Ibid., 137.

52. Feasley's observation was actually made by Gaddis's Paris girlfriend during the period when they "participated in what Miss [Margaret] Williams called the imitation of Greenwich Village, and since Gr Vil is a traditional imitation of the left bank . . ." (letter to Edith Gaddis, 17 June 1949 [*L* 142]).

53. Carr, 467.

54. De Kay interview.

55. Broyard, "Remembering William Gaddis in the Nineteen-Fifties," 13.

56. E-mail from Mark Lewis to Moore, 1 November 2010. Moore contacted Parker in 1984 and was able to obtain a few (but not all) of Gaddis's letters to her before she went silent.

57. As told to Moore in a letter dated 2 February 1984 (*L* 139).

58. Not quite so romantic when he was Bast's age, Gaddis himself would meet in a neighboring farmhouse with a woman whose company he once shared with his boyhood friend Arvid Friberg, Friberg's son recalled (in a letter to Moore and in the author's conversation with him, 14 November 2011).

59. Gaddis in Denham's memoir comes off much better than many of his near contemporaries. "Mailer," she writes, "demonized the wife so she 'deserved' to be killed by the husband. Women were to blame for everything and macho novelists delighted in doing them in (Mailer), impaling them (Pynchon), trashing them (Donleavy), demeaning them (Roth and Bellow), weakening them (Styron), brutalizing them (Robert Stone, Jerzy Koszynski)" (195). That is the view of someone who knew several of the listed writers intimately.

60. Muriel, who moved among artists all her life, was no more impressed by truth claims than by appeals to social relevance: "The arts are not to be trusted," she wrote in terms that apply to Gaddis's accretive, palimpsest method, which she could have observed over their sixteen years together: "Because they are too careful. Art itself fixes everything. The artist says 'I'll do it this way, no that way, no another.' He edits, he halts, he changes. This is not truthful—he withholds. He's a sneak. He figures things out. He changes his mind. He's not truthful. He says maybe—if he's smart-alec—that he's searching for truth. But it's a truth to please him. His truth. And maybe his truth is false" (*E* 237).

61. As Gaddis told Laurel Graeber upon publication of *A Frolic of His Own*, he would rather that "the reader be entertained than manipulated into crocodile tears." Whenever he's writing, he goes on to say, he would "stand back a step or two and see the eventual tragicomedy—the ridiculous nature of how we spend our time getting and spending" (22).

62. Gaddis himself was moved to write in support of his New York senator, Daniel Patrick Moynihan, who had questioned the Reagan administration's clandestine support of the anti-Communist forces in Nicaragua. Gaddis laments that the United States is still practicing covert support of terrorist groups a full decade after the "1973 War Powers Resolution passed following public disclosure of our secret assaults in Cambodia and Laos" (letter of 11 April 1983 [*L* 393]). The continued, continually self-defeating use of wide-open, "covert" activities into the era of the Iraq War, and its reflections in current American fiction, is explored by Timothy Melley in his books *Empire of Conspiracy* (Ithaca, N.Y.: Cornell University Press, 2000) and *The Covert Sphere* (Ithaca, N.Y.: Cornell University Press, 2012).

## Chapter 6

1. Barney Emmart, 5 October 1955. Emmart himself had settled around the same time, by March of 1955, into family life and he would report how "Nina croons softly over your picture" in that month's issue of *Time*: "Mr. Dworkin," the photographer and their mutual acquaintance, "Mr. Gaddis. And Nina swooning over how handsome. . . . Just a typical family scene at home." In the same letter, Emmart asked, "Are you still sure you want to get married?"

2. A. D. Emmart, 4 September 1955.

3. From Majorca, 19 October 1955. Graves wrote a blurb for *R* that was eventually published on the back cover of the 1962 Meridian edition: "The precision of William Gaddis's style is most unusual in his generation of writers. And

I am astonished that one who shows himself so familiar and up-to-date with the mountain of filth, perversions, falsity, and boredom revealed in *The Recognitions*, should have managed to keep his head clear and his heart warm, and his report readable" (quoted in Green, 86). In a letter to Gaddis of 14 January 1955, Graves said he "wrote that testimonial right off after spending a couple of hours sampling the book" and on further reading he remarks, more pointedly, at how the book "throws America back slap in its own face at great length, and with faithful reportage and rambles emphatically on and on with that despairing sense of wasted time and money which makes America what it is (but with Willie Gaddis always ahead of the game himself). I shall be very surprised if it doesn't get hailed—'hailed' is the only word—as the great American novel of the 50s."

4. Letter dated 19 April 1955; second page (and signature) missing.

5. From H. L. Marks, 17 July 1955.

6. Letter dated June 1955.

7. Letter dated November 1955.

8. Letter from Rufus L. Foshee Jr., from Tuscaloosa, Alabama, 1 November 1955.

9. Letter from Bill Corrington, 15 August and 10 September 1955.

10. From New York, 11 June 1955.

11. Author unknown; Gaddis read this one aloud in November 1976 at the McCarthy Arts Center recital hall, as reported in *The Michaelman* 7.

12. From William Hoopes of New York, 22 September 1955.

13. 20 July 1955; underlining in the original.

14. "Otto Friedrich 1929–1995." The document, dated 24 May 1995, was "Read by Lisel Friedrich for Mr. Gaddis, who was unable to attend the Memorial service due to illness." A facsimile is available online at http://ottofriedrich.com/wp-content/uploads/2014/03/William-Gaddis-Tribute.pdf.

15. Berkley interview, 56.

16. Melville, *Pierre*, 376.

17. There are further dimensions to the metaphor of the "shelf." The *Torschlusspanik* referenced in *J R* and *Agapē Agape* is about (literally) the fear of doors closing. Other definitions reference the aging bachelor's fear of being left on the shelf. An author who, like Gaddis, could see his books bound as "Penguin Classics" editions that nonetheless sold fewer than three hundred copies yearly might well feel the panic that comes from having guarded too well the "larger" and "private" book of his life.

18. Harnel, cited in note 13 above, 20 July 1955.

19. Letter to Edith, 27 December 1948 (*L* 119). Gaddis at age twenty-six was not immune to "a vain Delight at being called to the attention of the Great, in any fashion. And so now, Evelyn Waugh actually knows that I exist."

20. In the late 1950s when Pynchon was there, Cornell did not yet have a formal creative writing program. But Baxter Hathaway had already begun conducting workshops that Pynchon attended. Hathaway told me, in the eighties when I was at Cornell, about how the class gave a surprised standing ovation after Pynchon read one of his stories aloud.

21. Moore reminds us: "Pound didn't care for *Ulysses*, and regarded *Finnegans Wake* as unreadable" ("Sheri Martinelli," 35). Of course Gaddis insisted throughout his life that he never read *Ulysses*.

22. Ibid., 36.

23. To Edith Gaddis, 4 August 1942 (*L* 35).

24. Tyree cites these passages by Thoreau and Emerson in an essay originally published in 2004 and archived on the Gaddis Annotations website.

25. Tyree cites Emerson's classic essay in the 1862 issue of the *Atlantic Monthly*.

26. Safer, 73.

### Chapter 7

1. To Pat Gaddis, from the Columbus Hotel in Miami, Florida, undated but probably early sixties.

2. To Patricia Black, 29 October 1954 (*L* 217).

3. To Judith Gaddis, 13 March 1979.

4. Marian's complaint is echoed by Muriel Murphy when she speaks of "the strain of the shut-off, shut-in atmosphere of a writer's indentured household," and that presumably was true whether the terms of indenture were set by corporate work (which Gaddis held for most of his two marriages) or by a wealthier partner (or "roommate," as Muriel would speak of her time with Gaddis during their years together from 1979 to 1995) (*E* 59; 119).

5. Gaddis's writings for Pfizer in particular are concerned with making better managers of pharmacists, who contribute much to the shops where they stake some front space, but the "profession is pharmacy, not merchandising. Today, prescriptions and other health aids account for barely half his business. His strong point is not the managerial know-how needed to build up the front of the store. And that is where things are happening" (WU box 135, page 4). Chetwynd remarks that Gaddis did "a lot of writing about this," the theme of management overtaking the autonomy of professionals.

6. To Sarah Gaddis, undated late 1950s.

7. To Sarah Gaddis, 8 December 1986.

8. "Educational Technology Shapes the Future . . . Are You Ready?" (unpaginated); title page reproduced in *RSP* 31.

9. To Frank Kelley, 9 July 1958.

10. Interview with Paul Ingendaay, 18–19 December 1995, East Hampton, Long Island.

11. Ibid.

12. Should any doubt remain as to the biographical source of Gibbs's rant, here is how Gaddis would often recall his situation with the publisher of *The Recognitions*: "I was trying to get the rights back after ten years from the man who was running Harcourt . . . , and you couldn't buy it [in bookstores] . . . it was going for around $300 a copy . . . but they insisted it was still in print. Eh, that meant there were four copies in a warehouse somewhere. . . ." New York State Writers Institute reading, 4 April 1990.

13. "The Novelist and His Mentor."

14. Project summary is given by Ali Chetwynd in "William Gaddis's Education-Writing and His Fiction: A Fuller Archival History."

15. Schiller, Dworkin, Gaddis, "Challenge of Science Series: Problem Areas and Research Goals" (WU).

16. Ibid.

17. Yōkichi Miyamoto, *Eigo seinen* 122 (1 December 1976), translation by Heidi Yamamoto commissioned and quoted by Moore in his *Reader's Guide* (28n66).

18. Interview with Marie-Rose Logan and Tomasz Mirkowicz, 25 June 1981.

19. WU I-23/4.

20. Immanuel Wallerstein distinguishes the modern world system much as Wallace Stevens had distinguished modern poetry ("It Must Change," as he entitled the second section of his long poem "Notes toward a Supreme Fiction"). Wallerstein understands the compulsion to change as a dual legacy, deriving from two imperatives: (1) an economic "imperative of the endless accumulation of capital" that generates, in turn, "a need for constant technological change, a constant expansion of frontiers—geographical, psychological, intellectual, scientific"; and, (2) the political imperative, propagated by the French Revolution, "that political change was not exceptional or bizarre but normal and constant" (*World-Systems Analysis: An Introduction* [Durham: Duke University Press, 2004], 2, 3–4).

21. Gaddis sent the letter by registered mail to his house in Massapequa on 27 August 1956: "the idea itself was older with me than that, though I should have no evidence of how much older. I started to develop this idea into a short novel no later than March 1956; and so far as I know it is one entirely original with myself, in substance and treatment" (*L* 227–28).

22. Pennebaker shared this recollection with Sarah Gaddis in an e-mail dated 4 February 2013.

23. Letter to John D. Seelye, 10 May 1963 (*L* 250).

24. WU folder 474, 2 February 1963, I-1.

25. "Education Technology Shapes the Future: Are You Ready?" Unpaginated spread 3. In *J R*, Gaddis would concoct a project under the direction of former grade school coach Vogel, who sets out to "teleport" a man, J R's former teacher, Dan diCephalis, from "the company's Texas installation" to "an undisclosed receiving point somewhere in Maine" (689). One motivation for sending either a man or a message across long distances is, in cyberneticist Norbert Wiener's words, to extend "man's senses and his capabilities of action from one end of the world to another" (*The Human Use of Human Beings,* 133). But there is also a literary allusion to Henry David Thoreau, who observed a century earlier, in chapter 1 of *Walden,* how "We are in great haste to construct a magnetic telegraph from Maine to Texas; but Maine and Texas, it may be, have nothing important to communicate." Moore first noted the allusion in the *Explicator* 47, no. 1 (Fall 1988): 55, and I elaborate on this theme in "The Cybernetic Metaphor in William Gaddis's *JR*."

26. "Customer Awareness," 5 (WU).

27. "Treatment for a Motion Picture on 'Software'," *RSP* 25.

28. A number of critics have observed the more or less filmic quality that displaces conventional plotting and narration in *J R*. Michael Levine takes this notion further by arguing that Gaddis's novel is literally to be read as a film: While many have noted a "refusal of narrative" (to the point where George Steiner notoriously called the book "unreadable" in his *New Yorker* review), Levine focuses on the way Gaddis removes the exposition from subjectivity altogether in its use of filmic technique.

## Chapter 8

1. Clune, 23 (hereafter cited parenthetically).

2. Published the same year as the collection *Paper Empire: William Gaddis and the World System*, Clune's book participates in a turn away from the critical commonplace that systems are *represented* by Gaddis, as objects that exclude subjectivity. Rather, in the terms of such philosophical thinkers as Martin Heidegger and Niklas Luhmann, the world system is the shape (or enframing) that an embodied, collective subjectivity can take in the present.

3. Here I am following Hal Foster, in his perspicuous review of Gaddis's final fiction, "Long Live Aporia!"

4. Letter to John and Pauline Napper, 4 July 1968 (*L* 268). Earlier, in a letter of 4 May 1961 to Charles Monaghan, he admitted: "I so greatly envy you London, 2 visits convinced me (10 years ago) it and the people the only place that makes sense for me; but supporting a wife-and-two on Fleet street pay . . . I'm too old I guess to dare it now" (*L* 241).

5. "J R Up to Date," *RSP* 62, headnote.

6. Spice, 8 (hereafter cited parenthetically).

7. http://groups.yahoo.com/group/gaddis-l/.

8. Letter to Sarah Gaddis, 23 January 1988. He added, tellingly, "that's the advantage of a fiction, that one can go back and insert, clarify, rewrite, until it's a whole" (*L* 448, correcting "it's whole").

9. Gaddis's psychic distance from his homeland is given in a letter already cited (in chapter 3) to Edith Gaddis, 4 May 1948. Here again he recognizes the escapism of his dream of permanent residence in Spain: "Because I am an American, and my whole problem lies in American society; that is, in thinking it out, in understanding where that country has gone all wrong, and perhaps eventually being able to contribute something on the way to right it. . . . It would not do to stay in this good land" (*L* 103).

10. Letter to Edith Gaddis, 29 May 1950 (*L* 149).

11. Ruth Beardsley Kingsbury to Edith Gaddis (undated letter 1930 or 1931).

12. Kinney recalls how at Piermont the "single-car garage was built into the house, helping to form the building's square ground floor. Either he transformed the garage into a study, or a previous owner had."

13. He also completed, a quarter of a century later, the actual work that Gibbs is struggling with: *Agapē Agape,* published posthumously in 2002. Again, the published work is a reduction of the earlier project, and not nearly so compelling as *J R*, but nonetheless the aesthetic transformation offers something different, something not capable of being captured in Gibbs's analytic prose. *The way to the creation*, representable in fiction, is something that cannot be indicated so clearly even in an extensive scholarly-journalistic treatment, which Gaddis had tried on and off over a period of fifty years, as can be seen from the boxes of notes and abandoned drafts, a selection of which are excerpted in the appendix to *RSP*.

14. Dick Reisem, letter to William Gaddis, 27 May 1970, cited by Chetwynd.

15. Kinney. The initial contract, for *J R* and *Agapē Agape* combined, was with Holt, Rinehart & Winston and ran from 1963 to 1969, two years after the finished manuscripts were to have been submitted.

16. Kinney. In fact, the marriage lasted until 1977, nine years altogether and two years past the publication of *J R*.

17. Letter from Aaron Asher, 12 April 1973.

18. Gaddis would itemize his finances periodically in handwritten notes to himself; this one is dated 2 January 1976. He had just turned 53.

19. New York State Writers Institute reading, 4 April 1990.

20. To Judith Gaddis, 28 October 1977.

21. To John Napper, 13 October 1977 (*L* 327). The majority of his letters to the Nappers are addressed to John and his wife Pauline; this one went to John alone.

22. Letter to Edith Gaddis, 24 June 1950 (*L* 150). At that time he'd expressed a similar interest to Napper himself in a letter sent from Majorca on 27 September 1950: "I'm firmly considering life in London for a couple of months, and I'd certainly like to see you about that. Spain has done its work for the moment" (*L* 162).

23. To John Napper, 13 October 1977 (*L* 328).

24. To Judith Gaddis, 28 October 1977.

25. Ibid.

26. To John Napper, 13 October 1977 (*L* 327).

27. Ibid. "As a literary artist," Kinney supposes, "he was a driven man and, I've no doubt, often hard for a woman to live with; Judith was a bright, pretty young woman—who wasn't?—who may simply have wearied of living in his shadow with little to show for it materially or what she needed to supply her own self-esteem and future."

## Chapter 9

1. That and the equally notorious "binders full of women" could only have been spoken by a man who has ceased to recognize his employees or his interlocutors as fully subjective beings. Not to mention "those people" who deigned to ask candidate Romney's wife questions in news conferences.

2. Wolfe, 215.

3. "J. R., or the Boy Inside" was the title given to an early version of the novel's first forty-four pages, published in the *Dutton Review* 1 (1970): 5–68.

4. As Gaddis at Harvard began to devote himself more to his writing for the *Lampoon*, he also began to realize that the courses he'd been taking in psychology were not for him. In his first year he hadn't minded the class where they saw a film "of a dog with half a brain!! Boy they have everything here." But by his third year he was "beginning to realize what this psychology course is! No kidding—the reading is *incredible*! Trying to explain and form theories for personality—which I have decided is quite futile. I don't know why the devil I ever got involved with it" (letter to Edith Gaddis, 4 October 1942 and 17 February 1944 [*L* 38, 52]).

5. Kornbluh, 98.

6. Trollope, *The Way We Live Now* (cited by Kornbluh, 99).

7. "Why do we write? out of indignation? outrage?" (letter to Stanley Elkin, 12 March 1979 [*L* 344].)

8. Letter to June R. Cox, 24 January 1983 (*L* 388, where the headnote states Cox was "then Research Director of the Sid W. Richardson Foundation and

researching her book *Educating Able Learners: Programs and Promising Practices* [Austin: University of Texas Press, 1985]").

9. "It goes fast," Gaddis told me at our 1988 meeting in the East Seventy-Third Street apartment he shared with Muriel.

10. Among whom I would have to include myself in "The Compositional Self in William Gaddis's *J R*."

11. In "Tradition and the Individual Talent," Eliot had written of the artist's "continual surrender of himself as he is at the moment to something which is more valuable. The progress of an artist is the continual self-sacrifice, a continual extinction of personality" (*Selected Prose of T. S. Eliot* [New York: Harcourt, 1975], 40).

12. Letter to Sarah Gaddis, 8 December 1975.

13. To Sarah Gaddis, 21 July 1987 (*L* 436).

14. Gass, "Memories of Master Gaddis," 153.

15. Letter to Sarah Gaddis, 5 August 1986.

16. "I was surprised to hear of his 'impeccable dress' at his memorial," Kinney wrote, "but later learned that he had become a 'sartorial model' during his years living with Muriel."

17. Letter to Sarah Gaddis, 31 January 1986.

18. Consistent with his retreat from confrontations at home through two broken marriages, Gaddis was himself "aware of the part of my own delinquencies & clumsy & so often futile attempts to keep the peace." The phrase is mentioned in a letter to Sarah of 23 August 1990 (*L* 468).

19. "The Pen and the Sword," 17 April 2005, 31. In spite of his distaste for public displays, whether they came from Mailer, "the women" who protested their exclusion from the PEN conference, or the Reagan administration, Gaddis did once intervene forcefully in the politics of his own literary profession: he joined with thirty-seven former winners and judges of the National Book Award to protest changes made by the Association of American Publishers to the American Book Awards. "In the past," the authors' statement read, "the National Book Awards were made by a jury of the winners' peers; novelists selected the winning novel, poets the volume of poems, historians the work of history, and so on." That enabled on occasion choices of books, such as Tim O'Brien's *Going after Cacciato* (Delacort Press) and Richard Beale Davis's *Intellectual Life in the Colonial South, 1585–1760* (University of Tennessee Press), "which had not been ballyhooed by large publishers and were not necessarily well known." The changes to the award structure meant that titles would be submitted by publishers, not authors; and nominations would be made by committees formed by publishers, booksellers, and distributors, and librarians as well as authors. The changes seemed to Gaddis and the other signatories "designed to make sure that no more shockingly non-commmercial choices are made in the future."

20. As recalled by Sarah Gaddis in conversation (July 2010).

21. Sonia Johnson, "Read and Not Heard: Gaddis at the National Book Awards."

22. Moore, Wallace review (141), cited by Johnson, ibid.

23. To Judith Gaddis, 28 October 1977.

24. LeClair, *The Art of Excess*, 102.

25. Not to overdo the myth of a new media democracy, but anyone who measures patterns of activity on Twitter and Facebook can observe a fairly

predictable phenomenon: those who are tweeted and friended tend to be those who are tweeted and friended. See for example Matt Kirshenbaum's account of Twitter's role in bringing participants in the so-called Digital Humanities into an awareness of themselves as a "community": "What Is Digital Humanities and What's It Doing in English Departments?," in *Debating Digital Humanities*, ed. Matthew K. Gold (Minneapolis: University of Minnesota Press, 2012, 415–28).

26. My own book-length study, *Postmodern Sublime: Technology and American Literature from Mailer to Cyberpunk*, argued that such contemporary gestures beyond the limits of self and language could be understood in the long tradition of the sublime, with technology marking the space of resistance to the literary imagination that had once been identified with nature. This too is consistent with Gaddis's own strategy of avoiding failure through its representation in fiction, and avoiding the need to talk about oneself by making a theme of avoidance. Yet the sublime too, traditionally, has been deeply gendered, as we see already in the ancient Greek writer Longinus when he speaks of the impassioned poet as someone "pregnant with a thought," a rhetor who is capable not of merely persuading an audience but overpowering them; making them feel as if they themselves had "created what they only heard." The conceptual creativity that carries the sublime masculine poet, and his listeners, outside themselves is contrasted often in Longinus (and throughout later variations on the sublime) to the *procreative* power of an embodied, feminized nature—the ineffable power that, like the Goddess in Robert Graves, was so central to Gaddis's formative vision of gender differences, as we saw in chapter 5.

27. Gaddis had complimented DeLillo on the appearance of this novel in 1997, first mentioning another book DeLillo had sent him, *The Physics of Baseball* (1900), by Yale professor of physics Robert K. Adair: "dear Don, the 'physics' of baseball is an astounding piece of work & as though served up for my nefarious purpose, many thanks for going to the trouble of getting it to me; as for the generously signed copy of your new grand entry I think you know the measure of my appreciation, very best regards, Gaddis" (27 September 1997 [*L* 523]).

28. LeClair, "Me and *Mao II*."

29. Letter to Sarah Gaddis (date unknown).

30. The draft chapters of *The Pale King* gathered by Wallace's editor Michael Pietsch engage corporate mechanisms (and not just symptoms of corporate "culture") and Gaddis is mentioned there as "an immortally great fiction writer" (75). Franzen had similarly intended the title of his novel *The Corrections* to echo *The Recognitions* and Franzen in that novel references a fictive website named gaddisfly.com. We do get different views of the state by a number of different characters in both novels by Wallace and Franzen but not until *The Pale King*'s depictions of the corporatization of the Internal Revenue Service do we have a level of detail comparable to *J R* and in synch with the impersonal, small, even boring details that determine our situation in a corporate culture.

## Chapter 10

1. Letter to Judith Gaddis, 13 March 1979.

2. Mazza, iii.

3. The essay appeared posthumously in *RSP* 115–19.

4. Gaddis cites a steamy passage from a then-forthcoming novel by the congressman, which was not among the NEA submissions although, in Gaddis's opinion, "of those hundreds of manuscripts I read none, not one, descended to this level of trite vulgarity by Newt Gingrich tentatively aimed for the best-seller lists in the spring, when from over a thousand submissions for grants in poetry the NEA will award twenty-one, and those in creative writing will probably fare similarly" (*RSP* 118).

5. David Madden's 1971 volume *Rediscoveries* is a good example of this generosity on the part of mostly imaginative writers, reclaiming fictions (such as Madden's own reclamation of *The Recognitions*) that were important to each contributor's own development. Heide Ziegler's 1986 volume *Facing Texts*, which paired original short works by imaginative writers with commentary by literary scholars, was another noble attempt to bridge the divide between the two professions, housed as the scholars and writers often were within the same English departments. Nonetheless, it generally has proven much harder bringing creative and critical talents, who may have offices next to one another, onto the same page. The more fluid arrangement of text on screens and in databases carries a promise for the uniting of these two separate literary practices. See, for example, the awkwardly named but accurate and encouraging title for the ELMCIP database in Europe, "Electronic Literature as a Model of Creativity and Innovation in Practice": http://elmcip.net/knowledgebase.

6. In his memorial talk for fellow novelist and Glenn Gould biographer Otto Friedrich, Gaddis suggests that competition, not money, is the root of evil in America.

7. Gaddis himself was far less generous in his assumption about what motivates such writing, though his definitive position statement, which can be found in the papers, appears undated and it is not clear who is addressed. It is presented in caps:

I HAVE NO INTEREST IN OR SYMPATHY FOR "BECOMING FAMOUS" OR PRODUCING "BEST SELLERS" AS CRITERIA FOR STUDENTS WHO WISH PERHAPS NOT TO WRITE BUT TO 'BE WRITERS' IN A SEARCH FOR, AS YOU NOTE, "FAME & FORTUNE". THE TALENT & PERSEVERANCE DEMANDED BY THE WRITING OF WORK THAT WILL LAST IS A DIFFERENT THING. WG

A more nuanced expression of the distinction between the "young who want not to 'be writers' but to write" appears in a letter of reference sent to Robert Coover and the Creative Writing Program at Brown University, 19 June 1993 (*L* 489). Gaddis also addresses, in a letter recommending Joseph McElroy for a position at Queens University, his disposition toward the phrase "a writer's writer," which is simply a matter for him of mutual recognition among fellow practitioners: "he is certainly someone we who read his work hold in high esteem" (undated draft, circa 1993.) Though Gaddis never offered copy for jacket blurbs, which were addressed to a general audience and so contributed more to fame than to the common practice of a working guild, he was quite generous with recommendations addressed to specific people or organizations and supporting practitioners known to him personally and professionally. In this sense, Gaddis could be said to have shared completely his friend William Gass's view that "in this business to have the respect of those you respect is the only reward. And that reward is quite enough."

8. To Judith Gaddis, 2 May 1980.

9. To Judith Gaddis, 13 March 1979; Gaddis habitually misspelled "Susann."

10. In *A Vision of His Own* Wolfe points out how Jawaharlal ("Jerry") Mad-har Pai "voices some of Gaddis's best wit, as in 'reviewers are delighted to be referred to as critics unless they're on the run, then they take refuge in calling themselves journalists' (217)" (266). But this character, known familiarly as Mud-pye, is shown to be a pretender, a dark body that is of use to his white employers in his blue chip law firm. He is called a "real red brick university product all English tailoring really full of himself" (241). But he also, as Wolfe notices, "sounds some false notes. An English gentleman wouldn't say 'old sport'; perhaps Mudpye for-got that he learned the expression from a crook in an American novel. Nor would he clean his butter knife with a napkin at a private luncheon (356). His saying 'high marks' (356, 365) to show approval or praise also reveals false breeding, the correct English pukka-sahib term being 'full marks,' as Gaddis expects us to know" (265–66). Sonia Johnson, as we have seen, argues that Gaddis's elusiveness makes it hard to evaluate his attitude toward gender. The same, it would seem, can be said for race—although the theme of men trying to "pass" and not coming up to East Coast Ivy League standards is clear enough and would appear to be consistent. It turns up not only in this late treatment of Madhar Pai but in the early depiction of Anatole Broyard as Max in *The Recognitions* (see note 10, chapter 5).

11. Letter to Sarah Gaddis, on his impending divorce from Judith, 8 August 1977 (*L* 293).

12. Letter to Warren Kiefer, 28 July 1974 (*L* 293).

13. "—Look Liz, we've got to get a system. At least you brought [the mail] in, good. Now there's got to be a place for it. If I'm going to get any kind of an operation going here we've got to get a system, I've got to know where the mail is when I walk in, you've got to get a pad there by the phone so I can see who . . ." (13). Six "got to"s in the space of four sentences. Of course Liz will never do any of these things that she was never brought up to do as the daughter of a multi-national financier (a suicide; we're given to understand that he was in many ways no less disorganized than his daughter). The only system Paul will achieve in the novel, when he is explaining his schemes with a series of arrows and circles on a scratch pad, is a viable (albeit accidental) rendition of the Battle of Crécy (as Lester notices when he finds the page among the litter by the phone).

14. To Matthew Gaddis, 17 September 1970 (*L* 275). In so many ways Gad-dis resembled the private, philosophically minded pianist Glenn Gould, who in the early sixties composed a ditty with the lyric, "So you want to write a fugue? You've got the urge to write a fugue? You've got the nerve to write a fugue? Well don't you curse and sweat and fight it, just go and sit straight down and write it." The narrator of *Agapē Agape* mentions the biography of Gould written by Gaddis's lifelong friend Otto Friedrich. Gaddis taught at the University of Con-necticut (Storrs) in 1967.

15. To Sarah Gaddis, 17 September 1970 (*L* 276).

16. To Sarah Gaddis, January 1969 (*L* 270).

17. To David Markson, 5 March 1970 (*L* 272). That assistance at placing a finished work of fiction, the gift of a teacher to a student, was offered in part as an alternative to the practice of supporting fellow writers with jacket blurbs (a favor Markson had asked for his own novel of 1970, *Going Down*). Among family and

friends, pedagogy came more naturally to Gaddis than acts of overt promotion—and he closes his letter to Markson by advising the younger novelist not to "confuse" his own work with the apparatus of blurbs and hack reviews and marketing that accompanies a book on its first appearance: "I as much as any & perhaps more than many am vividly aware of the exaggerated pain of every reviewer's stab or even patronizing applause; but Jesus Christ looking at it all what's become of the Hicks Geismars Sterling Norths, nothing left but a whine in the air somewhere. I remain or rather, The Recognitions does" (*L* 273). He'd turn down Alice Denham similarly when her first novel *My Darling from the Lions* appeared in 1967, this time saying he didn't "think anyone's figured out the chemistry of book sales." It was, for Denham, "A polite rebuff that broke my heart. A quote from Gaddis could've been a gold-engraved invitation to the ball, guaranteeing serious review attention. Not sales but critics with influence. And he knew it" (*SBB* 283).

18. Letter to John and Pauline Napper, 1 November 1975 (*L* 299).

19. Gradschools.com accessed online 12 June 2012. http://www.gradschools.com/search-programs/creative-writing/united-states.

20. In a letter to Matthew (29 December 1973), who was going to be reading Housman, Eliot, Yeats, and Creeley in an undergraduate English class, Gaddis recalls Creeley "one night in my room in Adams House bloody head in hands having just turned his mother's car over in a ditch—of such things are poetry made? (You tell me at the end of the course)" (*L* 283).

21. Conversation with William Gass, St. Louis, Missouri, February 2010.

22. To Sarah Gaddis, 14 October 1978 (*L* 341).

23. Letter to Edith Gaddis, 4 May 1948 (*L* 102). In Panama, working on the Locks, he spoke of "this sort of paripatetic life" (13 March 1948) and tries to alleviate, by acknowledging, Edith's likely concern "that the fine education you gave me is producing nothing but a hemispherical bum, (let's say vagabond, sounds nicer)" (28 December 1947 [*L* 79]).

24. Letter to Judith Gaddis, 18 March 1977 (*L* 319).

25. Not for nothing did David Lodge entitle his 1984 novel *Small World*, and base his main academic character on the person of Stanley Fish, who would become known less for substantial contributions early in his career to Milton scholarship and more for his development of the academic star system at Duke and the University of Illinois at Chicago. The terms "inner-directed" and "outer-directed" Gaddis had found in David Riesman's classic sociological study *The Lonely Crowd* (1950), and he applies them specifically to himself (a mostly inner-directed artist) and young J R, the entirely outer-directed youth and budding businessman, who took all his literal instructions from what he saw others visibly striving for in their own lives. Of course the eleven-year-old's keen attention, unmitigated by adult concerns or even a self-conscious sexuality, makes him much better than adults at the accumulation-by-dispossession game.

26. To Sarah Gaddis, 14 October 1978 (*L* 341).

27. Ibid.

28. To William Jovanovich, 15 April 1970 (*L* 273).

29. Letter to Richard Hazelton, 12 March 1979 (*L* 345).

30. George Hunka, e-mail to the author, February 2012.

31. Kevin Begos, conversation with the author, August 2010, the source of subsequent quotations.

32. Recalled by Bigelow in an e-mail to the author, 2 May 2011. Bigelow would become a recognized innovator in the field of electronic literature that emerged with the Internet and in some ways extends the aesthetic of 1970s post-modernism, with its episodic, nonlinear and filmic enfoldings.

33. *All Fall Down* (Coffee House Press, 2009). The slogan is a reprise in the collection's final piece, a novella called *The Translator*. Caponegro told me that she "borrowed the actual graffiti verbatim from the wall of a Bard building circa 1977 where someone had penned it in homage to the glamorous Liza Wherry, and I employed it as analogous homage to the fictive (blonde) Liza with whom my fussy narrator is obsessed (and who is allegorically the book he is translating)."

## Chapter 11

The chapter epigraph is from a letter to Sarah Gaddis, 21 December 1987 (*L* 446).

1. Letter to Edith Gaddis, 7 April 1947 (*L* 66).

2. Letter to John and Pauline Napper, 1 March 1952 (*L* 200).

3. To Sarah Gaddis, 17 September 1987 (*L* 441). Elaine's is the famed Upper East Side hangout of artists, film stars, and writers.

4. Undated letter from 1957 to John Jacobs, Text Editor, *American Illustrated*, United States Information Agency. Gaddis tells Jacobs that "the novel I was writing, back when we pulled the competitive spirit together in 'Racing Cars in America', came out over a year ago, and for a first novel with a $7.50 price tag did better than some of us expected."

5. Judt, A19.

6. To William Gass, 3 August 1979 (*L* 348).

7. Ormonde de Kay interview.

8. "Do you remember my rude remarks about a 'painter' I'd heard about splashing paint on broken dishes with a $1 million a year guarantee from his NY gallery?" Gaddis asked Sarah in a letter dated 5 August 1986. "So of course here is Julian Schnabel a neighbor (he's about 33), white Mercedes & black Rolls, hugely impressed by THE RECOGNITIONS, asked me over to look at his work last week (& he's rather a loner, wife & a couple of small children, asked suggestions for a name for the latest, a boy born last week, I suggested Saul, he decided Vito)."

9. Letter to John Napper, Hallow'een 1991 (*L* 474). Sarah conveyed in conversation (June 2012) that Gaddis thought "Julian would be doing exactly what he's doing even without the success." Like many of his generous remarks on his friends' character, this one could apply equally to himself.

10. Bair, 489–90; the two quotations that follow are from p. 489. Critic Frederick Karl, a neighbor of Gaddis's, once told Steven Moore that he was the one who recommended Gaddis for the MacArthur, but the foundation likely welcomed several recommendations.

11. To Sarah Gaddis, 3 December 1978 (*L* 342).

12. To Sarah Gaddis, 8 September 1969 (*L* 271).

13. To Sarah Gaddis, 24 April 1969.

14. What was most distasteful to Steinberg and the roughly two hundred *New Yorker* contributors and staff who drafted a letter of protest was the appointment as editor of Robert Gottlieb, who had just left Gaddis's publisher, Knopf.

John Updike did not sign, knowing well enough that the gesture against the magazine's corporatization would be futile. Gaddis for his part had been scheming for ways to get out from under obligations to Gottlieb for his "next book" after *J R*. As early as 1976, a year following *J R*'s publication and several years before he would seriously start on a next novel, Gaddis had this to say to his agent, Candida Donadio: "I hope we can avoid any quid pro quo with Gottlieb regarding my 'next book'. In other words, giving up or giving in to something in exchange for his not pursuing any claim to a next book he might have under §14 of our agreement, which reads as amended: The Author agrees to submit to the Publisher his next book-length work before submitting the same to any other publisher. What might we have that he might want? First of course repayment of the $5000. December loan which was excluded from the *J R* contract, and which he has every right to have back off the top of any deal we should make" (letter dated 1 June 1976 [*L* 313]). One notes Gaddis's scrupulousness about the need to repay his debts, and a tendency perhaps to overestimate the convolutions in thought of a business associate and possible adversary: "Of course Bob is very shrewd (and frankly at this point I don't know if he's anything more than that), and may very well have exactly this trade in mind waiting for us to broach the matter of taking the next book elsewhere, as I have by now every reason to believe he would be glad to see us do, anyhow."

15. 4 January 1993 (*L* 483).

16. To John and Pauline Napper, 30 March 1986 (*L* 422).

17. To James Cappio, 5 January 1990 (*L* 459).

18. This is the final version of the passage that Gaddis sent to Steinberg, overleaf on the letter of 4 January 1983, typed in multiple variations with strikeouts and corrections.

19. Remarks to the New York State Writers Institute Seminar, 14 April 1994.

20. *The Art of Excess*, 102.

21. Wolfe, 256. The next quotation is from the same page.

22. Wolfe, 262.

23. Wolfe, 257. Here are some examples: "Thus when Christina looks up from a letter she is reading aloud and speaks her own thoughts, the shift is only indicated by a comma (23). Later, during her and Harry's fifty-mile drive from Manhattan to Wainscott, Gaddis recounts a great deal of conversation but describes no scenery. Still in Wainscott, some weeks later, a car pulls away from Oscar's house and returns four sentences—and three hours—later. This concentration compels our attention" (ibid.).

24. Gaddis incidentally mentions in a letter to his German translator Paul Ingendaay (25 August 1989) that the name Eigen in *J R* recalls Musil's *Mann ohne Eigenshaften* (*The Man without Qualities*) (*L* 457). The presentation of men without qualities arguably is consistent with the literary project of creating fictions without narratives. Musil is cited also, along with the other authors named in this paragraph, by British philosopher Gaylen Strawson in his provocative intervention "Against Narrativity," *Ratio* (new series) 17 (4 December 2004). Online at http://lchc.ucsd.edu/mca/reviews/against_narrativity.pdf.

25. A term used by Gaddis in an undated letter (November 1975) to David Markson, in reference to Christopher Lehmann-Haupt, the regular fiction reviewer for the *New York Times* (who had panned books by both authors) (*L* 299).

26. Wertheim, 445.

27. Ibid.

## Chapter 12

1. To Sarah Gaddis, 24 March 1995.

2. The last letter in Moore's *Letters*, when Gaddis declared the work "sort of compleat in itself, ie with a beginning middle & end," is dated 1 September. But even here, he mentions a "diatribe" on the Pulitzer prize that is "done but not the right p[l]ace" (to Gregory and Judith Comnes [*L* 528]). He eventually worked that into the version he left at his death.

3. Letter to Steven Moore, 7 April 1983 (*L* 392).

4. *Concrete*, 3.

5. Firbank's novels are among the earliest of Susan Sontag's "Canon of Camp" in *Against Interpretation* (1966). Firbank's frank "frivolity" among mostly upper-class characters may have been what Gaddis aspired to in early iterations of *The Recognitions*, with titles such as "Blague," "Vanity," and "Some people who were naked." (One of Firbank's novels is called *Inclinations*, rhyming with Gaddis's title.) The frivolous quality (a kind of "abandon") was never wholly left behind although fun and games, writ large across the culture, are shown steadily, systematically to support, rather than subvert, larger tendencies in the culture and the world system toward "control" (to again cite the terms from Toynbee that ultimately shaped Gaddis's world vision).

6. As he told Matthew Gaddis.

7. O'Donnell, 176.

8. Matthew's written comments were included with the typescript of *Agapē Agape* that I received from Viking Press while drafting the afterword to the book.

9. "O Heaven, Heaven, Heaven! / Who's robbed me of myself / Who's closer to myself / Or can do no more with me than I ever can?" *Complete Poems and Selected Letters of Michelangelo*, trans. Creighton Gilbert (New York: Random House, 1963), 7.

10. Gould's biographer (and Gaddis's old friend) Otto Friedrich was also much on his mind during the composition of *AA*. Already ailing in May 1995, Gaddis had been unable to attend Friedrich's memorial service at Saint Peter's Church on Lexington Avenue, but his words of remembrance (read by Friedrich's daughter Liesel) clearly place Friedrich among the select few who could, and did, "do more," inasmuch as he was always there, writing, producing, and providing for his family while the rest of the Village and Paris expatriates were "busy talking about the novels we were going to write and excuses for not writing them, while he was doing it, doing the work. [. . .] Thus I can hardly say he was an inspiration, but rather something nearer a living rebuke to our laziness, our excuses, the disorderly conduct of our lives in general." Friedrich shared Gaddis's "dim view of the human comedy" and he too had "no use for sentimentality," but he also showed a "warm generosity of spirit [. .]. for those whose work and efforts he respected, and I have always counted myself immensely fortunate in believing I was among that 'happy few.'" Gaddis's closing words could serve as an epitaph for himself: "And so, as they said of the architect, if you want to see his monument look around you. At his life, at his books and their extraordinary range, but most of all I think at [. . .] those children screeching and scrabbling through that

tiny cottage," the one on Long Island that Friedrich rented from Gaddis's family in the 1950s, "and what they have made of themselves today from what he gave them, and what they gave to him."

11. 13 October 1977 (*L* 327).

12. Tolstoy, *The Kreutzer Sonata*, 144.

13. Ibid., 304.

14. Matthew's recollections of the evening were communicated to the author at a meeting in New York City in the spring of 2000. John Sherry also mentions the drink and cigarette on the final night. Sherry knew that both had been forbidden because of his friend's emphysema, but he also wondered whether Gaddis "ever really stopped" smoking. Sherry's recollections, first published in *Hamptons Country* (June 1999), are archived at the Gaddis Annotations website. Thomas Girst also recounts Gaddis's last day in the article "Every Box Bears a Pearl: The Children of American Author William Gaddis Reveal His Literary Estate," *Frankfurter Allgemeine Zeitung*, 17 May 2001, 8.

# WORKS CITED

## Primary Works

### BOOKS BY WILLIAM GADDIS

*Agapē Agape*. Afterword by Joseph Tabbi. New York: Viking, 2002.
*Carpenter's Gothic*. 1985. New York: Penguin, 1989.
*A Frolic of His Own*. New York: Poseidon Press, 1994.
*J R*. 1975. New York: Penguin, 1993.
*The Letters of William Gaddis*. Edited by Steven Moore, with an afterword by Sarah Gaddis. Champaign, Ill.: Dalkey Archive Press, 2013.
*The Recognitions*. 1955. New York: Penguin, 1993.
*The Rush for Second Place: Essays and Occasional Writings*. Edited by Joseph Tabbi. New York: Penguin 2002.

### INTERVIEWS

Abádi-Nagy, Zoltán. "The Art of Fiction CI: William Gaddis." *Paris Review* 105 (Winter 1987–88): 54–89.
Berkley, Miriam. "PW Interviews: William Gaddis." *Publishers Weekly*, 12 July 1985, 56–57.
de Vree, Freddy. "The Second Belgian Radio Television Interview." Conducted May 1988.
Graeber, Laurel. "A Carnival of Disorderly Conduct." *New York Times Book Review*, 9 January 1994, 22.
Helgesen, Sally. "Every Day." *Bookletter*, December 1976.
Ingendaay, Paul. "Agent der Veränderung. Ein Gespräch mit William Gaddis" [Agent of Change: A Conversation with William Gaddis]. *Rowohlt Literatur Magazin* 39 (1997): 64–92. Conducted in English (18–19 December 1995), published in German. Unpublished English translation by John Soutter.
Logan, Marie-Rose, and Tomasz Mirkowicz. "'Kto do utworu przychodzi z niczym . . .' Z Williamem Gaddisem rozmawiają" ["If You Bring Nothing to a Work . . .": An Interview with William Gaddis]. *Literatura na świecie* 1, no. 150 (1984): 178–89. Conducted in English (26 June 1981), published in Polish. Unpublished English translation by Julita Wroniak.
Thielemans, Johan. "The First Belgian Radio Televsion Interview." Conducted August 1984.

## Secondary Works

Alberts, Crystal, Cristopher Liese, and Birger Vanwesenbeek, eds. *William Gaddis, "The Last of Something."* Jefferson, N.C.: McFarland, 2009.
Bair, Deirdre. *Saul Steinberg*. New York: Doubleday, 2012.
Bernhard, Thomas. *Concrete*. Translated by David McClintock. 1984. Chicago: University of Chicago Press, 1986.

Brown, Nicholas. "Cognitive Map, Aesthetic Object, or National Allegory. *Carpenter's Gothic*," 151–60. In *Paper Empire: William Gaddis and the World System*, edited by Joseph Tabbi and Rone Shavers (Tuscaloosa: University of Alabama Press, 2007).

Broyard, Anatole. *Kafka Was the Rage: A Greenwich Village Memoir*. New York: Carol Southern Books, 1990.

———. "Remembering William Gaddis in the Nineteen-Fifties." *New England Review* 17, no. 3 (Summer 1995): 13–14.

Carr, Virginia Spencer. *Dos Passos: A Life*. Evanston, Ill.: Northwestern University Press, 2004.

Chetwynd, Alistair. "William Gaddis's Education-Writing and His Fiction: A Fuller Archival History." *Orbit: Writing around Pynchon*, forthcoming 2015.

Clune, Michael. *American Literature and the Free Market, 1945–2000*. Cambridge: Cambridge University Press, 2012.

Coe, Jonathan. "American Fiction: A Law unto Himself." *Guardian*, 21 June 1994. Online at http://www.williamgaddis.org/frolic/frolicrevjcoe.shtml.

de Kay, Ormonde. Interviewed in December 1993 by Charles Monaghan. Online at http://www.williamgaddis.org/reminisce/remdekaymonaghan.shtml.

Denham, Alice. *Sleeping with Bad Boys: A Juicy Tell-All of Literary New York in the 1950s and 1960s*. Las Vegas, N.V.: Book Republic Press/Cardoza Publishing, 2006.

Foster, Hal. "Long Live Aporia!" Review of *Agape* and *The Rush for Second Place* by William Gaddis. *London Review of Books*, 24 July 2003, 13–15.

Franzen, Jonathan. "Mr. Difficult." *New Yorker*, 30 September 2002. Reprinted in *How to Be Alone*, 238–69. New York: Picador, 2003. Online at http://adilegian.com/FranzenGaddis.htm.

Gaddis, Sarah. *Swallow Hard*. New York: Atheneum, 1990.

Gaddis Annotations, The. http://www.williamgaddis.org/.

Gass, William H. Introduction to *The Recognitions* (New York: Penguin, 1993), x–xv.

———. "Memories of Master Gaddis." *Conjunctions* 33 (1999): 151–55.

Gates, Henry Louis, Jr. "The Passing of Anatole Broyard." In *Thirteen Ways of Looking at a Black Man*. (New York: Random House, 1997): 180–214.

Graves, Robert. *The White Goddess: A Historical Grammar of Poetic Myth*. 1948. Amended and enlarged edition. New York: Farrar, Strauss and Giroux, 1966.

Green, Jack. *fire the bastards!* Edited by Steven Moore. Normal, Ill.: Dalkey Archive Press, 1992.

Handy, Adelaide. "Steam Plant Purchasing Agent Finds Fascination in Her Work: Edith Gaddis's Shopping List Ranges from Huge Mechanical Shovels to Miles of Iron Pipe." *New York Times*, 6 April 1941, "Society News," D4.

Huizinga, Johan. *Homo Ludens: A Study of the Play Element in Culture*. Boston: Beacon Press, 1971.

Johnson, Sonia. "Read and Not Heard: Gaddis at the National Book Awards." June 27, 2012. Online at http://web.archive.org/web/20130924055107/http://blog.lareviewofbooks.org/post/26037833279/read-and-not-heard-gaddis-at-the-national-book-awards.

Judt, Tony. "My Endless New York." *New York Times*, 8 November 2010, A19.

Kabel, Philip. "The Road That Leads to Somewhere." Essay-obituary of Samuel E. Williams and Robert Dickinson Way. Newspaper title and date unknown (ca. 1937).

Kerouac, Jack. *The Subterraneans*. In *Road Novels 1957–1960*, edited by Douglas Brinkley, 463–559. New York: Library of America, 2007.

Kinney, Harrison. "Reminiscences of William Gaddis." 1999. Online at http://www.williamgaddis.org/reminisce/remhkinney.shtml.

Konstantinou, Lee. "Too Big to Succeed: On William Gaddis's 'J R.'" *Los Angeles Review of Books*, 28 October 2012. Online at https://lareviewofbooks.org/review/too-big-to-succeed-on-william-gaddiss-j-r.

Kornbluh, Anna. *Realizing Capital: Financial and Psychic Economies in Victorian Realist Form*. New York: Fordham University Press, 2014.

LeClair, Tom. *The Art of Excess: Mastery in Contemporary American Fiction*. Champaign: University of Illinois Press, 1989.

———. "Me and *Mao II*." Lecture given March 1993 at Case Western Reserve's annual "Discussion Day." Online at http://perival.com/delillo/meandmaoii.html.

Leggett, John. *Ross and Tom: Two American Tragedies*. New York: Simon & Schuster, 1974.

Levine, Michael. "Screenwriting: William Gaddis's *J R*." *The Journal of Narrative Technique* 28, no. 1 (Winter 1998): 21–42.

Looks, Bernard. "The Novelist and His Mentor." Online at http://metacog.org/dworkin/article.html.

Mazza, Cris. "Looking Beyond Moi." *Other Voices* 45 (2006): iii.

McGurl, Mark. *The Program Era: Postwar Fiction and the Rise of Creative Writing*. Cambridge: Harvard University Press, 2007.

Melville, Herman. *Pierre; or, The Ambiguities*. 1852. New York: Knopf, 1930.

Moore, Steven. Review of *Infinite Jest*, by David Foster Wallace. *Review of Contemporary Fiction* 16, no. 1 (Spring 1996): 141–42.

———. "Sheri Martinelli: A Modernist Muse." *Gargoyle* 41 (1998): 28–54. Online at http://www.stevenmoore.info/martinelli/smartinellimodmuse.shtml.

———. *William Gaddis*. Expanded edition. New York: Bloomsbury, 2015.

Murphy, Muriel Oxenberg. *Excerpts from the Unpublished Files of Muriel Oxenberg Murphy*. Edited by Evan Goss. XLibris Corporation, 2008.

O'Donnell, Patrick. *Echo Chambers: Figuring Voice in Modern Narrative*. Iowa City: University of Iowa Press, 1992.

Park, Ed. "The Precognitions: On the Posthumous Trail of W. G. Sebald and William Gaddis." *Voice Literary Supplement*, Fall 2002. Online at http://theunarchivable.blogspot.com/2007/09/piece-on-sebald-gaddis-and-bernhard.html.

Pennebaker, D. A. "Remembering Gaddis." *Conjunctions* 33 (1999): 157–60.

Puffenbarger, John. "Ernest Williams School Touched Many West Virginians." May/June 1999. Online at http://wvmea.tripod.com/jp99-5.htm.

Ravitch, Michael. "On William Gaddis." *Yale Review* 92, no. 2 (April 2004): 151–63. Online at www.michaelravitch.com/Gaddis.html.

Rushdie, Salman. "The Pen and the Sword." *New York Times Book Review*, 17 April 2005, 31.

Safer, Elaine B. "Ironic Allusiveness and Satire in *The Recognitions*." In *William Gaddis*, edited by Harold Bloom, 71–100. Philadelphia: Chelsea House, 2004.

Smith, Dinitia. "Gaddis in the Details: Is America Finally Ready for the Literary Wizard of the Hamptons?" *New York*, 3 January 1994, 34–40.

Spice, Nicholas. "Is Wagner Bad for Us?" *London Review of Books* 35, no. 7 (11 April 2013): 3–8.

Stade, George. "Mailer and Miller." *Partisan Review* 44, no. 4 (1977): 616–24.

Tabbi, Joseph. "The Compositional Self in William Gaddis's *J R*." *Modern Fiction Studies* 35, no. 4 (Winter 1989): 655–72.

———. "The Cybernetic Metaphor in William Gaddis's *JR*." *American Notes & Queries* 2, no. 4 (October 1989): 147–51.

———. *Postmodern Sublime: Technology and American Literature from Mailer to Cyberpunk*. Ithaca: Cornell University Press, 1995.

———. "The Processual Page: Materiality and Consciousness in Print and Hypertext." In *The Future of the Page*, edited by Peter Stoicheff and Andrew Taylor, 201–30. Toronto: University of Toronto Press, 2004.

———. "The Technology of Quotation: William Gaddis's *J R* and Contemporary Media." *Mosaic* 28, no. 4 (December 1995): 143–64.

———, and Rone Shavers, eds. *Paper Empire: William Gaddis and the World System*. Tuscaloosa: University of Alabama Press, 2007.

Taylor, Mark C. *Rewiring the Real: In Conversation with William Gaddis, Richard Powers, Mark Danielewski, and Don DeLillo*. New York: Columbia University Press, 2012.

Tolstoy, Leo. *The Kreutzer Sonata and Other Stories*. Translated by Louise and Aylmer Maude and J. D. Duff. New York: Oxford University Press, 2009.

Tyree, J. M. "Henry Thoreau, William Gaddis, and the Buried History of an Epigraph." *New England Review* 25, no. 4 (September 2004): 148–62. Online at http://www.williamgaddis.org/critinterpessays/tyreegaddisthoreau.shtml.

Walker, Christopher. "All in Order, Thanks." (London) *Observer*, 27 February 1994, 18.

Wallace, David Foster. *The Pale King*. Boston: Little, Brown, 2011.

Wallerstein, Immanuel. *World-Systems Analysis: An Introduction*. Durham, N.C.: Duke University Press, 2004.

Wertheim, Larry M. "Law as Frolic: Law and Literature in *A Frolic of His Own*." *William Mitchell Law Review* 21, no. 2 (1995): 421–56.

Wiener, Norbert. *The Human Use of Human Beings*. New York: Avon Books, 1987.

Wolfe, Peter. *A Vision of His Own: The Mind and Art of William Gaddis*. Madison, N.J.: Fairleigh Dickinson University Press, 1997.

## ABOUT THE AUTHOR

Joseph Tabbi is a professor of English at the University of Illinois at Chicago. He is the author of *Cognitive Fictions* and *Postmodern Sublime: Technology and American Writing from Mailer to Cyberpunk*, editor of the *electronic book review*, coeditor of *Reading Matters: Narrative in the New Media Ecology*, and founding member of the Consortium on Electronic Literature.